THE NAZI, THE PRINCESS, AND THE SHOEMAKER

My Father's Holocaust Odyssey

By Scott M. Neuman

Edited by Adi J. Neuman

*T*his book is dedicated to my father,

my family that lost their lives in
the Holocaust,

the Jews of Radziejow,

and all the Jews that were murdered by the Nazis.

TABLE OF CONTENTS

INTRODUCTION

This project began in 1981, in Chicago, when I became the proud father of my first child, a son. We named him Adi, meaning precious jewelry in Hebrew. My wife chose that name for its similarity in Hebrew to the name Azriel. For my father had specifically requested that in choosing our son's name, we remember his favorite brother, Azriel, who was murdered by the Nazis in the Holocaust.

A few nights after my son was born, as I watched him sleeping so peacefully, a thought appeared in my mind. "One day my son will grow up and ask me, 'What happened to Grandpa during the Holocaust?'" After mulling over this question, I realized that I was not even remotely prepared to answer. I had only minimal knowledge of my father's experiences in the Holocaust. When I was growing up, my mother had declared that we kids were never to bring up the subject – it was strictly taboo.

Only once did I ever hear my father speak of his experiences during the Holocaust. That was on a tour of Israel in February of 1968, which was a Bar Mitzvah gift from my parents. My father met another Holocaust survivor in the iconic Dan hotel in Tel Aviv and I sat nearby and listened in. For whatever reason, my father did not speak in Yiddish with this man, even though he always spoke in Yiddish with his "greenhorn" immigrant friends.

I still remembered a good deal of what my father told his friend. However, aside from that conversation, I had little

1

knowledge of his experience to impart to my son.

It was then I decided that, in order to preserve my father's story, I must write this book. So I mustered the courage and broached the subject with my father. As I spoke, he looked at me in a curious manner as if to say, "*Mah Pitom?*" (Hebrew for "what's this all of the sudden?") A moment later, to my complete surprise, he agreed without reservation to answer any question I might submit.

I conducted a series of interviews with my father in his house, the house I grew up in. Each session lasted about an hour, and it took several days to complete. During the interviews I used a tape recorder and did not take any physical notes. I did this in order to allow for a flow of information that was not subject to interruption or distraction.

In the interviews, my father recalled his story in chronological order, beginning with his childhood. He described his entire Holocaust experience, from Germany's invasion of Poland until his liberation by the Russian army in January of 1945. Finally, he spoke about his post-Holocaust experiences in Poland, Germany and America. As he spoke, I would only occasionally interrupt in order to clarify a question or request that he elaborate on a certain point.

I must confess that I was emotionally drained upon finishing our last session. I was also disappointed in myself that only now did I realize the magnitude of my father's suffering as a result of the Holocaust.

At the conclusion of the final interview, I stared at my father, feeling proud that I was the son of such a man. As I had discovered, my father's experience was unique and extraordinary, even among Holocaust survivors. I enthusiastically told him that his survival was nothing less than a miracle. I declared that it would be a tragedy if his account was lost, and that it should be publicized for for the benefit of our family, the Jewish people, and any person interested in the trials and tribulations of the human condition.

I then asked his permission to publish his experiences.

I could tell by the look on his face that he was pleased with my reaction. I'm sure that he was thinking that he was no different than any other Holocaust survivor. He saw nothing truly special about his life that others would find interesting. But still, he was pleasantly surprised that I thought his story was worthy of retelling. So he answered with the modest reply, "Whatever you want to do is O.K.."

I was excited to begin. After hearing my father's incredible Holocaust story, I knew that it would read even stranger than fiction. His improbable story of survival could only have been the result of divine intervention. It felt as if I had been entrusted with a sacred treasure.

The next day I started to put pen to paper. As the pages piled up, I began to realize that I was inadequately prepared to author such an important project. In fact, after reviewing the initial drafts of my father's account, it was clear that I was not even remotely doing justice to his unbelievable story.

I became so frustrated and despondent from my lack of progress that, without consulting my father, I stopped working on the project. I lied to myself by saying that it was just a temporary break, necessary to allow my creative juices to begin flowing. Mercifully, my father never asked me about my progress. As more and more time went by, I continued to rationalize that I had not abandoned the project, rather, I had merely put it on the "back burner."

Time flew by quickly raising two children. After many years of hiatus, I resolved that I would complete my long-abandoned project. My father had already passed away in 2003, but I still felt the need to make good on my pledge.

As my immediate family can attest, once I put my mind to something, I become obsessive about it. My entire family was glad that I was finally going to complete the project, because for a long time I had been giving them a collective headache by repeating the mantra that one day I would finish the book.

I came up with an unusual idea to help restart the project. I would begin modestly by telling my father's story, piece by piece, through a website. The first step was to create the site. Luckily, I found the perfect ally in this project, my son, Adi. He was now in his early twenties, and had experience designing websites. I figured I could use my parental power of guilt on him. So I told him, "I need you to create a Holocaust website dedicated to your grandfather, his family, and the destroyed Jewish community of Radziejow."

I explained to him that such a website would be a perfect way to fulfill the commitment that I had made to his grandfather. The ultimate goal of the website would be to memorialize the daily life and history of the once-thriving Jewish community of Radziejow. The website would somehow create a virtual Jewish Radziejow.

During this monologue, I noticed that he had a strange look on his face. I gathered he was thinking that it was not easy to be a son. Still, after putting forth my vision of the website, he stared into my eyes with an incredulous look on his face and simply responded, "Anything else?"

My first thought was, "Success!" My second thought was that since his response was so "positive," he had left open the door to further exploitation. So I decided to run by him an idea I had for the website.

"Your grandfather and I agreed that his family's building in Poland was unjustly stolen from him. So shouldn't the website give the Poles of Radziejow an opportunity to correct this injustice?" I said these words in a sarcasting but somewhat convincing tone.

My son had over the years become an observant Jew. He took seriously the commandment of honoring one's father and mother. I, embarrassingly, had waited thirty years to show proper honor to my father, whereas my son immediately set out to create this website that was just a wild idea in his father's mind.

My son methodically created the technical structure that would serve as the foundation of the website. At various times, he would ask for my input. One day he asked me what web address I would like. I thought about it for a moment, then, remembering the bit about getting my family's building back, I replied, "What better name for this website then Polandinjustice.com."

Of course I knew that, barring some sort of apocalyptic event, the Poles would never return the Naiman property. Rather, I thought that in order to be compelling, the website needed a vehicle for telling the story of my father's lost world. The Naiman building's ownership was a central theme of the website. It represented how Jewish property had been systematically looted by Nazis, and how that theft had later been legitimized by the Polish government after the war. Furthermore, the current lack of a Jewish presence in the Naiman building, and in Radziejow in general, illustrates how the once vibrant, thriving Jewish community of Poland had been utterly destroyed by the Nazis.

After creating the website, my son and I soon became the custodians of a great deal of previously lost evidence regarding my father, his family, and the Jews of Radziejow. For example, we were able to obtain an official handwritten document in German that listed the names of all the Jews living in the Radziejow ghetto a short time before its liquidation. Many of those names were hauntingly familiar. They were the names of my father's extended family, as well as many names that I had heard my mother and father talk about when I was growing up. I remembered that some of the survivors were living in distant parts of the United States, Canada, France, and Australia.

More evidence arrived by e-mail. A child of a Holocaust survivor living in Toronto sent us a photograph from the late 1930's of the entire Jewish community of Radziejow, along with local Polish officials, at the dedication of the Beis Rochel Synagogue. This was the synagogue where my grandfather conducted the holiest of all prayer services, *Neilah*, on Yom Kippur. A Polish travel agent later sent us a picture of the Beis

Rochel Synagogue after it was destroyed by the Nazis.

Other photographs we received depicted Jews as they were forced to live in the ghetto, complete with the cutout Jewish stars that they were ordered to wear on the front of their clothing. One showed Jewish men conscripted to forced labor being marched out of Radziejow. These slave laborers were accompanied by a sharply dressed mounted German police officer.

Of particular interest, we obtained a photograph of the entire contingent of German occupation forces at a ceremony in Radziejow's Market Square. We even received photos from the librarian of the Radziejow library that depicted the German troops that were sent to liquidate the ghetto.

Finally, a Polish photographer sent me a picture of the Jewish cemetery where my grandparents and great-grandparents on my grandmother's side were buried. Unfortunately, the cemetery no longer exists. It was partially dismantled during World War II, and after the war it was transformed into a cement quarry. Today, it is a park. This is only a partial list of the amazing discoveries that stemmed from the website.

After maintaining the website for a number of years, I decided that the time had come to actually write the book I had planned. I reasoned that in the meantime I had become older and wiser, and my writing skills had improved. Furthermore, I had now a good deal of background material and information to supplement my father's account.

The first step was to locate those long-forgotten cassette tapes recorded in the early 1980s. After some searching, I found them in a torn plastic grocery bag at the bottom of a bedroom closet. Upon finding them, my first impression was that the cassettes would not work. Their expected longevity had long passed, as they were now over thirty years old. I put one of the cassettes in an old tape recorder that was laying around in the same closet, plugged it in, and, to my surprise, it played flawlessly.

My plan was that the book would be a precise retelling

of my father's experiences before, during, and after the Holocaust. The account would be told, for the most part, through his eyes, and supplemented by the accounts of other survivors from his hometown of Radziejow. In addition, I would include enough historical background to allow the reader to understand my father's account in the proper context.

Just like a computer's code can become corrupted, memories can change over time. This book is a retelling of how my father remembered events that took place more than forty years prior, and therefore the descriptions in this book may not always be 100% accurate. Thus, I apologize to the reader in advance for any details that may not be an exact depiction of what happened.

The material used to write this account comes from several sources. First and foremost, my personal interview of my father in the early 1980s. The interviews produced five 90-minute audio cassettes. Second, my father's interview by the Shoah Foundation that was founded by Steven Spielberg. This interview, conducted by Margaret Liftman for Survivors of the Shoah, Visual History Foundation, took place in his house in June of 1996. Third, similar videotaped testimonies of about ten other survivors from Radziejow. Fourth, the book *A Promise Kept to Bear Witness*, written by my "Aunt Yetka." My aunt, whose real name is Joyce Wagner, published her account in 2007. Fifth, my cousin Lenny Marcus's documentary about Radziejow produced for Public Television of Boston. Sixth, personal interviews that I conducted with Holocaust survivors that had lived in Radziejow. Seventh, material provided by the Radziejow Library including photographs of the German occupation of the town during World War II. Finally, extensive research on Radziejow and the Holocaust from historical accounts and websites including *Virtual Shtetl*.

For genealogy research, I was greatly assisted by a website called Geni. With the help of Geni, combined with other resources, I was able to construct a family tree dating back to the 1750s. For me, that was astounding, equivalent in some way to those blue-blooded Americans that date their lineage to the landing of the Mayflower in Plymouth, Massachusetts.

In this book, Ben Neuman is referred to as Binem or my father depending whether I am telling his story or whether I am speaking directly to him. Binem was his name in Poland, though he was also referred to by his nickname, Bineck. The name stayed with him when he left Poland in 1946 until he became an American citizen in 1955 and adopted the name Ben. However, he continued to be Binem to all his Yiddish-speaking "greenhorn" friends. Even my mother, a native-born American, would occasionally switch back and forth from Ben to Binem. When I was growing up, I made it a point to "zone out" the name Binem because it reminded me that my father was some kind of foreigner. I only called and thought of him as "Dad." As I grew older, the name Binem appealed to me because it created a link between myself and the lost world of my father.

It should be noted that after the Holocaust, my father found peace with God. As he grew older, he became more and more observant. He made sure that his children received a Jewish education, his sons had Bar Mitzvahs, and he paid for several trips for his children to go to Israel. All these efforts were made in order that his children remained Jewish. He understood that, against all odds, he personally survived the horrors of the Nazis relatively unscathed. He knew that his surviving the Holocaust was nothing less than a miracle, and only God has the capacity to perform miracles. Thus, he re-served his hatred for Hitler and his co-conspirators.

My father would say that people killed Jews, and these people were the Nazis and their anti-Semitic helpers. These helpers included many Polish citizens. Still, he could not hate all Poles, because there were many that endangered their own lives to save him. Even more confounding was that he couldn't hate all Germans, because he encountered a few Germans that also helped him survive.

It will never be known exactly why my father survived

when others, including nearly his entire family, were slaughtered. In my opinion, my father survived because he was either destined to survive from the very beginning of the Holocaust, or he earned the right to survive by his actions during the war.

His odyssey is sprinkled with true miracles and unbelievable events. For those who read this book and conclude that he was just lucky, I most vehemently disagree.

Jews celebrate yearly the holiday of Purim, as described in the *Megillah*. In the Purim story, Haman, an evil tyrant akin to Hitler, attempts to destroy the Jewish people, but is thwarted by a series of "fortuitous" events. As explained by the classical commentaries, though each individual event that was necessary for the Jews' salvation could be explained rationally, the hopelessly improbable combination, seen as a whole, is an undeniable testament to the Almighty's intervention to save the Jewish people.

The series of improbable events that led to my father's survival, in a similar manner, simply cannot be rationalized by luck or ingenuity or any other logical explanation.

The purpose of this book is to memorialize my father's life as well as the Jews of Radziejow that were murdered by the Nazi scourge. Today, Jewish Poland as it was before the Holocaust is no more. There is not a single Jew remaining in Radziejow. All that remains of the world of the Jews of Radziejow are the descendants of the survivors scattered throughout the world. The children of the survivors and their children are living examples of Hitler's failure to destroy the Jewish people.

My father's journey ended with his death on Holocaust Remembrance Day in the Spring of 2003. The date of his death is a reminder to me that, had he been murdered during the Holocaust, I would not exist. When I visit my father's grave, my eyes always focus on two words on his gravestone that best describe his life:

HOLOCAUST SURVIVOR

THE TOWN OF RADZIEJOW

R adziejow is a small town in north-central Poland. It sits idyllically on a hill, surrounded by the countryside's picturesque greenery and rolling fields. Dotting the landscape are farmhouses, barns, haystacks, cottages, and even mansions on large estates.

Spring turns Radziejow and the surrounding countryside into a kind of Garden of Eden. The forests turn green and the crops in the fields begin to grow. This continues until autumn, when the harvest season arrives. Golden stalks rise towards the sky, covering the fields like a dense forest. Peasants scurry around as they cultivate their fields. All this among a cacophony of sounds such as the humming of buzzing insects. To top it off, the sweet fragrance of wild flowers permeates everywhere.

When the harvest ends, the countryside completely transforms. Winter arrives and the fields become a barren wasteland. Still, the fond memories of the lush forests, the smell of the wild flowers, and the vitality of nature affords the citizens of Radziejow solace to await spring, when the cycle of life renews.

Radziejow is located a relatively short distance from one of Europe's major rivers, the Vistula. It is within a few hour's drive of Poznan, Lodz, Danzig, and Warsaw. As a result of this central location, over the past few centuries Radziejow has been a sort of national football for Poland's neighbors, having often changed possession from neighboring Russia to Germany and back again.

The history of Jews living in Poland dates back to the thirteenth century. King Kazimierz III and then later King Boleslav of Poland granted charters that invited Jews from around the world to live in Poland. The charters contained specific provisions meant to attract Jews, including the promise of religious freedom. This was significant at a time where Jews were being expelled from several European countries. Even in countries where they had not been expelled, European Jews were almost universally oppressed. Poland's new charters were seen by many Jews as a gift from God.

Interestingly, it has long been said that the very name Poland, or *Polin* in Yiddish, has a hidden significance for Jews. The first syllable, *Po*, means "here" in Hebrew. The second syllable, *lin*, is similar to the Hebrew word meaning lodging place. A prominent rabbi even went so far as to remark that God knew one day the Jews would be exiled from *Eretz Yisroel* (the Land of Israel). To protect his people, God hid away in Heaven a portion of the land of Israel so when the time came and the Temple would be destroyed, he would place this piece of *Eretz Yisrael* in Poland so it could serve as a resting place for the Jews during their exile.

Historical accounts referencing the town of Radziejow date back as early as the twelfth century. About three hundred years later, Jews began to settle in the town. One historical account states that a Jewish synagogue was located in Radziejow in the early 1500s. Later that century, around 1546, a king's edict ordered that all the town's Jews be banished from living in the town. Two centuries later, the Jews returned. By the 1770s, Jews made up approximately five percent of the town residents. Those Jews were restricted to living and doing business along Torunska Street, which became a main street.

The Jews of Radziejow engaged in a variety of professions and businesses. By 1862, Jews were no longer required to live in the vicinity of Torunska Street. By then, the street had become known by Poles and Jews as "Yiddishe Street" (Jewish Street). Even with this newly granted freedom, Jews, for the most part, remained in the area of Yiddishe Street. The reason for this is simple: Jews enjoy living and working together. Likewise, they loved to be around the familiar sounds and smells that could only be found on Yiddishe Street.

Jewish religious life can be demanding, with its thrice-daily communal prayer times along with many food restrictions. So for the Jews of Radziejow, it was convenient to live close to the *shul* (house of prayer), kosher bakery, and kosher butcher shop. It was a delight for them to simply stroll along Yiddishe Street and take in the sweet smell of breads that were baked fresh daily, except, of course, on *Shabbos*, the Jewish Sabbath. Likewise, the Jews enjoyed haggling at the kosher butcher shops. The familiar sound of animals awaiting *shechita* (kosher ritual slaughter) seemed to shout in the ears of a Jew, "I'm home!" Even the unpleasant smell of those same animals created a certain sense of comfort. In short, the Jews of Radziejow felt secure and at ease among their *lantzmen* (Jewish relatives or friends).

At the turn of the twentieth century, Radziejow was part of Russia. The Russian occupiers were notoriously anti-Semitic. Russian soldiers would often make special visits to Radziejow for the sole purpose of harassing the Jews. They did this by pulling on the beards of religious Jews, among other degrading acts. These bullies had one purpose, to humiliate the hated Jews.

In an act of sheer desperation by the town's Jewish leaders, a delegation was sent to Germany, whose border at the time was about 30 miles away, to beseech the German government to take control of Radziejow. At that time, Germany was led by the Kaiser. After receiving this request, he ordered the German army to take control of the town. The German justification for this border seizure, among, of course, other considerations, was ostensibly to protect the Jews. And the

Jews, in fact, felt much safer under the protective umbrella of Germany.

Some decades later, when when Russia invaded Poland from the East in the beginning of World War I, many Jews actually fled to German-controlled territory because, historically, the Germans had treated Jews better than the Russians.

After Germany's humiliating defeat in World War I, Poland regained its independence. As per the terms of the armistice agreement imposed by the victorious allies, German territories and lands were taken away. The area surrounding Radziejow was incorporated into the newly established country of Poland. At that time, the population of the town was about 7,000 people. The Jewish population was less than 1,000.

In November of 1917, Vladimir Lenin, leader of the Communist revolution, took control of Russia. War broke out when the Communists attacked the nascent Polish Government. The war began in 1919 and ended in 1921. In a decisive battle, known today as the Battle of Warsaw, Poland was victorious. Many historians agree that this decisive battle essentially ended Communist plans to sweep across Western Europe.

During the war with Russia, the Jewish community of Poland was threatened with a particularly virulent strain of Polish anti-Semitism. A group of rabble-rousing nationalists claimed that the Jews had never fully assimilated into mainstream Polish society and therefore constituted a fifth column. They made the audacious accusation that the Jews had collaborated with Russia to help in its fight against Poland. Such sentiments reached Radziejow, where locals branded the Jews as traitors. These anti-Semites pointed out that in recent local history, the Jews had petitioned a foreign government, Germany, for their own benefit.

Motivated by greed, and under the guise of patriotism, city officials of Radziejow arrested several prominent Jews. These Jews were falsely charged with treason for their al-

14

leged collaboration with the Russians during the war. It was irrelevant to the persecutors and prosecutor that the accused Jews were never even involved in politics. This was a age-old scheme used by anti-Semites to extort money from the Jewish community. In this case, the plan was to implement a newly established criminal statute to justify the arrest of Jews and charge them with the capital crime of treason. Government officials dropped the hint that if the Jews were to pay a ransom the charges would be dropped.

The ransom demanded was the then-astronomical sum of 100,000 zlotys. When the Jewish community complained that this amount was impossible to raise, the officials doubled down and made it clear that if the Jews failed to pay the ransom, the hostages would be killed. To understand the enormity of the ransom demand, one need only review official documents that estimate the total value of all Jewish community property in Radziejow in 1938 as 18,000 zlotys. These crooked town officials demanded a sum over five times that amount.

The Jews of Radziejow, like many Jews throughout nearly 2,000 years of exile, painfully realized that the only way to save their innocent *lantzmen* was to somehow find a way to pay the ransom. The Jews that were appointed to collect the ransom by the *Kehillah* (Jewish Community Governing Committee) made it clear that if they failed to collect the ransom, the community would have to bear the guilt of standing by and watching the execution of innocent Jews. Left unsaid was the understanding that the hostages' execution would not be the end of this tragedy. The execution would in all probability be immediately followed by a *pogrom* (a violent, organized anti-Semitic riot) against the whole Jewish community. So, against all odds, the money was collected and presented to the extortionists before their arbitrary deadline expired. The hostages were subsequently released.

A short time after their release, the *Kehillah* filed a formal protest with the national government. To the credit of the new government of Poland, an investigation was conducted to determine the facts surrounding the payment of the ransom. The investigators concluded that malfeasance was perpetrated by several town officials. This resulted in an actual judicial proceeding. Evidence was presented to determine whether the Jewish community of Radziejow should be compensated as a victim of governmental corruption.

After a lengthy trial, the Court, to the consternation of a good many of the town's Poles, and to the surprise of all, ruled for the Jews. The Court ordered the local government to return the entire amount to the Jewish community.

MY FATHER AND
HIS FAMILY

My father was born in June of 1919. His Polish name was Binem Najman, and his Hebrew name was Simcha Bunim Naiman. Binem's parents were Shimon Naiman and Hinda Naiman (Pocziwy). Shimon was born in the town of Piotrków Kujawski, which was located about six miles south of Radziejow. Shimon's father's name was Moshe Naiman, and his mother's maiden name was Maria Braun. Moshe Naiman was a doctor that died in a plague. Unfortunately, we have no information about Binem's grandmother.

Shimon, Binem's father, was one of twelve children. The oldest sibling was named Hirsch. Hirsch was followed by Masha, Markus, Perel Gitel, Michal, Mindia Leczycka, Nachman Nachum, Israel Ber, Rivka, Shmuel, Avraham Yaakov, Shimon, and Mendel. At one time Shimon's brother Hirsch lived in Radziejow, because he married a woman from the town named Bajia Leszcynska. He and his wife had eight children. It is unclear whether Hirsch continued to live in Radziejow because my father never mentioned him in his interviews.

Shimon Naiman

My father said regarding Shimon's side of the family that they were not close. However, Manes, a cousin of Binem from his father's side and also a Holocaust survivor, lived in Radziejow and was among Binem's closest friends. Binem also mentioned that he had several cousins that were in the Polish Army when Germany invaded Poland. He said that those that were not killed during the invasion were captured and later murdered by the Germans.

Hinda was Binem's mother. Her maiden name was Pocz-ciwy. Her father's name was Baer, and her mother's name was Miriam. The Pocziwys had lived continuously in Radziejow since the 1700s. Hinda's grandmother was Hana Lajerowicz and her grandfather was Shimon Lajerowicz. Her great-grand-father was Jacob Gradowski and her great-grandmother was Maya Gradowski.

Hinda Naiman

Hinda was one of eleven children. The oldest was Hudis Wagner. Hudis was followed by Hinda, Max, Shimon, Izrael Szymcio, Hudes Rivka, Sam, Izrael, Gitel, Chava, and Chaim. Hinda's brothers and sisters lived in Radziejow. Sam, Izrael, and Max emigrated to the United States prior to the Holocaust.

Listing of the names of Binem's relatives here serves two purposes. First, to document the roots of the Naiman family and Binem's life in Radziejow. Additionally, it gives some hint as to the scope of the destruction created by the Nazi nightmare known as the Holocaust. A quick calculation reveals that both Hinda and Shimon came from families of ten to twelve siblings. Shimon and Hinda had eleven children, and each of their siblings had a similar number of children. Many of their children already had children prior to World War II. Only a handful actually survived the Holocaust.

These were typical large Jewish families who were almost completely wiped out in just one of many hundreds of similar villages that existed in rural Poland. A quick mathematical projection shows the sheer number of Jews murdered by the Nazi menace and the unbelievable scope of the Holocaust tragedy.

In historian Anthony Beevor's great work, *The Second World War*, he describes the approach of Soviet war reporter Vasily Grossman, stating that "the duty of survivors was to try to recognize the millions of ghosts from the mass graves as individuals, not as nameless people in caricatured categories, because that sort of dehumanization was precisely what the perpetrators had sought to achieve. In the same way, we attempt here to bring life to the individuals in our family who were murdered in the Holocaust.

Baer Poczciwy, Binem's grandfather on his mother's side, was by profession a horse trader. His reputation in the community was that of honesty and integrity in all his personal and business affairs. He was so honest that a incident he had with government authorities became folklore among both Jews and Poles of Radziejow.

At the border crossing between Russia and Poland, Baer had been asked by a guard if he had any contraband in his possession. He answered no. The guard proceeded to search Baer's belongings and discovered an undeclared bottle of contraband whiskey. Baer had truly forgotten about the bottle, but he realized that it appeared that he had lied to a government official. Baer thought fast and grabbed the bottle of whiskey from the startled customs official, drinking it in one giant gulp before the official could protest. The contraband was gone. A crowd of government officials and border guards surrounded the now inebriated Baer. After discussing the matter between themselves, they concluded that there was no evidence of contraband. With a smile on their faces, they let Baer pass. Thus, Baer maintained his reputation for honesty and never breaking the law.

Many skeptics believe that honesty and success in business do not go hand in hand. Even the skeptics had to admit that Baer was the exception to this rule. He was an example to both Jews and Gentiles. He was well liked and became one of the wealthier Jews in Radziejow.

Baer was rich enough to afford to arrange for his four daughters to marry Torah scholars. In the Orthodox Jewish communities of Poland, a *shidduch* (betrothal) of one's daughter to a Torah scholar was more prestigious than marrying a wealthy man. The best place for a father to find such scholars were in the Talmudic academies known as yeshivas. Baer was committed to marrying all of his daughters to Torah scholars. He traveled across Poland visiting the top yeshivas to find matches for his daughters from the very best *talmidim* (students).

Once he located a suitable prospect, he would offer the young man a generous financial package. This unusual method enabled him to entice three budding *Talmidei Chachamim* (Torah scholars) to court his daughters. For example, Gitel, Hinda's sister, married a red-bearded scholar named Hersh Jacob Witowski who came from a rabbinical family. Hersh supported his family by running a grocery store in Radziejow. Hersh's daughter, Holocaust survivor Joyce Wagner, said that her father was known to be the best *ba'al tefillah*, or leader of prayer services, in town. Unlike many Orthodox fathers, Hersh insisted that Joyce be given a Jewish education. Moreover, he was a large donor to the opening of Beis Yaakov Girls School in Radziejow.

Grave of Baer Poczciwy

Miriam Poczciwy, Binem's grandmother, was a pious woman who was beloved by the community. She was known for her generosity, especially for her efforts to help poor brides have weddings with dignity. She would raise money for the bride's dress, dowry, and wedding feast. As a result of her many contributions to the community, she was loved and respected by all the Jews in Radziejow.

Years before the outbreak of World War II, Baer passed away. Miriam's sons had immigrated to the United States. They insisted that she come to live with them in Milwaukee, Wisconsin. Since the brothers were all successful businessmen, they made sure that her life in the United States was extremely comfortable.

Miriam lived with her sons in Milwaukee until just before the beginning of World War II. To everyone's shock, she demanded that her sons send her back to Poland. Her sons tried to tell her that Jews from Poland and the rest of Europe were fleeing for their lives to the United States. Miriam didn't care. Instead, she gave them two reasons for wanting to move back to Poland. First, she maintained that the United States was not kosher enough for her. Second, she wanted to be buried next to her husband, Baer, in the Radziejow Jewish cemetery. I was also told by Gilda Wagner, the great granddaughter of Miriam, that a third reason for her return was to help care for the children of one of her sickly granddaughters.

Shimon Naimon was considered a *lamdan*, a learned scholar, and was among the best students at his yeshiva in Piotrkow. Baer offered him a deal that a yeshiva *bocher* (unmarried student), couldn't refuse. In exchange for marrying his daughter, Hinda, he promised to pay room and board at the Yeshiva for five additional years of study, and then set him up in the business of his choice.

The engagement was completed, and soon after Shimon and Hinda were married. As per the agreement, Shimon continued his studies. After five years of intense Talmudic studies, Baer set up Shimon in the shoe and leather business in Radziejow.

Shimon was quite successful in the leather business. As the business grew, so did the family. Shimon and Hinda had eleven children. Rivka was the oldest, followed by Harry, Masha, Max, Machel, Gucha, Ruta, Shmiel, Azriel, Binem, and Malka. His sister Ruta died at the age of 19 just before the outbreak of World War II when she choked to death on a chicken bone.

Naiman Family

My father once pointed out that the Jewish tendency to have large families created a sort of pension plan for their parents. When children were old enough, they were trained in the family business. Eventually they would take over the business, and the father and mother would retire. The children, in turn, were expected to support the retired parents during their old age. My father mused that in this system, elderly parents lived quite happily in a secure family environment without ever having to work again.

Due to this well-established system, Jewish boys from a very young age generally knew what their future would hold. Most boys would refrain from seeking out a different profession, for to do so would mark them as rebellious and ungrateful.

Shimon was a pious man. Every waking hour was spent devoted to learning and following the Torah. He was Radomsker Chassid. Radomsker Chassidim comprised a large sect with thousands of followers throughout Poland. The group was led by the Radomsker Rebbe, Rabbi Shlomo HaKohen Rabinowicz. The name "Radomsker" was derived from the name of the town in Poland where the Rebbe lived, Radomsk.

The Radomsker Rebbe was thought to be the richest rabbi in Poland. As a result of his great personal wealth, he was not beholden to donations, as he himself provided the bulk of the funds for maintaining the group's institutions. It is said that he gave half of his personal fortune for the upkeep of the sect's several yeshivas of higher Torah learning. He was also known for his extensive personal library, which was renowned among Torah scholars throughout the world.

It was the philosophy of Radomsker Chassidim that members that were scholars should remain in their own communities. This is in contrast to many Chassidic groups at that time, which encouraged scholars to live near the movement's Rebbe. The Radomskers emphasized constant Torah learning and avoiding distractions, such as local Jewish politics.

Radomsker Chasidim for the most part were businessmen that spent as much time as possible studying the Talmud. They were modest in lifestyle but generous both financially and spiritually. At a minimum, Radomskers tithed their gross income. Many pious Jews in Radziejow were Radomsker Chassidim.

When Binem was a young boy, he traveled with Shimon on several journeys to the city of Radomsk. There Shimon would arrange a private audience with the Radomsker Rebbe. Having a private audience with the Rebbe was considered a great honor for a Chassid. The Rebbe was believed to be endowed by the Creator with *Ruach Hakodesh*, divine inspiration. When a Chassid presented him with a personal problem, the Rebbe had the ability to combine his intellectual and spiritual powers to help advise him on how to deal with the challenge.

These private audiences were difficult to arrange. To have a private meeting with the Radomsker Rebbe, one began the process by writing out the problem. Then the note, along with a donation, was brought to the Rebbe's personal *Shammes* (assistant). Binem described the *Shammes* as a giant man with flaming red hair. The *Shammes* would consult with the Rebbe to determine whether he would meet with the supplicant. If the Rebbe agreed, the Chassid would wait his turn to be called into the Rabbi's private study for the consultation. This waiting period could take several hours.

Binem remembered one such audience with the Rebbe. It was the day his father took him on a journey to request an emergency meeting with the Rebbe. Shimon's daughter, Masha, was in the midst of a difficult pregnancy. She was a delicate woman of small stature. Her doctor felt that the pregnancy was very risky for Masha, and that her body would not be able to withstand the pangs of childbirth. Shimon, of course, was extremely distraught by this prognosis. Without delay, he rushed to Radomsk to ask the Radomsker Rebbe what should be done.

After an intense discussion, the Rebbe advised Shimon what seemed to Binem to be a preposterous solution. He told Shimon to buy a chicken and donate it to the poorest family in Radziejow. The Rebbe assured him that once this was accomplished, all would be well.

Binem remembered thinking that the Rebbe's solution to this life-threatening problem was questionable at best. Shimon, on the other hand, felt that if the Rebbe told him that the problem would be solved if he gave a chicken to a poor family, there was no reason to second-guess the Rebbe's advice.

So the first thing Shimon did when he returned to Radziejow was rush to buy a plump, healthy-looking chicken. He then made inquiries and determined which family in Radziejow was most in need. Shimon then cheerfully gave the chicken to that family. Having fulfilled the advice of the Rebbe, Shimon was satisfied that the problem had been solved. Time proved that the Rebbe's advice had been sound, as Masha actually had an easy birth.

It is interesting to point out that the Radomsker Rebbe, may his soul rest in peace, died a martyr's death several years later. During the liquidation of the Warsaw ghetto, the Nazis, in a surprise roundup, stormed into the Rebbe's apartment in the heart of the ghetto. He was there with his daughter and son-in-law. The soldiers ordered the Rebbe to come with them, and he refused. Clearly, it was his position that a Jew does not take orders from the enemies of God.

The Rebbe told them, "You are planning to kill me, so do so now, because I am not cooperating with you."

The Nazis again ordered him as well as the married couple to follow him. The Rebbe replied, "I am ready to die here in my room and not in a gas-wagon."

The Nazis in the room were infuriated. As a result of the Rebbe's righteous defiance, one of the outraged Nazis shot him in the head, and then shot and killed his daughter and son-in law.

Before World War II, two of Binem's older brothers immigrated to the United States: Harry in 1921, and Max in 1924. According to Harry's son Don, a retired English professor, Harry decided to leave Poland after an anti-Semitic incident that took place at his high school. Harry was the top student in his class. One teacher, a known anti-Semite, gave the class an assignment. Harry failed the assignment. The student who sat in front of Harry, who was considered one of the least intelligent students in the class, received a mark of excellence for the same assignment. After receiving his grade, Harry had a verbal confrontation with the teacher. Harry attacked the teacher for having made anti-Semitic statements in the past. This particular teacher had for many years expressed his anti-Semitism both in his words in the classroom and his attitude toward the Jewish students.

When the principal of the school confronted Shimon regarding his son Harry's behavior, Shimon sided with the school authorities. Shimon knew that if the argument escalated, Polish authorities would likely become involved and the government would inevitably side with the school. So, in order to maintain the balance of peace between the Jews and the government authorities, Shimon forced Harry to apologize. Harry, being a proud young man, was upset with his father's reaction. When Harry continued to argue his position, Shimon slapped Harry's face.

That day, Harry decided that he had had enough of Poland. He told his mother Hinda what had occurred. Hinda made arrangements with her relatives in America to assist. The relatives sent Harry a boat ticket for him to come to Milwaukee. Hinda then arranged with her father to bring his wagon to the Naiman building the night before the boat's departure, and wait under Harry's bedroom window. When the wagon arrived, Harry climbed out of the window and made his way into the wagon. Grandfather and grandson then travelled to the Port of Danzig, about fifty miles away. The next day, Harry boarded a ship bound for the United States.

According to my father's version of events, Harry left Poland because he was nearing draft age for service in the Polish Army. Army service in Poland was very difficult for Jews because of rampant anti-Semitism among soldiers and officers. Therefore, Shimon decided that Harry should leave Poland to live with his relatives in the United States.

Whatever the actual reason, Harry made his way to Milwaukee, Wisconsin to join his uncles and cousins from Radziejow. They helped him with both employment and housing. Harry was bright, a hard worker, and had excellent business acumen. He became a highly successful entrepreneur. He operated a number of businesses over the years and eventually owned a large retail garden supply complex. He married Ida, and had two children, Donald and Helene.

By the time Max, another of Binem's brothers, decided to go to America, the process had became more complicated. The immigration policy of the United States had changed. A strict immigration quota now limited the number of new immigrants allowed to enter. So Max decided to try his luck in Canada. Max gained Canadian citizenship by becoming a soldier. Still, his dream of joining his brother in Milwaukee remained. For several years, he actively sought entry to the United States.

Eventually Max was successful in attaining legal immigration status to the U.S., and not long after he was drafted this time into the American Army. He eventually settled in Los Angeles and owned a successful non-kosher butcher shop. He married Marcella and had three children, Sheldon, Helene, and Mark. My mother told me that the children's Hispanic nanny was a fervent, proselytizing Jehovah's Witness. Needless to say, two of the three children eventually converted to Christianity. Mark became a Jew for Jesus, and Sheldon became a Seventh Day Adventist. Their sister, Helene, remained Jewish.

Shimon Naiman was constantly asked to take on a leadership role in the community. However, he had no interest in engaging in local Jewish politics. As a rule, Radomsker Chassidim were known for their total devotion to the study of Torah. Shimon's main interests were Torah and his family, followed by his business.

Still, he did not neglect his community obligations. Shimon was the head of Radziejow's *Chevra Kadisha* (Jewish burial society). In Judaism, care for the dead is considered to be the greatest kindness one can give to his fellow man, for a dead person can neither show gratitude nor return a favor. Jewish laws concerning this ritual are complex and require a scholar to ensure that all aspects are properly carried out. Moreover, it is preferred that the man in charge of the *Chevra Kadisha* be pure in his devotion to the tenets of Judaism.

Shimon was also the trustee of the town's *Beis Din* (Jewish court). When Jews in Radziejow had civil legal disputes, those grievances were not brought to the town's secular court, rather, the dispute was decided by the Radziejow's Jewish Court. Torah law was the only law used to administer justice in this court. When money was at issue, the Court required that the amount of money in dispute be deposited with a third party. Even though there was an actual Jewish Bank in Radziejow located on Yiddishe Street, Shimon was the preferred person to hold the funds by both the court and the litigants. The reason was simple: everyone trusted him. The people of Radziejow would joke that even the Rabbi couldn't be trusted with the funds, lest after the case he say, "I already spent the money."

Shimon's reputation as a pious, God-fearing man was such that he was held in high esteem by not only the Jews of Radziejow but also the Poles. The Gentiles living near Market Square were delighted as they watched Shimon walk to shul every Friday evening. All the shops had already closed for the coming Sabbath. When Shimon emerged from the Naiman building on his way to shul, he was dressed in his best clothes in order to honor God's day of rest. Since Shimon was a wealthy man that spent his money freely to perform *mitzvot* (God's commandments), his Shabbos clothes were likely the finest available in Poland at the time.

To the average Pole, he was quite a sight to behold, with his long black dress jacket made of the finest silk. The jacket, known as a *bekishe*, is still worn by Chassidim today. On his head was a shiny, black, cantor-style hat made of silk. And, of course, being the owner of the largest shoe store in town, he wore high boots made of the very best quality leather available. Due to his sterling reputation, the Poles never subjected him to the usual anti-Semitic taunts or attacks that even the Rabbi of Radziejow had to endure. When I asked my father why Shimon was immune from the usual anti-Semitic behavior of their neighbors, he simply replied, "Of course he was never subjected to any taunting - he was respected."

Shimon's daily routine was set in stone. No matter what the season, he would wake up promptly at five o'clock in the morning. He would ritually wash his hands, get dressed, and then descend the stairs to the kitchen to prepare a cup of tea. Armed with his cup of tea, he would move to the parlor to continue studying the Talmud and its commentaries from the place he left off the previous night. He knew where he stopped by the bookmark he placed between the two portfolio pages of the tractate of the Talmud he was studying. For the next nearly two hours, he would study without interruption. At a few minutes before 7 a.m., he would replace the bookmark and close the book. He would then put on his coat, say good-bye to anyone in earshot, and then walk directly to the shul.

At shul he would don his *tallis* (prayer shawl) which was beige-white with black stripes, along with his black leather *tefillin* (ritual phylacteries). After ensuring that the strap was wrapped seven times around his arm, and that the *tallis* covered his head, he was ready to begin to *daven* (pray) with the required *minyan* (quorum of ten men). *Shacharis* (morning prayers) lasted for about an hour.

Once concluded, he returned to his residence, walking directly to the kitchen. He would then ritually wash his hands, say a blessing over a slice of bread or roll, then partake into a full breakfast prepared by one of his daughters. After eating and saying *birkas hamazon* (blessings after a meal), he would walk from the kitchen located in the back of the building down the long hallway to the door that opened to the store. The store opened promptly at 9:30 a.m. and remained open until 6:00 p.m. He would briefly leave in the afternoon to walk over to the shul to recite the midday prayers called *Mincha*. Upon closing the store for the evening, depending on the time of year, he would walk back to the shul for *Maariv* (evening prayers).

After the short service, he would return home to eat supper. When he finished, he would return to his specially designated chair located in the parlor and continue his studies from the point he left off in the morning. He would study non-stop until midnight. This was his schedule every day of the week until Friday evening, when it was time to celebrate the ushering in the Sabbath.

Occasionally, Shimon would have to reluctantly deviate from his routine in order to deal with family or community responsibilities. Shimon did his best to keep the outside distractions to a minimum. His main goal in life was to live by the rules of the Torah as practiced by his Chassidic sect, the Radomskers.

As Shimon's shoe and leather business continued to grow, he decided to relocate to a larger building. In the same year Binem was born, 1919, Shimon bought half of a building at a prime location in town, opposite one of the corners of Market Square. Although it was not on Yiddishe Street, a number of Jewish shops were located on the four sides of Market Square. Many of these store owners' sons were either friends of Binem or relatives such as the Levys, Markowskis, Frankenbergs, and Rosenbergs.

Market Square was famous for its flea and farmer's markets. Every Wednesday, with the exception of Jewish holidays, the market bustled with people. It was a joyful day for both the Jewish merchants and Poles. The Jews opened dozens of stalls in the square to display their wares. Even the Naimans had a booth, despite the fact that their store faced Market Square.

From the surrounding farms, scores of farmers and their families would travel to Radziejow to shop or operate a booth in the farmers' market. While in town, the farmers would buy shoes, clothing, and other items. The standard currency at that time was the zloty, however, bartering was sometimes conducted. A typical trade for the Naimans might be one or more live chickens for a pair of shoes.

Shimon's new building was large enough to accommodate both the business and a respectable and comfortable living quarters. So the family moved to the residential area of the building that was located behind the first floor storeroom as well as on the entire second floor. This expansion caused Shimon's business to become the largest of its kind in Radziejow

The Naiman building had three exterior entrances. The

main entrance for the store faced Market Square. A door on the side street opened into the Naiman's living quarters. Finally, there was a back door from the living quarters that led to the yard. At the rear of the store was a stockroom, which stored shoes and boots of different sizes, leather products, and machinery, along with tools used in the making and repairing of shoes. There was also a workspace for a shoemaker that made the leather tops for shoes. In the back of the storage room was an interior door that connected to a narrow hallway that led to the Naiman's living quarters.

The living quarters on the first floor consisted of a parlor, dining room, and a kitchen. Attached to the kitchen was a large pantry that was covered with a removable roof. During the holiday of Sukkot, the roof was removed and replaced with branches, creating a sukkah. The area became a dining room for all meals, as Jewish law requires all meals on Sukkot must be eaten in a sukkah. To many Jews in Radziejow, the Naiman Sukkah was considered the ultimate in convenience since it was attached to the kitchen.

The backyard was approximately 25 feet by 40 feet. Located near the rear was a wooden shed and outhouse. The shed was used to store coal and wood. Before Jewish holidays, the shed was transformed into a coop for poultry that were housed and fed in the shed. However, these birds were "free range," as the chicken and geese were able to run around the fenced-in yard. When needed, a chicken or goose was taken to the shochet (kosher slaughterer) on Yiddishe Street. A shochet is essential in a Jewish community, as, without his vital services, a Jew cannot eat meat. Meat was considered a luxury for the Jews of Europe, and Sabbath and holiday joy was symbolized by the eating of meat.

The upper floor of the building consisted of several bedrooms. Shimon's children slept according to their gender, two to a bed. Binem shared his bed with his brother, Azriel, who was a few years older than him. The two slept in the same bed together for nearly twenty years.

The building still stands today with the address being 5 Rynek. Rynek Street continues to be one of the main streets in Radziejow.

As I mentioned earlier, many of the Jews living in Radziejow were related. The Naimans had many aunts, uncles and cousins living in the town. I tried to elicit from my father the names of all his relatives in the town. Every time I did this, he would make excuses, saying, for example, he just couldn't recall. I wondered whether his subconscious was blocking this information as a way to protect him from having to deal with the full scope of the tragedy that he experienced, as the vast majority of his relatives were murdered during the Holocaust.

My father still had pleasant memories of his favorite uncle, Uncle Israel. Israel was Binem's mother's brother. He operated a very successful bakery. Anyone looking at Uncle Israel would immediately recognize that he had the look of a storybook baker. Uncle Israel was a big man, both tall and wide. He weighed well over two hundred and fifty pounds. He always had a smile on his face, and his jolly demeanor was infectious.

Uncle Israel's bakery was considered by both Poles and Jews to have the best baked goods in the area. He was well known for his tasty breads. Filling his bakery's display case was an excellent selection of different specialty breads. His two most popular items were his signature rye bread and his perfect Kaiser rolls.

Uncle Israel had a special love for Binem since he was the youngest of his sister's Hinda sons. Hinda died when Binem was only a few years old. As a result, Uncle Israel always kept an eye on him.

One day he decided that because Binem was a frail child, it was his responsibility to "put some meat on his bones." As a result, Uncle Israel insisted that Binem accompany him on his pickup and delivery route. As Binem grew older, this tradition continued during Binem's school vacations. Binem would ride shotgun on Uncle Israel's horse-drawn buggy during his daily flour purchases from the farms surrounding Radziejow. Uncle Israel always made sure that there was a big bag of rolls on the buggy seat for the two to nosh on. He would laugh and say in his jolly tone, "Eat, eat!" When Binem felt too full to eat even one more mouthful, Uncle Israel would continue to urge him, saying, "fat is healthy!"

Besides owning the bakery, Uncle Israel had a thriving grocery store. Near the front of the store there were several different candies and sweets that always attracted kids. For this reason, Binem was considered by his friends to be the luckiest kid in Radziejow. Uncle Israel gave Binem carte blanche to take as much candy as he wished. As a result, Binem and his friends all agreed that their favorite hangout was Uncle Israel's grocery store.

Before the beginning of World War II, Uncle Israel made the hard decision to leave his beloved Radziejow and emigrate to the United States. There he would join his two brothers, Max and Sam, in Milwaukee. Uncle Israel's bakery and grocery store were taken over by Binem's aunt and uncle, Hersz and Gitel Witkowski.

As a boy, just about every day, Binem would steal time away to play soccer with his friends. His father was against sports because he felt that they were a waste of time. He would admonish Binem by explaining that his time would be better spent in pursuit of Torah studies and not by running around and trying to kick a ball. He repeatedly told Binem, "When you grow up, you will be sorry for not studying harder."

I asked my father, "Nu? (was he right?)"

He replied, "Looking back on it, I wish I studied harder."

At the time, Binem did not care about the consequences of his lack of dedication to study. His father tried to avoid the subject, at least most of the time. And when it was brought up, Binem could never really be angry with his father because he understood that Shimon was a Torah scholar and he wanted him to follow in his footsteps.

It was not as if Binem had a great deal of time to waste. His day started at seven o'clock in the morning. After begrudgingly waking up, he would reach near his bed for the cup of water designated for ritual hand washing. This is a *mitzvah*, or Jewish commandment, known in Yiddish as *negel vasser*. With his hands dripping wet, he would get out of his bed to go to the washbasin and wash his face. Afterwards, he would dress in the clothes laid out for him by his sisters, then rush downstairs to the kitchen where a warm breakfast again prepared by one of his loving sisters would be waiting for him. After eating a hurried meal, Binem would rush to public school trying his best not to be tardy. School started promptly at eight o'clock.

Public school attendance was a mandatory requirement of the Polish government. The curriculum included math, reading, geography and history. The classes were mixed with Jews and Poles, both boys and girls. The majority of students were not Jewish, coming from the town itself and the outlying farms. Classes lasted until one o'clock in the afternoon.

After school, Binem would hurriedly walk home with his friends. Always on guard for ambushes by gangs of Polish youth, the Jewish boys walked together, feeling there was strength and security in numbers. And this security was needed for good reason. The Polish boys seemed to enjoy fighting, and especially fighting with the Jewish boys.

When I asked him to explain, Binem said that the Polish farm boys were mostly anti-Semitic because their parents were anti-Semitic. They were constantly looking to cause trouble with the Jewish kids. Ironically, Binem reflected on this and then stated that from his personal experience during the dark years of the Holocaust, some of these same "bad apples" eventually matured and actually helped him to survive.

Returning to his schedule, when Binem arrived at his

home he would go straight to the kitchen for lunch, again prepared for him by one of his sisters. After he finished his meal, he recited *Birkat Hamazon* (Grace after Meals). Then in a rush, he ran off to Cheder, which was Hebrew school. Cheder started at two o'clock in the afternoon and ended at seven o'clock in the evening. There he studied Mishna, Tanach and Gemorah, i.e. Jewish Law, the Bible, and the Talmud. Like the rest of the *kinder* (kids) his mind would wander, thinking about friends and things to do when he had some free time. After an exhausting day, Binem would return home and promptly sit down in the kitchen to eat dinner.

Binem was usually exhausted by the end of the day. If it was his choice, he would had preferred to have some free time or just nod off to sleep. But Shimon had different plans for his youngest son. Right after dinner, like an alarm clock, Shimon would summon Binem to join him in the parlor. Shimon would reach for one of the large leather-bound volumes of the Talmud and open it to the *daf*, or page, of where he last left off. Binem, being the youngest, had the obligation of this honor to study with his father, one of the most learned scholars in Radziejow. The reason for this exclusive honor is that Binem's brothers were already too old for Shimon to force them to participate. As a result of his being forced by his father to learn with him, Binem loathed this part of the evening. But, because he respected his father, for many years he never openly complained.

That changed when Binem reached his early teenage years and started to rebel. This rebellion was a slow and painful process because of his deep respect for Shimon. Binem began to complain in a roundabout way. He would sometimes mutter to himself in front of his father, "Why do my friends have more free time then I do? Why don't my friends have to study after dinner like me?" It took some time, but at age 15, Shimon eventually relented.

As the youngest son, Binem was always last in receiving privileges. For example, each week his sisters prepared the Shabbos cholent, a hot meat and bean dish. Also, they baked the family favorite, sweet noodle kugel. All baking and cooking was done prior to sunset because these activities are forbidden on Shabbos. However, in order for the cholent and kugel to be kept hot, they had to be kept in an oven large enough to hold the pots. Most Jewish households were equipped with small, primitive stoves, so the community would use the large ovens in the kosher bakery for keeping food hot over Shabbos. After the Naimans' Shabbos food was finished cooking and baking, it was placed in marked pots and transported by wagon to the kosher bakery that was located a few blocks away.

Binem's problem was that using a horse for transportation on Shabbos is strictly prohibited by Jewish law. So, Binem, because he was the youngest, had an embarrassing chore on Sabbath morning. Just prior to the Shabbos day meal, he was required to walk over to the bakery and *shlep* (carry) the heated items two blocks to the Naiman's kitchen. Among the Jewish youth in general, and Binem's friends in particular, anyone that performed this task was laughed at and derisively called the "Shabbos Kugel *Schlepper.*" It was considered a menial task done on a day when everyone else was enjoying themselves. As far as Binem was concerned, it was degrading. This feeling was unfortunately reinforced by Binem's friends as they stood near the bakery waiting for Binem to shlep the pots. As soon as he appeared his friends would crack up with laughter as they repeatedly shouted at Binem, "You are a kugel *schlepper.*"

One cold Sabbath morning, Binem was returning from the bakery with the pots, when suddenly in a moment of complete, overwhelming frustration, he rebelliously dropped both pots, causing the contents to spill all over the dirt-covered street. Binem, knowing full well the ramifications of this outrageous act, returned to the house with the two empty pots in hand. His sisters were understandably upset. However, to Binem's astonishment, when Shimon was told that there was not going to be a hot meal because of what Binem had done, instead of being angry and punishing him, Shimon was thoughtfully reticent. He seemed to know the reason behind Binem's "negligence." As a result of Binem's act, Shimon changed the rules so that all of his sons were required to participate in carrying the Shabbos food back from the bakery.

The majority of Radziejow's Jewish elderly were *frum* (religious). Many of their children, including adult children, were not. Still, out of respect for tradition, most of the Jewish townspeople, at least in public, observed the laws and traditions of the Sabbath. Of course, this had ramifications for the non-Jewish population. Since the vast majority of merchants were Jewish, the town business district was literally shut down Friday afternoon and reopened on Monday. Non-observant Jews and Poles alike could not shop on the Sabbath, because all stores were closed.

Even with the short work week, the Jews of Radziejow were financially better off than most of their Polish neighbors. While the peasants owned or held leases of the lands around Radziejow, the Jews of Radziejow owned and occupied a majority of the buildings used for commerce. As a result, Jews generally lived in better housing. The Poles recognized this, but found solace by mocking their Jewish neighbors, saying, "We own the streets, while you Jews only own the buildings."

Most Jews did not live near Market Square, so on the Sabbath the square was empty of commerce and transformed into a park for the Jewish community. It took on a festive atmosphere. Jews would promenade through the square on their afternoon walks that were part of their Shabbos routine. Jewish children would play soccer and other games in the center. Friends and relatives would meet to *shmooze* (talk). For the most part, the Sabbath was an idyllic day.

From an early age, whenever Binem was on vacation from school he would work in the family's shoe and leather store. In fact, everyone in the family worked there. With so many family members working, one might assume that the Naiman store was the only shoe store in town. However, there were in fact at least six other shoe stores in Radziejow. Competition was fierce to attract the limited customer pool. Amazingly, all the shopkeepers remained friends.

Binem's tasks included stocking the shelves, dusting the shoes in the display window, and, most importantly, waiting on customers. To increase customer flow, Binem would often be told to stand outside and watch for "live ones to reel in." Binem was able to spot these potential customers instinctively. They were usually farmers in town for the day. Binem would spring into action when they were within a few shops of the Naiman store. He would rush up to them and start a conversation. The farmers were both polite and amused as Binem would detail the amazing bargains available. Many times Binem was successful in getting the family to cross the threshold of the shop. Sometimes he would even physically pull them in. Once inside, the chances of making a sale increased manifold.

Binem reflected, "I did a very good job at pulling customers in. They weren't annoyed with me, in fact, they enjoyed it. For them it was a type of entertainment."

The only obstacle for Binem was the fact that all the shoe stores used the same method for increasing customer traffic into their shops. This resulted in confusion when members of a large family would be dragged into different stores at the same time.

The Naiman shoe store was also a wholesaler of different materials and tools that were essential for shoemakers. The store catered to both Polish and Jewish shoemakers around Radziejow. In Poland, shoemakers both made and repaired shoes. One of the keys to the Naimans' success was that their reputation for having the lowest prices on the different grades of leather and materials associated with the construction of shoes. Shimon, and then later Shmiel, who took over

general operations when he came of age, also had a strong relationship with area shoemakers, so the Naiman store had a
virtual lock on the wholesale distribution of leather and shoe-
making materials.

JEWISH LIFE IN RADZIEJOW

T he Jewish community of Radziejow was located in a row of houses and businesses along Torunska Street, better known as Yiddishe Street. The street was comprised primarily of small shops on both sides of a gravel road. Most of the shops had living quarters above and behind the retail space. They were, for the most part, little more than shack-like structures, with some of the larger stores being made slightly more elaborate by their adorned display windows. There were no trees lining the side of the road. The vast majority of the traffic on the street was pedestrian, along with a handful of horse-drawn wagons. Few motor vehicles were to be found traversing Yiddishe Street, or, for that matter, Radziejow itself.

There were two Jewish houses of worship in Radziejow. The first was located across from the corner where Yiddishe Street began. The building was not only a place for prayer, but also a school where Jewish children would study in the afternoons after finishing Polish public school. Within the building there were two separate *minyanim* (prayer services involving a quorum of ten or more men aged 13 or older as required for Jewish communal prayer), one Chassidic and one Traditional-Orthodox. The *minyanim* were conducted three times a day, 365 days a year. The building had a large *Beit Midrash* (study hall) as well as classrooms.

The second synagogue, Beis Rochel, was built in the mid-1930s. It was located near the center of Yiddishe Street, approximately five blocks away from the first synagogue. Beis Rochel, during its short period of existence, served mainstream Orthodox Jews along with modern or progressive Jews, and even some who considered themselves secular. The strictly observant Jews remained loyal to the old house of worship and study.

The first and only Rabbi of Beis Rochel was Chaim Plotgevitz. He was the Rabbi of the old shul starting in 1926. Rabbi Plotgevitz had pro-Zionist political leanings. In fact, his son Menachem immigrated to Israel after the Holocaust and lived there well into the 1980s. Menachem operated a liquor store on the main business street in Tiberias, next to the Sea of Galilee. The previous Rabbi was Sziojma Grodzinski who served the community from 1919 until he left this position in 1924.

The Jews of Radziejow were close-knit, like a family. In fact, many residents were in some way related to the others. Jewish neighbors that were not actually related were still seen and treated as distant relatives. Everyone in the town knew each other's name and a great deal about their neighbor's private lives.

While the elders of the community were for the most part strictly observant Jews, many young people were already straying away from the traditions that had held Jewish communities together for thousands of years. Like the non-Jewish youth, young Jews were being drawn to the "isms" that became popular across Europe. One major difference, however, was that the Jews were not only restricted from joining many of these new movements, they were in fact the scapegoat for two of the new "isms," Fascism and Nazism. Therefore, Jews straying from Judaism either embraced exclusively Jewish "isms" such as secular Zionism and Bundism or universal "isms" such as Communism.

Zionism was the Jewish political movement based on the proposition that Jews must end their exile by returning *en masse* to the State of Israel. Only by living in their own country, Zionists felt, would Jews be capable of living normal lives. In addition, Zionists believed that Jews would have to learn trades other than commerce, such as farming, carpentry, and construction in order to build a new nation in Israel.

The strongest Zionist organization in Radziejow was Hashomer Hatzair. Along with its adult membership, the organization included a youth group which was a branch of the same Jewish youth group in Israel known as the Scouts. Hashomer Hatzair was a left-leaning socialist movement that was associated with the Kibbutz movement in Israel.

Zionists in Radziejow established a Jewish Public Library and Reading Room in 1929. The literature was, of course, of the kind that promoted building a Jewish State in Palestine.

Hashomer Hatzair established summer camps throughout Poland. Its leaders encouraged young Jews to learn modern Hebrew and acquire the skills necessary to help develop the Land of Israel, such as farming. The idea was that graduates would "make Aliyah" (move to Israel) and join a kibbutz in Israel. This secular movement emphasized communal living. In many ways, it was a shining example of communist philosophy in action. The camp emphasized that all its members, both men and women, would be involved in decision-making for the community, and that every job was equally important. In theory, the elected members of the governing board had no more rights and privileges than the camp cook.

Throughout Poland, Hashomer Hatzair emphasized engaging Jewish youth, and therefore many of its activities were geared to entice young people to join. Members met once a week to learn the new Zionist songs and dances and listen to lectures about life in the Land of Israel. The group's goal was to build lasting relationships and a strong comradery among its members.

The highlight of being a member of Hashomer Hatzair was summer camp. The three-week retreats would be located on farms throughout Poland. During the day, the youth would learn skills necessary for life in Palestine, with an emphasis on hard physical labor. For many of these young Jews, this was a new experience. Jewish parents, in general, pampered their children to a very late age. When actual hard physical labor was needed around the house or for business, it was usually done by hired Poles. To many of these spoiled youth, the novel idea of working with one's hands was a new and pleasurable experience. With a pastoral camp setting and no real adult supervision, it was a very attractive vacation.

At night, after a hard day of work, the youth would be brought together to sing and dance. The camps stressed equality of the sexes. For many observant Jewish teens, this was a dream come true, since at home separation of the sexes was absolute. Here at camp, it would be their only opportunity to experience joint activities with the opposite sex. Orthodox parents that knew of this were appalled. But what could they do? They were at a complete loss of how to counter this twentieth century assault on traditional morals.

The Hashomer Hatzair movement was a Zionist variation of the philosophy of Communism. Both philosophies promised to create a utopian society. For many young Jews, this was a great draw. For thousands of years, Jews have awaited the Messiah, whose coming would usher in the Messianic Era. To many Jews it seemed that man had waited long enough, and it was now up to mankind to create a utopian society. Communism offered one alternative method to bring about this change. In the communist vision, Jews and Gentiles would abandon their religious differences and replace it with a political philosophy advocating the equality of man in which all workers would seek to create a just society.

Some young Jews were intellectually drawn to the idea that wealth should be shared to benefit all of society. They joined communist organizations such as the Union of Polish Youth and the International Red Aid as well as other communist-inspired community groups. In Radziejow it was no different. Jewish communists operated openly in Radziejow.

Jews that adhered to the communist philosophy maintained that if everyone is equal, then it stands to reason that anti-Semitism would end. This pie-in-the-sky approach fooled many Jewish youth, while most of their parents were understandably skeptical.

Bundism, not to confused with the religion of Buddhism, was a socialist secular Jewish movement. Its philosophy emphasized Jewish culture as opposed to the Jewish religion. The Bund was essentially a Jewish national political party that advocated the rights of Jews to be an accepted minority in European politics. The Bundist allegiance was nationalistic to the country they lived in. Therefore, for the most part, they were anti-Zionists and anti-communists because these groups pledged their allegiance to other outside entities. Bundists were very active in the community. The Bund established a Radziejow chapter called The Workers' Association of Physical Education.

The Orthodox Jews of Radziejow ignored these new ideas and focused on the time-tested traditions of the Torah, as elucidated by the Oral Law. As per tradition, observant Jews prayed that God would send a redeemer in the form of the Messiah to usher in an era when all Jews will return to live in Israel and worship at a rebuilt Temple in Jerusalem. These devout Jews prayed that God would continue to protect the Jews in exile until the Messiah would arrive.

From the beginning of the twentieth century, a new world of social upheaval had emerged in which traditional values were being pushed aside and replaced by new values. It was no different in Radziejow. Many families watched as members left the community to start new lives in other parts of Europe, the United States and Israel. Many young Jews had adopted the dress and language of the Gentiles and expressed opinions that were antithetical to everything their parents believed in. After a while, many of the pious Jews decided that it was a waste of effort to try and convince their children of the errors of their ways. So, for the most part, they were silent. The pious remained pious as they watched their children follow different paths. At the same time, they continued to pray silently to the Almighty that their children would return to the ways of the Torah.

Even with all these fundamental transformations occurring throughout Europe and in Radziejow itself, the Jewish community infrastructure remained intact. The Jews of Radziejow maintained a central authority to control both the civil and religious life of the community. It was as if the Jews had their own government operating within the government of Poland. The Jews held yearly elections to choose their governing board. In 1936, the community voted in a seven-member board, comprised of four Zionists, two Bundists, and one Orthodox Jew.

The Board was responsible for managing the community budget. Revenues were collected in the form of taxes from the Jews residing in Radziejow. The amount collected was based on a careful consideration of each individual family's ability to pay. Still, when a Jew would receive his bill, he would often contact the Board to try, as my father put it, to "chew down" the assessment. The Board of the Kehillah (community) used the funds collected to maintain the various Jewish institutions, fund holiday celebrations, and, of course, pay the Rabbi's salary. Also, the Board was responsible for representing the Jews of Radziejow in just about all dealings with Polish government officials.

Divorces and marriages, as well as monetary disputes among Jews, were brought before a Jewish court. The tribunal consisted of the Rabbi and a few learned individuals in the community. The decisions of the Court were final and respected by all. Anyone that disregarded the ruling of the court faced the prospect of excommunication, which included not being permitted to be buried in the Jewish Cemetery. This punishment was rarely, if ever, imposed. Just the thought of the possibility of such a penalty kept all litigants in line.

The Orthodox controlled other institutions, such as the organization Gemilus HaChesed. It distributed charitable funds, ran an interest-free loan society, and was responsible for the Chevra Kadisha, or Jewish burial society.

Social activities were limited, as Radziejow was a relatively small rural town. Still, the community maintained a Yiddish theater. There was also a sports club called Maccabi. The club established a soccer team in 1930 that competed with both Jewish and Polish teams.

In the 1900s, the majority of trade in goods and services in Radziejow was controlled by Jews. A virtual monopoly was held on certain goods, For example, leather was essential in the production of many products such as shoes, belts, overcoats, purses, and wallets. Shimon built up his leather goods business to be the largest of such enterprises in the Radziejow area.

Jews were also bakers, tailors, barbers, glassmakers, shoemakers, and painters. Survivor Roman Rogers's family sold bicycles, bicycle parts, sewing machines, farm equipment, and cow milking machines. Other Jews owned a variety of stores featuring general merchandise, food, and hardware. There were also watchmakers and silversmiths, as well as other types of artisans. The town's only doctor, Dr. Paniski, was Jewish.

Jews were also involved in finance. There was a Jewish bank. Roman Rogers's brother was a securities broker. He specialized in the purchase and sale of Polish Government bonds issued on a regular basis starting in 1920.

Many of the Jews in Radziejow enjoyed their wealth by buying the latest inventions. For example, Roman Rogers was from a wealthy family that owned two businesses, one in Radziejow and another in a larger town located twenty miles away. The Rogers always had the most cutting-edge products available in rural Poland. He remembered that among his family's more interesting possessions were a motorcycle and a Ford Model T.

A favorite spot for the young and old was the kosher delicatessen located a few doors down from the Naiman Shoe Store, one of two restaurants in Radziejow. Survivors in Toronto told me that my father and friends would hang out at this restaurant. While enjoying a tasty *haimishe* (homemade) sandwich with friends, they would tell jokes and schmooze about the latest news.

The shul was the official place where Jewish men gathered. There they prayed together three times a day. Before services and after, the less pious among the participants would *kibbitz* (talk) with one another about their lives, both their triumphs and failures. During times of illness and tragedy, they would console one another. When a death occurred in the community, the shul members would rally behind the bereaved, bringing the family of the deceased meals and whatever else was needed, such as monetary assistance and interest-free loans, to help ease the burden.

When there were *simchas* (happy events), the Jews would celebrate together. There were always engagements, weddings, circumcisions, and bar mitzvahs to attend. Gifts were generously given to make sure that the recipient understood the invitee was truly thankful to be included in the celebration. Survivor Henry Gronow remarked that the celebrants often had to restrict the list of invitees to only closest relatives, otherwise it would be necessary to invite all the town Jews to every affair.

For Jews in Radziejow, Shabbos (Saturday, the Sabbath day) made the toils of daily life worth living. Preparation started Thursday when the wives and older daughters went to Yiddishe Street to purchase baked goods, meat, vegetables, and other ingredients for cooking. Thursday night and Friday morning, Jewish women cleaned their houses and cooked for the *Shalosh Seudos* (three meals required on the Sabbath). Just prior to Shabbos evening, Jews closed their shops and went home to put on their finest clothes. The women lit the Shabbos candles and set the table as the men walked to the shul on

Yiddishe Street.

In shul, the men exchanged pleasantries concerning the week until services began. The *Kabbalat Shabbat* prayer service was highlighted by the singing of *Lecha Dodi*, ushering in the Sabbath bride. After *Maariv* (evening prayers), the men returned home to the first of three festive meals. The father blessed his children then made *Kiddush* (Sabbath blessings over wine). Then the family would ritually wash their hands and wait silently until the father made *HaMotzi* (blessing over the bread). The family then ate the best meal of the week. During the dinner, men sang *zmiros* (special songs for the Sabbath).

The next morning, men, boys, and some women went to shul for the morning service. As they prayed, they gave thanks to God for all the blessings He had bestowed upon them during the week. After services, the family gathered at the dining room table to enjoy the second festive meal. The main dish was cholent, a bean or barley-based chili-type preparation with meat or potatoes, which was served piping hot. The men again sang special *zmiros*. Afterwards, it was quite common to see entire Jewish families, when weather permitted, promenade down Yiddishe Street. The more adventurous leisurely hiked in the adjacent fields and forests. Some of the majestic green hills surrounding Radziejow were cautiously avoided, because vagrant squatters would occasionally attack Jewish wayfarers. In fact, many Jews feared visiting the Jewish Cemetery, because the road leading there passed these dangerous hills. Other Jews would take a peaceful Shabbos *schluf* (nap).

In the late afternoon, men would return to shul for the *Mincha* service. When they returned home, the family sat together and sometimes hastily ate the third festive meal. After *Birkat Hamazon* (grace after meals), the men went back to shul for evening prayers. Once a month, services were followed by the blessing on the new moon. Then the men returned home and the family gathered around the table to hear the father conduct the *Havdalah* service. Spices for smelling were passed around, and a multi-wick candle was lit. When the father was finished, he drank the special cup of wine leaving just enough to douse the candle's flames. This service formally ended the Sabbath and ushered in the new week. In Radziejow, most Jews had an additional day off of work because of Blue Laws prohibiting working on Sunday.

When Binem was four years old, his mother, Hinda, passed away at the relatively young age of 52. She died of unknown causes. She was a true *Eishes Chayil* (valorous wife). Her life was dedicated to her husband and children. Even in her last days, despite suffering from a terrible illness which was most likely pneumonia, she manned the Naimans' outdoor booth in Market Square. When she died, Shimon was grief-stricken. Hinda was the only woman he had ever loved. She had bore for him eleven children: six sons and five daughters. She had worked side by side with Shimon in the store, while at the same time caring for the needs of their large family. After Shimon finished the thirty day mourning period, someone asked him if he planned on remarrying. Shimon answered him, "I have only one wife."

In accordance to his faithful love for Hinda, Shimon never remarried. Her grave and its monument stood as what Shimon wanted to proclaim as eternal testimony of his devotion and love for her. Some years later, as a direct result of Nazi and Polish anti-Semitism, not only the monument but even her actual body was desecrated and destroyed.

When a Jew in Radziejow died, he or she was taken to the Jewish cemetery. It was located to the south of the town, in the countryside near the road to the nearby town of Pitrokow. The cemetery was located on a large parcel of land. It consisted of a graveyard and a large adjacent building that was used both as shelter and a place where bodies were ritually cleansed according to Jewish law before burial. During the time of the ritual cleansing, the Book of Psalms was recited and repeated by a *shomer* (guard) until the burial. The *shomer* was usually a relative of the deceased or an especially holy member of the community who performed the task sometimes voluntarily and sometimes for pay. As the cemetery grew in size, a six-foot-high chain-link fence topped by barbed wire was installed to protect the grounds.

The graveyard consisted of graves marked with *Matzevos* (grave markers). They were made of wood, granite, or marble that ranged in height between three and six feet. Since the Jewish population was small, anyone visiting a beloved one's grave was comforted when he glanced at the adjacent graves and read the names on the headstones of the deceased that were once their neighbors.

Hinda's monument, as compared to all the other grave markers, was considered by all a remarkable work of art. It was built so it would tower over the entire cemetery. It was comprised of a large marble base topped with an intricately carved wood pillar crafted to resemble the *Etz Chaim* (Tree of Life). At approximately eighteen feet high, it stood out as the outstanding monument in the cemetery. In fact, since it could be seen from great distances, locals used it for navigation.

The monument seemed to beg the question: why would the Jewish community permit a mourner to erect such an ostentatious edifice? The answer is simple: Shimon Naiman. Shimon was a Torah scholar known to everyone as a humble and pious man. He was anything but a braggadocio. So the administrators made an exception. They realized that the monument represented Shimon's last statement, an unabashed proclamation to the world that cried out to all who saw it that Shimon painfully mourned the passing of his wife.

After Hinda died, the responsibility for the day-to-day supervision of raising the two youngest children, Binem and Malka, fell upon their sisters. Shimon's daughters did their best to continue the pattern of childrearing that Hinda so expertly executed during her lifetime. One problem that confounded the sisters was that Binem was a poor eater. The sisters tried various methods to encourage Binem to eat, but all failed. Mimicking Uncle Israel, the sisters would say, "We must put some meat on his bones!" No matter what the sisters cooked to entice him to eat, Binem would just pick at his food. As a result, he was considered an undersized, sickly child.

When Binem reached the age of seven, he was required by law to attend Polish elementary school (*szkoła podstawowa*). Compulsory education was mandatory until the age of 14. This caused Shimon much concern. He knew by law that Binem must attend school. On the other hand, he was being constantly told by both his sons and daughters that Binem was just too frail to be able to withstand the daily schoolyard brawls instigated by the Polish youth against the Jewish children. Unfortunately, the Jewish elementary school in Radziejow had closed just before Binem was born. The closure was a great loss to the Jewish community. The Jewish elementary school had taught a curriculum that was acceptable by the Polish government and had allowed the Jewish children to learn in a safe environment.

Shimon made a decision. In order to protect Binem, he

sent him to live with his older daughter Rivka (Regina), who was happily married to Yaakov Fleishhocker and living in the nearby town of Lipno. In Lipno there was a Jewish elementary school. Binem remained with his sister until he finished the second grade. By then, Binem's eating habits changed. As a result, he grew into a strong boy that was ready to withstand the anticipated harassment he would encounter when he was scheduled to begin public school in Radziejow that fall.

The Jewish young boys donned caps to public school instead of the yarmulkes that they wore at home. Jewish schoolboys knew that a yarmulke was a tempting treat for their Polish classmates playing in the schoolyard. Once a yarmulke was spotted, Polish kids would compete to be the first to grab it. But grabbing away the yarmulke was only the beginning. The Polish kids would then play a perverse game of keep-away by tossing the yarmulke from one to another as they watched with glee as the helpless Jewish boy tried to retrieve it. Rarely would he be successful in intercepting the yarmulke; however, when recess was just about to end, the game would be concluded when a Polish classmate threw the yarmulke to the ground in disgust, with the accompanying derogatory slur *Zid* (Jew)!

Polish youth, especially those from the outlying areas of Radziejow, would form gangs. Binem commented that the typical gang member ranged from mentally slow to just plain dumb. These gangs' main recreational activity was attacking Jewish pupils. Among the Jewish boys it was known that a lone Jew was a guaranteed target for harassment. So, to counter this, Jewish classmates made it a priority to stick together in a buddy system. This mutual defense strategy worked best when the buddy system consisted of at least five boys. The plan was to show a formidable united front and, if need be, to fight as a team. No matter how weak or frightened the Jewish boy was when his group was in a schoolyard skirmish, he would fight to the best of his ability.

Total decisive victory against the aggressors was not

possible. If they were too successful in fighting back, the older Polish students that were watching would come to the aid of the younger ones. In contrast, Jewish older pupils reacted differently. They never came to the aid of the younger boys because it would only escalate the problem.

I asked my father, "Didn't your older brothers come to your aid?"

He smiled, "They had their own problems."

Deep down, the Jewish boys knew that they were ultimately no match for their physically superior gentile opponents.

My father explained, "When we were ten Jewish boys walking together and we saw two Polish kids with a stick crossing our path, we would say to each other, 'Run, we're outnumbered!'"

This strategy of Jewish mutual defense resulted in lifelong relationships among the members. The boys would always hang out with one another even when there was no actual threat. Upon graduation from public school at the age of 14, the boys continued their friendship. Even after the Holocaust, those that survived remained lifelong friends no matter which country they eventually settled. This comradery remained because it was forged in the furnace of suffering and occasional triumph.

The Naiman family members often discussed the anti-Semitism in Radziejow. Verbal attacks were routine. Stones were regularly hurled at Jews as they walked outside of Yiddishe Street. Even the Rabbi was not immune from such attacks. There was little the Jews could do but endure.

Fortunately, the Jewish community were able to bribe local law enforcement for protection. The Jewish shopkeepers were very liberal in showering gifts and money on policemen when they entered their establishments. This curried their favor, ensuring the officers would quickly intervene to protect the Jews from threats when necessary.

Radziejow survivor Ann Goldman Kumer confirmed

that even as a female pupil she was not immune from the anti-Semitism to which the boys were subjected. She remembers cringing when a Jewish classmate received a high grade on a test or homework. There were sneers from the Polish pupils as they said in an undertone that the only reason that pupil received a high grade was because he was a *Zid*.

In the Naiman home, Binem remained closest to his brother Azriel. During the day, when not in school, Azriel and Binem were constant companions. Azriel was a child prodigy. His ability to solve complex math problems was uncanny. He was grudgingly considered a genius by his teachers, for he would often correct their mistakes. At some point Azriel's math teacher started to doubt his own computations. In order to avoid being corrected in class, this teacher would consult with Azriel before presenting certain difficult math problems to the class.

At age thirteen, Binem became a secret member of the Hashomer Hatzair Zionist youth group. Radziejow survivors such as Jack Marcus, Ann Goldman Kumer, Roman Rogers, and Joyce Wagner fondly remembered their experiences as members of this organization.

Binem felt forced to keep his membership secret from his father. The reason for this was his father was religious, and Hashomer Hatzair was a secular socialist movement. Not only that, Hashomer Hatzair advocated that return to the Land of Israel would be achieved through Jewish action. Shimon was deeply opposed to this philosophy. Though Orthodox Jews had quietly been returning to Israel for hundreds of years, most of these Jews were non-politically motivated rabbinical scholars that settled in the holy cities of Tiberias, Safed, and Jerusalem. They had no intention of building a Jewish state; their return was an expression of personal religious devotion with no connection to nationalist aspirations.

The Zionists differed in that their ultimate goal was to establish a country for the Jews as soon as possible. Orthodox Jews were not all against this concept, but they were concerned that the Zionists were for the most part not God-fearing Jews. Shimon adhered to the traditional view the in-gathering of exiled Jews from *Gallus* (the Diaspora) would be initiated by the Messiah. When the Messiah would actually come was beyond man's ability to predict, however, as famously codified by the Jewish sage Maimonides (the Rambam), a Jew must believe that the Messiah is coming imminently, and even if he delays one must still wait.

A compromise position for some believing Jews was articulated by Rav Avraham Isaac Kook (1865-1935), the first Chief Ashkenazi Rabbi during the British Mandate. Rav Kook believed that the Zionist movement was part of God's plan in bringing about the Messianic Era. Of course, he would have preferred that the Zionists acted in accordance to God's commandments. Still, Rav Kook honored the *Halutzim* (Zionist pioneers) for reclaiming the land in order to set the groundwork for the future spiritual redemption.

Binem's friends were active participants in the secular Zionist group, and that placed Binem in a dilemma. Whenever Binem hinted to his father that he wanted to join, Shimon was quick to reply that Binem was forbidden to be associated with people who did not respect God's commandments. Shimon tried to explain to his son that the group he wished to join was anti-religious and promoted values that were not in accordance with Jewish law. His favorite proof was that mixed folk dancing took place. In Shimon's opinion, any organization that promotes such behavior was antithetical to the sacred law. Binem listened and nodded, but inwardly did not agree.

By 1939, the year Poland was invaded, Hashomer Hat-zair had grown to an astounding 70,000 members in Eastern Europe. With the rise of Nazi Germany in the late 1930s, the group urgently shifted its focus from the training of agricultural workers for the settlement of Palestine to that of mutual defense of the coming onslaught of the Nazi juggernaut.

Binem knew that eventually his father would discover

his defiance. On the one hand, Binem respected his father and abhorred the idea that he was acting against his wishes. On the other hand, he was a typical adolescent that wanted to think and behave like the other young Jews of Radziejow. So, against Shimon's direct orders, Binem would sneak out at night and attend these Zionist gatherings in order to have a "good time" with his friends.

Binem became quite involved with Hashomer Hatzair. As summer approached he knew that a showdown was inevitable. The Hashomer Hatzair organized a three-week sleepover summer camp, which Binem and his friends were required to attend. Binem procrastinated to commit as he was afraid of Shimon's reaction. Binem had already graduated from public school and was expected to work daily in the store with his brothers and sisters. He knew that they would cover for him if Shimon, who was by now retired, would unexpectedly enter the store. But surely his lack of attendance at religious services and Shabbos meals would attract Shimon's attention.

When his friends had all already signed up for camp and the final date for applying was approaching, Binem summoned up the courage to ask his father.

"I decided that I'm going to the Hashomer Hatzair camp," Binem said.

Shimon's answer was that he would not be allowed to attend, period.

Binem was visibly upset. "Why can't I go, all my friends are going?" he asked.

Shimon replied, "If you go, you will skip *davening* (prayer services), and you might even be served *chazir* (pig), God forbid."

Binem understood, for in his heart he knew that his father's concerns were probably true. Still, he was resolved not to take this refusal as the final resolution of this matter. In Binem's mind, if he did not attend he would no longer be respected among his peers.

Binem had a contingency plan. He staged a protest in

the form of a hunger strike. He announced his intentions in front of the entire family. Binem stopped eating. Binem's sisters later, in private, convinced him that he didn't actually need to stop eating, rather he needed only to appear as if he was on a hunger strike. Binem thankfully agreed. He ate food that his sisters secretly supplied him, The sisters' motivation was that they were afraid, God forbid, that Binem would starve himself to death. Shimon never discovered Binem's cheating, so as the hunger strike continued Shimon became more and more distressed.

Shimon became so worried about the health of his youngest son that he began to waiver. He reasoned that, according to the Jewish Law, the concept of *Pikuach Nefesh* (life-threatening danger), required him to act. So he consulted the Rabbi, Chaim Platkiewicz. After a scholarly discussion, Rabbi Platkiewicz decided to get involved. Acting as a kind of arbitrator, as he was known for his own positive leanings towards religious Zionist philosophy, the Rabbi met with Binem. When he was done, Rabbi Platkiewicz told Shimon that he believed that his son was so determined to attend the summer camp, he would continue his hunger strike at the risk of ruining his health. The Rabbi explained that while Hashomer Hatzair was a secular group with a novel approach to Jewish values, its members were Jews and definitely not *Goyim* (Gentiles). It was his opinion that Shimon should consider allowing his son to attend the camp if Binem would pledge to eat strictly kosher food and *daven* (pray) three times a day as required by Jewish law.

I asked my father, "Did you daven every day, like you promised your father and the Rabbi?"

He replied with a smirk, "Only when I had a chance."

I pressed him for a more complete answer. "How often did you have a chance?"

Binem answered, "What was I to do? My friends would have laughed at me if I put on my tefillin."

So Binem attended the camp, whose attendees were

members of Hashomer Hatzair chapters located throughout Poland. The camp was operated as if it was a working kibbutz, and the campers were required to do farm work, attend lectures, and participate in evening social activities. For the first time in his life, Binem was free of religious obligations. He truly enjoyed the companionship and unity of purpose presented by the dedicated camp staff. Before the camp experience, he viewed his life through the black-and-white lens of Jewish existence as experienced in the village of Radziejow. The camp opened up a new vista that was bathed in the vibrant colors of a land which Jews were reclaiming after thousands of years of exile.

Binem remembered one particular staff member who he described as a strong, handsome man: Mordechai Anielewicz. Binem was impressed by the way Anielewicz naturally carried himself, and felt that this strapping young man exuded leadership. And Binem was right. Anielewicz became a legendary Jewish hero who was the face of Jewish resistance during the Holocaust. Anielewicz led Warsaw's Jewish underground that defied the unstoppable German juggernaut and managed to bloody the nose of the bully. He did this by first leading the ghetto fighters to assassinate Jews that actively cooperated with the Nazis. These traitors had acted for their own benefit at the expense of their fellow Jews. Anielewicz then planned and led a Jewish revolt that not only killed scores of Germans and their proxies, but also aided the Allied cause by forcing Germany to deploy vital war resources to put down the uprising.

Anielewicz's actions restored a sense of Jewish self-worth and nationalist pride that resonated around the world. His unequivocal martyrdom proved to both Jews and the Gentile world that there was a choice, an alternative way to die for those targeted by the Nazi extermination machine. Even today, his actions are referenced by officers of the Israel Defense Forces as a source of inspiration, proving that even when a situation seems hopeless there is always a choice to act valiantly.

Binem was not alone in being inspired by the camp experience. In fact, several of his friends made Aliyah to Palestine prior to the Holocaust. Those that had gone were miraculously untouched by the ravages of the Holocaust. One can see God's hand in this, because Palestine, which had been considered a dangerous place for Jews, turned out unexpectedly to be one of the safest places in the world for Jews during the Holocaust. Although Germany had plans to conquer Palestine, they were stopped in Egypt by the British in the famous battles at Al Alamein and Tobruk. As a result, Hitler put his plans to conquer Palestine on hold while continuing his conquests of Europe, Asia, and Africa. Moreover, Jews were even exempt from being drafted to fight the Germans, because the authorities of the British Mandate refused to allow Jews living in Palestine to serve in the British Army.

Binem's experiences at the camp and as a member of the Hashomer Hatzair had a profound effect on his adolescent years. Interestingly, when discussing the camp with my father's first cousin, Joyce Wagner, I had the feeling that she likewise felt that the camp was a turning point in her life.

For me, it was difficult to understand how a three-week camp could have such a lasting effect. When we discussed the camp, I watched my father's face change, which gave me the feeling that he was trying to find an answer deep in the recesses of his consciousness.

He said simply, "It was my best experience in Poland."

When Binem returned from summer camp, disaster struck the Naimans. The Naiman building was destroyed by a fire. The conflagration was accidental. The fire began in the neighboring carpentry workshop that comprised one half of the building, and spread quickly, eventually engulfing the Naiman's half. The family barely escaped with their lives. Many of their possession were burned in the inferno.

Like most provincial buildings throughout Poland, the building and their belongings were not insured. When the Naiman brothers Harry and Max who were living in the United States heard the bad news, they quickly sent enough money to rebuild the building, restock the store, and furnish the house. My father said that all of this was accomplished because at that time the dollar was very strong in Poland. In fact, enough money was sent to build an even better building.

The Jews of Radziejow were primarily focused on two goals. First and foremost was the observance of Jewish laws and traditions. Their other goal was to have a *parnosa* (earn a living). A good *parnosa* meant food on the table, a roof over one's head, and a sense of security against the hostile outside world. However, when opportunities for financial gain clashed with Jewish values, economic considerations took a back seat.

A good case in point was the town's domestic referral service. Most Jews in town, whether they could afford it or not, employed a maid. Ability to afford such a luxury didn't matter, because having a maid created the appearance of success. One enterprising Jewish woman capitalized on this symbol of status. This Jewish woman earned her living by finding maids among Polish women that lived on farms surrounding Radziejow. She received a commission each time she placed a maid with a homeowner. Her problem was that there were not enough homeowners to sustain this type of business. To solve this problem, her business plan called for a high turnover of maids. Thus, this shrewd woman schemed to have the maids constantly shuffling from one household to the next. She would solicit offers from other Jews to lure a maid away from her present job. The maid was happy to get a raise in pay and the woman was delighted when she received a new commission. The Jewish household that lost the good maid would then turn to the woman to find their household a new maid, and hopefully an even a better maid than the last one.

Everyone in town knew this shuffling of the maids was a bit of a scam. However, the Jews allowed this to continue. For they knew that the proprietor needed a means to support herself. And besides, shouldn't a good maid get a better salary? So no one protested or became indignant over the arrangement. Instead, it was viewed as just another reality of life in Radziejow. In other words, it became a tradition. And traditions were the lifeblood that kept the community together.

There were other local characters that helped keep the town's Jews smiling. For example, one of the more famous members of the community was Reb Yuko, a tailor by profession, but better known for being the *gabbai*, or beadle (Rabbi's assistant). He was praised for his devotion to community service. Reb Yuko was the manager of *Hachnosas Orchim*, the organization responsible for welcoming Jewish visitors. Radziejow had few hotels or inns for overnight visitors. Survivor Jack Marcus stated that his grandfather operated a type of inn about two blocks from his grandfather's home that housed up to six travelers. But the majority of itinerant salesmen staying overnight would go directly to Reb Yuko. He then assumed responsibility to arrange kosher meals and a place to sleep for the visitor.

Reb Yuko was entrusted with extraordinary powers. He was authorized to assign a Jewish household to board a guest. The way he did this was by issuing a voucher. On this form, which was issued under the official authorization of the Kehillah (local community council), was a place for Reb Yuko to fill in the name and address of a community member who would be obligated to host the visitor. While everything looked official, unofficially everyone knew that the Jews of Radziejow would gladly host a visiting Jew with or without a voucher. The reason for such hospitality was that hosting a visitor is an important mitzvah (commandment) from God. The Jews on Reb Yuko's list of hosts were always interested in doing a mitzvah. Still, Reb Yuko managed *Hachnosas Orchim* in a way that everyone would have an opportunity to share in this mitzvah.

Reb Yuko lived a pure, austere life and was considered to be the most humble of all Jews in Radziejow. As a result, he was a local legend. The more he tried to dissuade others from putting him on a pedestal, the more famous he became. He was considered by many of the townspeople to be a true *Lamed Vavnik*. Literally translated as "thirty-sixer," this refers to the Jewish tradition that in every generation there are thirty-six holy Jews that cause God to renew his covenant with humans not to destroy the world. No one knows who these *Lamed Vavniks* are, but that doesn't stop some Jews from guessing. In order to obtain this status, the person must be considered by God to be both pure and righteous. To many, Reb Yuko fit the bill. He was an extremely humble and honest man, and as far as the townsfolk were concerned, he was a saint without equal.

It was told that one day a rich Jew living in Radziejow approached Reb Yuko and made an amazing proposition. "Reb Yuko, I will give you ten thousand zlotys if you would only pledge that you will change places with me in the World to Come."

As expected by all, Reb Yuko refused the money. But what was surprising was why. He told the man that even if he offered all the money in the world it would not guarantee that God would honor such an exchange. Therefore he couldn't possibly take the money, because that would be the equivalent of stealing. And if he indeed stole this man's money, then what good would the agreement be, because the man would be changing places with a thief. "Who knows? By taking your place in the world to come, I might be far better off than you!"

Being careful not to completely disappoint the rich man, he gave the man an alternative. "You would be better off just giving the money to charity."

Another well-known personality was Shmeil Zeifer, a teacher at the Jewish Academy in Radziejow. He was a secular, assimilated Jew that taught non-religious subjects, and was an excellent teacher by all standards. The students loved his stories and his personal interaction with them. However, he was not without his detractors.

The religious parents wanted Zeifer to be fired, but they

reluctantly agreed to allow him to teach secular subjects. They did so only because all Jews in Radziejow felt that the times were changing. Many young adults were no longer clinging to the old traditions. They could not blame Shmeil Zeifer for this change. He was merely one of the early "converts." The pious Jews remained pious, but had little choice but to allow their children to explore the new sources of secular knowledge. Zeifer allowed them to do so in a safely protected Jewish environment, as opposed to the dangers inherent in sending their children to Polish public school.

Another character associated with the school was a man whose name was Shverek. He was better known as "Yisroel with the Clopper". His job was to ring the bell to call the children to school. Both children and adults anticipated the ringing as part of the natural flow of a day in Radziejow. People would even arrange their schedules according to the sound of his bell. Yisroel's predictable bell-ringing gave the Jews of Radziejow a sense of security and continuity.

Another colorful character of Radziejow was Calman Hirsch. He was a poor man that always had a smile on his face. When Calman smiled, all of Radziejow's Jews smiled with him.

Also, there was Toiver Guluf (Guluf the Deaf Guy). The story of how he had become deaf was well-known in Radziejow. A roofer by profession, he was contacted by a member of the church during a terrible storm. He was told that the church's roof had been damaged and was leaking. Guluf was fearless, and would work even which it was raining. He also only used a minimal amount of safety equipment.

Guluf braved the weather and went to work. Unfortunately, while in the midst of the repair, he slipped and slid from the apex of the roof landing head first on the ground below. He was terribly injured but eventually he recovered. As a result of the fall, he lost his ability to hear. Thus he received the nickname, Toiver Guluf (Guluf the Deaf Guy). Of course some of the Jews said that he was deaf because God punished him.

I asked my father, "Were they right?"

He answered, "A Jew should not have anything to do with fixing a church."

The most prominent person in town was Rabbi Chaim Benjamin Platkiewicz. He replaced Rabbi Sziojma Grodzinski who served from 1919, the year that Binem was born, until 1925. Of the many rabbis that served the Jewish community of Radziejow over its long history, the most admired was Rabbi Mazur, who had served during the late 1880s until the early part of the 1900s.

When Rabbi Platkiewicz was hired by the Radziejow Jewish Community, he either purchased or was provided a house that was located about six blocks away from the old shul. After settling in, he learned that the house was not in an ideal location. On occasion when walking to shul, he would be harassed by unfriendly Polish neighbors, often juvenile delinquents. For example, one Sabbath day he was walking to shul for the morning service when a few young ruffians made a game of running up to him and pulling on his beard, then making a swiftly escape.

The Rabbi viewed these antics as degrading, but was at a loss as how to deal with the situation. He took solace in the fact that throughout history Jews had been similarly tormented by the uncivilized members of their host nations. Unfortunately, his house placed him in a location where some of the most anti-Semitic townsfolk lived. He decided to quietly endure the occasional acts of aggression and degradation, perhaps viewing them as being a sort of divine test. One wonders if these anti-Semitic acts ultimately influenced the Rabbi's embrace of Religious Zionism.

Although anti-Semitic aggression occurred all year long in Radziejow, one Polish holiday called Dyngus Day posed a real danger to Jews. Dyngus Day was celebrated on the Monday after Easter. For Poles, it is a day of fun. The historical origin of the holiday dates back to 966 A.D., when the Polish Prince Mieszko was baptized. According to tradition, boys sprinkle girls with water as a sign of fertility and purification. Girls were permitted to retaliate the following day by throwing dishes at the boys. The Jews of Radziejow were not privy to the details of the holiday, but were well aware that anti-Semites used the holiday as an excuse to splash water on Jews, both male or female. The more water, the better! When a Pole splashed a Jew on Dyngus Day, it was done with malicious intent.

Every Dyngus Day, the Rabbi of Radziejow was splashed with water when he walked to shul. But one year, an audacious anti-Semitic woman dumped an entire bucketful of water on Rabbi Platkiewicz while several Poles watching the incident laughed. For the next three days, when the Rabbi walked past his Polish neighbors on his way to shul, the Poles remembered the incident and would laugh at him. On the fourth day, things changed radically. Not only did the laughter stop, but a strange feeling of remorse was seen on their faces. The woman, who had become a local celebrity for dousing the Rabbi, had suddenly died of unknown causes. Many believed it was punishment from God for disrespecting a holy man. The neighborhood Poles came to a silent understanding that it was a dangerous thing to bother the Rabbi. From that day on, the Rabbi was spared the degradation of being the target of stone throwers, beard pullers and water splashers.

In 1935, the four sons of the late Rabbi Mazur, the former spiritual leader of the old shul, made their annual pilgrimage to visit the resting place of their parents in the Radziejow Jewish Cemetery. These men lived in the city of Danzig, near the Baltic Sea, which was about 100 miles away from Radziejow. They were successful businessmen. In fact, they were so successful, they had become the richest Jewish family in Danzig and possibly all of Poland. Every year they would arrive on their Mother's *Yahrzeit* (anniversary of a death) to recite the traditional Kaddish prayer with a minyan of at least ten men in front of her gravesite. They would then invite the entire Radziejow community to join them in a celebration. Before the celebration ended, the brothers would make a substantial contribution to the coffers of the general fund of the Jewish community.

One year in the mid-1930s, the sons were feeling extremely generous and decided they would do something special to honor their parents. They requested a meeting with the leading Jews of the town. At the gathering, one son told the leaders that they would underwrite any project for which the community decided that there was a particular need. They emphasized that the cost of such a project was not to be an issue. The sons then solicited suggestions from each of the Jews in attendance.

One attendee thought it would be nice to build a Jewish hospital. Other equally important suggestions were made. When it was Shimon's turn, he stated the obvious fact that the present shul was too small to serve the needs of the Jewish Community. He pointed out that on Rosh Hashanah and Yom Kippur, there was not enough space to comfortably accommodate all those that wished to attend services. Shimon added that Rabbi Platkiewicz lived a considerable distance from the shul, and that the walk through the Polish neighborhood was not pleasant for the Rabbi. The dangers and insults the Rabbi had experienced in the past were not appropriate for the most distinguished member of the Jewish community. Shimon suggested that if a new shul would be built, it should include living quarters for the Rabbi and his family.

Upon hearing this proposal, the crowd in the room nodded in unanimous agreement. The Mazur brothers embraced the suggestion. What better tribute to their father, who was once the Rabbi of Radziejow, than to build a grand shul as a memorial. It was immediately decided to go forward with the project. The sons said that they would gladly pay the entire bill for the shul's construction.

Due to a variety of reasons, including local Jewish politics, it took nearly three years to construct the new shul. Upon completion, the new shul was spacious and solidly constructed. Attached to the shul was ample living quarters for the Rabbi and his family. The shul was named Beis Rochel. It is likely that the brothers named the shul after their mother.

Just a few years before the outbreak of the German invasion of Poland, the entire Jewish community as well as local Polish town officials turned out for the dedication ceremony. The photograph of the ceremony includes many of the Jews mentioned in this book including Frankenberg the mini bus driver, Shlomovich the tailor, Shpievak the tailor, Lubinski the wheat dealer, Zief, Rakowski, and Markowski, to name just a few.

Dedication of Beis Rochel

To many, it must have been the most joyous occasion ever experienced by the Radziejow Jewish community. Everyone marveled that they should be privileged to have such a modern shul. In contrast to the near non-existing building standards of Radziejow, Beis Rochel was built according to the best construction practices available at that time. Both Jews and Gentiles agreed the building was both opulent and structurally sound. For example, it was unusual for a building in Radziejow to be entirely out of brick. The contractor claimed that the building was virtually fireproof.

No one would have imagined that just a few years later the Nazis would order the burning of all the local synagogues in the region. In Radziejow, the fireproof construction of the shul caused a hiccup in the cruel Nazi plan. However, to finish off the destruction of the shul, the Nazis in charge of its destruction simply used dynamite.

POLES AND JEWS

The Poles living in Radziejow and the surrounding countryside were mostly ambivalent about the Jews. On the one hand, many disliked the Jews and viewed them as outsiders. Some priests continually ranted that the Jews killed Jesus. To the average Pole, the Jews did not act like Poles and certainly the Orthodox Jews did not dress like them. Orthodox Jews normally wore a black outfit and covered their heads with either a cap or yarmulke.

Furthermore, the Jews spoke to one another in a foreign language, Yiddish. That also perturbed the average Pole, since Yiddish sounded awfully close to German, the language spoken by their nearest enemy. Many times during commercial transactions between Poles and Jews, the Poles would hear the Jews speak to each other in Yiddish. Not only did the average Pole feel that was rude, it also made them wonder whether the two Jews were conspiring to cheat him.

The Jews also generally tried to remain as separate as possible from the mainstream population. For the most part, Jews never socialized with Poles. Many Poles assumed that the Jews believed that they were somehow superior to them despite the Jews being a minority in Poland.

On the other hand, some Poles looked at the Jews with admiration and sympathy. Jewish men appeared to them as loving husbands, excellent fathers, and good providers for their family. The Jews dressed conservatively and were quiet and reserved. Rowdy, drunken behavior was much less common among Jews than their Polish counterparts. Furthermore, many Jews seemed sincere and pious in their beliefs.

Those Poles that disliked the Jews had much in common with the other European anti-Semites. In fact, there were a number of thriving anti-Semitic movements across Europe. These movements specialized in spewing out an intense hatred of Jews and their religion. It is no wonder that the anti-Semitic rhetoric of Hitler was music to the ears of some Poles. When those same Poles heard that Hitler's personal thugs, the brown-shirts, were attacking both Jews and their property, these Poles were further emboldened to lawlessness, wanting to grab their share of Jewish loot. Moreover, the Catholic Church, of which nearly all Poles were congregants, continued to foster a negative view of the descendants of the Hebrews who they preached were responsible for the murder of Jesus.

Despite their differences, Poles and Jews surprisingly managed to remain civil to one another, because, in the final analysis, they had a mutually beneficial and even symbiotic relationship which made both groups dependent upon one another. The Polish Government understood this relationship and encouraged it. In most cases, the central government went out of its way to promote this relationship by acting as an honest broker between the two groups. Prior to the promulgation of laws that led to the boycotting of Jewish business in the 1930s, the government policy was one of tolerance towards the Jews. This position was out of step with mainstream opinion. Despite government efforts, the prevailing attitude of the typical Pole towards the Jews was that Poland would be better off without the Jews.

The Jews were not completely innocent in this matter. Many Jews, even the most liberal among them, viewed the Poles with suspicion. Interaction with Poles was kept to a bare minimum, and restricted primarily to business and government dealings. The suspicion was not purely paranoia. Anti-Semitic incidents were common throughout the history of the Jews in Poland. Still, despite these obstacles, the two communities lived most of the time side by side in relative peace, to their mutual benefit.

No matter how great the friction, the two groups always found common ground in business. The Jews needed the Poles for their agricultural products and raw materials. The Poles needed the Jews for goods and services. Thus, the two groups were integrated despite the various walls, both physical and spiritual, that separated them.

The separation of Jews and non-Jews in Europe was an arrangement that developed over centuries, from a time when the Jews of Europe were forced to live in designated areas called ghettos. The word ghetto is derived from the name of the area in Venice where Jews were restricted to live in the Middle Ages. Over time, the word "ghetto" became used to refer to any isolated Jewish enclave.

As Europe progressed, so did Poland. Laws changed concerning ghettos, and in many countries Jews were allowed to live wherever they chose. Anti-Semitism continued among the populace despite the changing laws. As a result, Jews were dissuaded from moving out of the perceived safety and comfort of the ghetto.

Well before the anti-Semitic culture of the Nazis took hold in Germany, there were extremist Poles that portrayed Jews as evil. They believed that Jews should be expelled from Poland. The history of Poles being involved in blood libels, extortion, random beatings, pogroms (violent anti-Semitic riots), and murder is too long to list here.

This hatred of Jews caused a bad reaction in a small minority of Jews. Some Jews claimed that they were taught in certain *Chederim* (schools) to despise the Poles. One of these Jews is quoted as stating, "Our rabbi insisted that we Jewish children spit on the ground and utter curses while passing near a cross, or whenever we encountered a Christian priest or religious procession...on the way to school we passed a Roman Catholic church and a Russian Orthodox church, and we spat, pronouncing the words found in Deuteronomy 7:26:

'Thou shalt utterly detest it, and thou shalt utterly abhor it, for it is a cursed thing.'"

This kind of behavior by Jews towards Poles was rare. Some Poles in Radziejow believed that Jews hated Poles. However, this was clearly not the case. The main reason why Jews maintained a separate community was that Jewish law encourages Jews to live in close proximity of one another. For example, a Sabbath-observant Jew is not allowed to travel by wagon or ride a horse on the Sabbath, or even walk outside of a town a certain distance. Therefore, in order to attend Sabbath services in Radziejow, a Jew had to live in walking distance of the synagogue.

The Sabbath was not the only reason for Jews to live together. Jews felt safe and comfortable participating in organized Jewish life which required constant interaction. For example, a Jew must *daven* (pray) with a *minyan* (quorum of ten) men, three times a day. Only by working and living in near proximity was it possible for the community to keep many Torah laws.

The Jews in Poland were on the constant lookout for zealous Polish anti-Semites. Although small in numbers, they were still very dangerous. These anti-Semites lived everywhere, including the small town of Radziejow. They would parrot the international watchwords of hate.

A favorite invective was that Jews were parasites, which was proven by the fact there were no Jewish farmers in the surrounding area of Radziejow. The anti-Semites contended that the reason Jews were not farmers was because they looked down on people that engaged in hard labor. These anti-Semites simply ignored the reasons behind the lack of Jewish farmers. The first being that only recently were Jews in Poland allowed to own land and work as farmers. Second, as stated earlier, Jewish law made it difficult to be a farmer and a practicing Jew. Finally, Jews contributed to Poland in other ways. Productivity in society is achieved by many different means that compliment and strengthen each other. Jews played a vital role in Poland in the manufacturing and distribution of goods and vital services. Without the Jewish businessmen that sold products to the general populous, production would have been far less effective for the lack of efficient distribution of manufactured goods.

For the most part, there was a complete disassociation of Jewish and Polish social life. Both the Church and the rabbinical leadership encouraged separation of the two communities. Rabbis discouraged interaction, lest it lead to assimilation. Many priests taught suspicion and even hatred of the Jews.

However, there was no real comparison between Jewish and Polish extremists. The Polish anti-Semites advocated pogroms, boycotts, and public denigration of the Jews. From time to time, the talk exploded into acts of violence that included physical attacks on Jews. On the other hand, Jewish extremism was limited to harsh talk and juvenile gestures.

One of the greatest fears of the Rabbis and just about all Jewish parents was assimilation. Throughout Jewish history, interaction and assimilation had always led to intermarriage. Thus, the Jewish community encouraged separation. The majority of Christians were also happy that the Jews practiced a kind of "voluntary isolationism," for they, too, did not want their children to marry Jews. "A Jew who married a Christian was anathema in both social circles."

It is important to emphasize that the majority of Poles and Jews did not hate one another. Rather, each group was basically indifferent of the other. The Poles had their way of viewing the world, and the Jews had their own way. "Jews maintained their own lifestyle and values and preferred to have only limited contact with the Poles, usually confined to business dealings. Little wonder, then, that Poles and Jews did not really know each other well, even though they had lived side by side for centuries... Ethnocentrism in Poland was a two way street"

It would also be unjust to assert that as a result of these

religious and political differences, all Poles were anti-Semitic. Many religious Poles bore no ill feelings towards the Jews. For the most part, they were involved in their own lives and were therefore indifferent towards these strangers in their midst. The Jews were a fact of life around them, being neither good nor bad. Similar to the way Americans view with curiosity the Amish and their lifestyle. One difference, however, is that the Amish choose to live on farms that are located separate from mainstream American society. The Jews in Poland, however, lived in close proximity to the Poles but kept their personal lives separate.

The older religious Jews that had business relationships with Poles kept the relationships strictly limited to commerce. They rarely, if ever, found themselves in a mutual social setting. On the other hand, Jewish children were required by law to attend public school with the Poles. What emerged was that some Jews developed social interactions with like-minded Poles inside schools and, on rare occasions, even outside of the school setting.

The Jews of Radziejow had some interest in Polish politics, such as that which related to Jews and commerce. On the other hand, Jews had little interest in Polish history, and even less in Polish culture. They were preoccupied with earning a living and observing the precepts of the Torah.

For example, when I asked my father to describe Radziejow's Town Square, he mentioned that displayed prominently in the square was a large statue of a Polish hero named Andrzej Kościuszko.

I asked, "Who was he?"

My father replied, "He was an officer that fought in the United States War of Independence. He was a very popular general in Poland because he successfully did battle with invading Tatars and the Turks." This answer proved the point, as Kościuszko was famous for battling the Russians, not the Tartars or Turks.

I asked him, "What was your opinion about Kościuszko?"

His answer came with a smile: "Jews didn't mix in politics." Later I realized that his smile and answer summed up the Jewish opinion of life in Poland.

THE WINDS OF WAR

In the early 1930's, a clear change in the relationship between Jews and Poles could be observed in Radziejow. Harsh sanctions against Germany after its defeat in World War I, widespread economic depression, and discontent among the working-class, among other factors, paved the way for the rise of fascist, anti-Semitic movements such as Hitler's Nazi Party. With Hitler's meteoric rise to power, some Poles in Radziejow were emboldened to express their own local brand of anti-Semitism.

The anti-Semites in Radziejow harassed Jews both physically and psychologically. For example, broadcasts of Hitler's speeches were often picked up on radios within Poland. A few of the more active Jew-haters proudly set their radios on their window sills with the speakers facing the street in order to force passing Jews to listen to Hitler's demonic voice, while shouting out the most despicable anti-Semitic vitriol for dramatic effect.

Though Radziejow had a reputation of relative religious tolerance compared to many communities in Poland, some of the local Poles embraced this new wave of anti-Semitism to the point that they actually perpetrated physical attacks against innocent Jews. These attacks often escalated to pogroms against the entire Jewish community.

The first widespread pogrom in Radziejow occurred at the end of a soccer match between the local Jewish team and a regional Polish team. The Jewish team won the game by a single goal. As a result, the irate Polish fans, without any provocation, attacked the Jewish spectators in the stands. The rioting soon spread from the stadium to Yiddishe Street. Luckily, the local Polish police mobilized quickly and established order by arresting several of the more violent Poles. Soon the riot petered out. The Jews lauded the police for their quick response.

A second incident that was even more disturbing started with a violent altercation between a Pole and a Jew. A Polish butcher was renting space from a Jewish butcher. The Polish butcher sold *treif* (non-kosher meat) in an area of the shop separate from where the Jewish butcher sold kosher meat. For whatever reason, the Pole at some point refused to pay his monthly rent. The Jewish butcher insisted that he pay his rent on time or leave. This resulted in a heated exchange between the two butchers that escalated into physical blows. The Jewish butcher was getting the upper hand in the fight when a crowd of Poles passed in front of the shop. The Poles were on their way home from daily mass. At that exact moment, the Jew had reached for a hammer and struck the Pole. With blood dripping from an open gash on his face, the Pole seized the opportunity and called out to the crowd that the Jews were trying to kill him. The crowd reacted violently and began attacking Jews walking down the street. In short order, a full-blown pogrom ensued. Again, Polish police raced to the scene to protect approximately 70 Jews who were attacked along Yiddishe Street.

It is important to point out that the police did not act entirely out of benevolence or even simply to uphold the law. Actually, the police vigilance was due to goodwill that had been carefully cultivated through bribes that Jewish shopkeepers had given to the officers. These bribes, for the most part, were not overt. For example, Jewish shop owners usually did not charge a "shopping" police officer for small items. Larger items were sold at greatly reduced discounts, so much so that the discount oftentimes resulted in the shopkeepers sustaining a loss from the transaction.

Even with police protection, the Jews of Radziejow were aware that their tranquil lives were being swept away in Europe's renewed atmosphere of hatred towards Jews. As the German power soared, some Poles increasingly pointed to the Jews as the source of all of Poland's problems. Acts of violence against Jews grew each year. In 1936, twenty-one pogroms and 348 individual acts of violence were perpetrated in the Bialystok region alone. In that same year, throughout Poland, seventy-nine Jews were killed and approximately five hundred were wounded from October to April. The following year, in the month of August, there were 350 physical assaults against the Jews of Poland.

Radziejow was no exception. Local thugs walked up to Jews and ranted the mantra, "Jew, Jew you better run before it's too late!" Or even more ominous, "You better go to Israel before we hang you!"

The main problem preventing Jews from escaping the obvious impending disaster was that, realistically, there was no place in the world for Jews to find refuge. It was apparent that no country was interested in taking in large numbers of Jews. The Jews of Radziejow, like the rest of the Jews of Europe, were trapped.

I asked my father, "Didn't the Jews talk about this new wave of anti-Semitism?"

He answered, "Talking about it with one another did not stop the growing fear among us, it only intensified it."

In the period after Hitler took control of Germany, the United States began to tighten immigration rules to the point where a very limited amount of immigrants were admitted under a strictly enforced quota system. The Naiman brothers living in North America, Harry and Max, watched the plight of European Jewry in horror. Together, they made a concerted effort to bring the family to safety in the United States. They filled out the required immigration forms and collected the extensive documents necessary to sponsor their family to immigrate to the United States. They even sent money to Poland to pay for the family's transportation expenses. However, all was for naught. Because of the strict quota, at the time Hitler invaded Poland, the Naimans were still on the long waiting list for the issuance of visas.

My father recalled that the plight of Polish Jewry became so desperate that an engineer in Warsaw organized a march of deliverance to Palestine. In this twentieth century version of the story of the Exodus, the engineer pleaded, "Every Jew should join this march to freedom."

His words convinced thousands of Jews to join him. Predictably, the Jews did not get far. After hundreds gathered at a designated starting point in Warsaw to begin their long trek, the Polish Government stopped the march because the participants failed to obtain the required transit visas. The government officials explained to the marchers that they needed visas to allow them to enter each country between Poland and Palestine. Then the Polish Police dispersed the marchers. This incident sent a shockwave throughout the Jewish communities in Poland. It was now crystal clear that the Jews were stuck in a dangerous situation that all knew was soon to become much worse.

Binem remembered how the Jews of Radziejow had discussed the event. Some had commented that even if the police hadn't intervened, the march was doomed from the start. It was completely disorganized. Basic requirements such as food, portable housing, medical supplies, and other provisions had not been prepared for the long journey. Others commented that even if they did have everything necessary to complete such a treacherous journey, it would have made little difference. Palestine was surrounded by hostile neighbors that would never had allowed Jews to pass through. The Arab mentality at the time of the march was to stop the expansion of Jewish settlements in Palestine. It was obvious that the marchers would have evoked a violent response that would have inevitably ended in tragedy.

The failure of the march illustrated to many Jews in Poland their overall helplessness. They realized there was nothing they could do to be proactive to stave off the impending disaster. That left the religious Jews to pray for divine salvation, while the secular Jews put their faith in the overall goodness of mankind to prevent Hitler and his ilk. And even if the nations failed to stop Hitler, many rationalized that, as bad as Hitler was, "The Jews had survived worse enemies."

Binem and his family were at a complete loss on what they should do in light of the ominous events. Some of the young Jews believed that although the elderly had little choice but to ride out the storm, the young should take a chance and run away from Poland. Binem, merely a teenager, refused to contemplate the thought of abandoning his family in this desperate hour. He reasoned that even if it was the most logical course of action, he was not of the age to make such a radical decision.

Just about all Jewish families living in Radziejow were having the same discussion. A general consensus emerged that there were no real options, so therefore the Jews of Radziejow would simply wait and see.

Shimon, now in his mid-sixties, had long rejected the idea of leaving Poland to join his sons in America. He understood from others that America was not religious enough for an observant Jew. He would point out that Hinda's mother Miriam actually returned to Poland after living with the family in Milwaukee, Wisconsin, because Jewish life was better in Poland.

Shimon reasoned that if an elderly woman was unafraid to return to Poland, things couldn't be as bad as people said. Moreover, he understood that the Naimans were very strongly tied to Radziejow. All of the family's roots were in Radziejow including many relatives, the building, and the business. It would be near impossible to sell the building and the business. If the Naimans decided to leave, they would have to walk away from their assets and livelihood. In addition, there were just too many Naimans to make the journey at one time. There were nine brothers and sisters living in or near Radziejow. Two of the sisters were married and had children. Moving was a logistical nightmare. And what if these doom and gloom predictions didn't occur? Wouldn't it be foolish to move and lose everything on the mere chance that Hitler might invade Poland? Finally, Shimon wanted to be buried next to his late wife, Hinda, who he still missed deeply.

It was not that Shimon was ignoring the looming danger. He knew that disaster was likely imminent. However, he understood that he was he was powerless to prevent it. So he did what he knew was best in such situations, he prayed that the Almighty would protect the People of Israel. He hoped by the merit of Torah study, God would be receptive to the prayers of Polish Jewry. Binem pointed out that Shimon never openly discussed his concerns during the family meetings. He felt that if he did, it would only increase the level of fear that all were experiencing.

Radziejow survivor Joyce Wagner, Binem's first cousin, stated that all was set for her family to join their relatives in Milwaukee. At the last moment, her father, Hersz, refused. He heard that in the United States Jews walked with their heads uncovered and actually worked on the Sabbath. That was too much for him to bear. He told the family that he rather risk facing the anti-Semites then to endanger his soul.

Shimon's family were further disturbed by the prophetic visions of Binem's older sister Masha. She was known as the family's poet because she was always writing poetry. One Shabbos, three years before the war broke out, the family was gathered at the dinner table. Without provocation, Masha suddenly erupted in a bone-chilling scream. The Naimans were startled. Masha's face had drained white as if she had been terrorized. She then tried to vocalize her thoughts, but all that could be heard from her lips was a whisper saying, "I smelled gas, poison gas."

The family members looked at each other, hoping that

someone could explain. Finally, she calmed down. One of the family members asked her what she was saying under her breath. She replied that she saw people around the house pumping gas through the walls in order to poison them. Binem at the time was seventeen years old. He and the other siblings were sure that she must be losing her mind.

During the days that followed, Masha's health deteriorated as she continuously spoke of her nightmarish vision. The family, feeling that there was no alternative, decided to consult Doctor Paninski. After examining Masha, the doctor said that she suffered from no physical malady. He suggested that she be examined by specialists at the regional mental asylum. The family reluctantly agreed over Masha's protests. There she was seen by a number of psychiatrists and underwent a series of tests.

All the psychiatrists diagnosed her condition as a form of mental trauma which they called shock. They believed her vision was the result of brain trauma. The psychiatrists explained that the only known treatment for this condition was electroshock treatment.

Shimon was aghast to learn the details of this horrific procedure. Moreover, he was skeptical in their diagnosis. He repeatedly asked the psychiatrists if the treatment was dangerous. The doctors responded that the treatment could be dangerous. Legally, in order for a hospital in Poland to perform this radical procedure, the administrating doctor was required to have a family member sign a release form which waived any right to hold the hospital and doctors responsible in the event that something went wrong. Normally the husband would be considered the closest family member, however, Shimon's son-in-law deferred to his father-in-law, as Shimon was a scholar and a man of experience.

Shimon was not convinced that this radical treatment would work, nor did he feel that it was safe to have an electric current shocking his daughter's brain. He had no need to consult his rebbe, the Radomsker Rebbe, because he had already concluded that he would not allow his daughter to be treated in such a manner. Therefore, Shimon refused to sign the waiver.

The doctors were not accustomed to having their expertise refuted. Still, since she was already admitted to the hospital, they agreed to allow Masha to continue to be observed and be treated using non-invasive methods. Masha stayed a number of days at the hospital. She hated it there. She knew what she saw and no one was going to convince her otherwise. So, in order to force her own release, she announced that she was beginning a hunger strike. Even during the hunger strike, she told family members that she continued to see visions of piles of Jewish bodies being burned. The administrators of the hospital concluded that the alternative treatments were not helping but rather exasperating her condition. That, coupled with her hunger strike, caused her to be discharged from the hospital.

When she returned home, Masha continually begged her family to attempt to escape from Poland. She said that they would be doomed if they did not flee. On one occasion, she suddenly became hysterical, imploring her family to run from the house because hidden within the walls were poison gas pipes. She said that the vents were behind all the pictures on the walls. The family patiently removed all the pictures to show her that there was nothing there. This did not assuage her distress. Her bizarre behavior continued even after the invasion of Poland by Germany. It was then that the family members agreed that her supposed insanity was in actuality true visions.

Binem, in hindsight, concluded, "She was prophetic! Masha was telling us what was going to happen to the Jewish people."

As far as the Jews of Radziejow were concerned, the main topic in the news was German expansionism. Hitler changed from a theoretical problem for Polish Jewry to a real threat when Germany annexed Austria in March of 1938. Hitler carefully gauged the reaction of world leaders in the wake of this clear violation of the Treaty of Versailles. He concluded that it evoked little response. So he decided to turn next to Czechoslovakia, where a region called the Sudetenland had a population that was predominantly ethnic German. After extensive diplomatic negotiations, Britain and France agreed not to oppose Nazi Germany's annexation of this territory. This agreement was recorded in the document known as the Munich Agreement. The Prime Minister of Great Britain, Neville Chamberlain, infamously declared to the English people that the agreement ensured "peace for our time."

Instead of placating Hitler's obsession for expansionism, the Munich Agreement only acted as a catalyst. The more Hitler saw weakness in the European nations' resolve, the greater was his appetite to control all of Europe. Hitler professed that he was now satisfied. But his thoughts and actions were the exact opposite of his words. Hitler's eyes now turned towards Germany's peaceful neighbor, Poland.

The government of Poland was now faced with what appeared to be an inevitable invasion by Germany. Poland had no choice but to mobilize its armed forces. Defenses were shored up and men were called up by the thousands.

Among those mobilized were over 100,000 Jews. The Naiman brothers were not among those ordered to report for military service. The Polish Army drafted men above the age of 21. Binem was 20. The two oldest brothers, Max and Harry, were living in the United States. Binem's remaining brothers living with him in Radziejow were Michael, Shmeil, and Azriel. Michael, known as Macho, had a medical deferment due to severe scoliosis, which caused Macho to be unusually short and have one shoulder much higher than the other. Shmiel indeed was registered to serve, and was about to be drafted. However, when the war began, he had yet to be called up. Binem's remaining other brother, Azriel, was over 21 years old, and thus eligible to serve. However, during the chaos before the war, the local officials in charge of the draft somehow failed to register him.

Hitler in his lust for power set out to conquer both Europe and Asia. He did this because he was a power-hungry megalomaniac. But he hid this from the German masses. Instead, he announced that the military was being used in order to supply the Fatherland with the natural resources and manpower required to fulfill Germany's destiny of becoming the most powerful nation on earth. Germany, he said was too small, and therefore the German people needed growing space to fulfill the national aspiration of a "Thousand Year Reich." The Nazis euphemistically referred to this fundamental German manifest destiny as *Lebensraum*. But what the term meant in actuality was aggressive territorial expansion driven by racism.

When Hitler decided to invade Poland, he believed that the European nations would either again cave to his aggression or be punished by German might. He felt that all of Europe was weak and had no stomach for war. Therefore, in his mind, all the nations that comprised Europe were ripe for subjugation and conquest.

In 1939, Germany's population was 69 million, with an additional 10 million new citizens following the annexation of Austria and the Sudetenland. On the other side of the border, Poland's population was just over 30 million. The vast majority of Poles, approximately 26 million, were Roman Catholics, with about three million Jews and an additional one million ethnic German citizens of Poland known as Volksdeutsche. Many Poles considered the Volksdeutsche as a fifth column for Germany.

THE NAZI INVASION
OF POLAND

On September 1, 1939, German forces invaded Poland. The Nazis manufactured a false pretext to justify this international aggression and blatant land grab. Germany alleged that Polish troops crossed the border and attacked the town of Gleiwitz in order to take out a "vital transmitter" that was set up at the local radio station. Of course, this was a complete fabrication. At the time of this pretext, Germany was fully mobilized to attack Poland from three directions.

Among the German troops that entered Poland were three SS Death's Head regiments of the Brandenburg Division. These were special forces units made up of German foreign nationals. The Death's Head regiments had a very different mission than that of the German Army. Their mission was to rid Poland of its Jewish population in a horrific manner, and they soon became infamous for the atrocities they carried out in Poland.

The Death's Heads were ruthless beyond one's darkest imagination. The mindset of these specially selected soldiers was that of complete unquestioning obedience to their officers. They were given orders to act with no mercy as they rained down wholesale slaughter on the Polish villages they entered. "As a result of these secret orders whole villages were burned to the ground. Peasants and Jews were executed mainly by mobile firing squads."

These actions represented the initial implementation of Hitler's public declarations that if war broke out, "...the result will not be the Bolshevization of the earth, and thus the victory of Jewry, but the annihilation of the Jewish race in Europe." Even during the early stages of the invasion, it became clear that Hitler's secret plan was being implemented with unimaginable cruelty. "Within two weeks, the Brandenburg (Death Head) Division had left a trail of murder in more than thirteen Polish towns and villages."

As the war progressed, Poland's government was systematically dismantled. The world watched in horror as the German bully decimated the brave but weaker Poles. Civilized people could not understand why Nazi Germany would commit such atrocities against peaceful Poland that for years had lived in harmony with its neighbor.

The German Army, or Wehrmacht, was nearly twice as large as Poland's army and much better organized. Germany fielded over sixty divisions and dominated the air with approximately two thousand aircraft. The German land forces constituted five armies making up a total of 1.5 million soldiers. It was a professional army commanded by capable generals. The Luftwaffe, Germany's air force, was made up of hundreds of the latest fighter planes and bombers. These included the infamous Junkers Ju 87, or Stuka, with its incredibly loud propeller-driven sirens. The German Army was therefore unquestionably the most powerful fighting force in Europe.

Poland had 39 divisions on paper, but in reality the Army could actually field much less. Moreover, its air force consisted of about 800 outmoded aircraft that were not even remotely capable of battling Germany's fighter planes. Unlike the Soviet-Poland War of 1920, Polish generals had no delusions that they could somehow defeat the German Army.

The German invasion began with fast moving armored tanks and mobilized artillery overrunning the Polish defenses before the soldiers were prepared to react. This new type of warfare became known as Blitzkrieg. With Polish troops powerless to stop this new war tactic, the Germans quickly overran the haphazard Polish defenses. The Polish soldiers manning these defenses were either wiped out or captured during the initial German onslaught. Those that managed to escape retreated in disarray. Attempts to organize and counterattack were in vain. The Polish army showed tremendous courage battling its larger, more organized, and more technologically advanced enemy. With over 2,700 German tanks to Poland's 800, the Poles were at a loss as to how to react.

On September 1, 1939, at the famous battle known as the Charge at Krojanty, Polish cavalry attacked a dispersed German infantry battalion only to end up fighting against German armored cars firing machine guns. The cavalry retreated, losing about a third of its 250 troops along with its commander. Still, the battle was considered a victory of sorts because it temporarily delayed the German advance. A myth was created about this battle in which the Polish Cavalry were imagined to have charged German Panzer tanks with the soldiers wielding lances and sabers. Regardless, just about all efforts by the Polish Army were tragic regardless of the brave efforts to defend the Polish homeland from the invading Germans.

Radziejow survivor Henry Gronow was a Jewish soldier in the Polish Army at the time of the invasion. He was drafted into the Polish Army in 1934 and served in a Polish cavalry unit. Three years later, in 1937, he received his discharge. When Germany entered the Sudetenland in Czechoslovakia in 1938, he was recalled for reserve duty. He was sent to the front line with orders to repel the German invasion force.

Gronow and his fellow soldiers witnessed the German Army's new tactic of *blitzkrieg*. First came wave after wave of fast-moving tanks supported by hundreds of Luftwaffe bombers and massive artillery support. The attack was then followed by tens of thousands of infantry troops and their support units. Gronow and his fellow soldiers were never prepared to stop such an overwhelming display of firepower. After three weeks of Poland's brave but fruitless resistance, he was captured by the Germans. He spent six months at the POW camp Stalag 2A that was located near Brandenburg, Germany before being returned to Poland and released.

On September 1, 1939, the day World War II broke out, the Naiman family was awoken by the sounds of a distant battle. Radziejow was a mere hour's drive from the border with Germany. The next few days left both the Jews and their fellow Polish villagers shaking in fear, knowing that at any moment the Germans would arrive. The top priority of the townsfolk was to get information regarding the events occurring around them. However, news was scarce from the Polish side, while the German radio broadcasts bragged of victory after victory. Just a few days later, on September 5, 1939, the Germans occupied the nearby town of Piotrkow.

The Jews of Radziejow soon learned from refugees what had transpired. "The Germans set fire to dozens of Jewish homes, then shot dead those Jews who managed to run from the burning buildings. Entering a building which had escaped the flames, soldiers took out six Jews and ordered them to run. Five were shot down, the sixth, Reb Bunem Lebel, died later of his wounds."

Refugees from all over Poland told similar stories, revealing the scope of the Jewish predicament in occupied Poland. The German Army was targeting Jews for humiliation and elimination. When the Jews of Radziejow heard these stories they were at a complete loss on how to react. Fathers looked at their wives and children and knew that they could not protect their families from the oncoming onslaught. "If the Polish Army with their tanks and guns could not stop these animals," they would ask, "what could I, a Jew, do?" As a result, depression, despondency, and hopelessness overwhelmed the Jews of Poland.

The Naiman family huddled in the basement and listened in terror as they heard the whistling of artillery shells along with small arms fire. The most frightening of all were the sounds from bombing raids of the Luftwaffe as they destroyed fortifications and installations and then followed up by strafing the Polish soldiers as they sought cover.

The Jews of Radziejow initially hid in their homes or wandered aimlessly down Yiddishe Street. Eventually there was a gathering in front of the shul. The Jews debated what was the best course of action. All agreed that the Germans had terrible machinations against them. With Radziejow being one of the larger Jewish towns close to the border, the Jews felt especially targeted. Still, there was some hope. The Polish Army continued its efforts to defend the border. Jews had observed soldiers digging fortifications around the town. However, some commented that as a result of these Polish fortifications, it was almost guaranteed that there would be a full scale battle over the town of Radziejow. There was a consensus that with the German juggernaut moving closer to Radziejow, the only course of action was to evacuate the town.

The Naimans had a family meeting to decide whether to flee or stay. They discussed the two options. If they chose to stay, then they would find themselves in the middle of the upcoming battle. If they fled, they would have to abandon nearly everything they owned and become refugees. But what else could they do, knowing how the Germans would treat them once Radziejow was occupied? So the decision was made to flee.

Transportation was almost impossible to arrange. Just about all of the horses, wagons, buggies, and motorized vehicles were either requisitioned by the Polish Army or were being used by their owners to flee. Finally, after much searching, a family member was able to procure a horse and a large wagon. The wagon was quickly loaded. Every inch of the wagon was critical. The wagon had to serve as both transportation for those family members that were unable to walk, as well as to carry vital items such as food, clothing, furniture, cooking utensils, religious items, and merchandise. Once they finished packing the essentials, there was not an inch of room to spare. After locking the doors of the Naiman building, the Naiman family hit the road unknown.

As they left Radziejow, the Naimans understood that they were now homeless refugees. The brothers, sisters, cousins, nephews, nieces, and uncles tried to cheer each other up as they followed on foot behind the wagon. On the wagon itself was the driver and next to him the family patriarch, Shimon. They left Radziejow with scores of like-minded townsfolk, both Polish and Jewish. Silently, all were asking themselves the same question: "When, if ever, would they be able to return?" Shmiel, being the eldest son of the Naiman clan, was their leader. He was responsible for the welfare of the group. He made his decisions after consultation with Shimon and other family members.

The Naimans had no plan or even any idea as to where they were going. Shmeil logically decided, and all agreed, that it would be best to travel east because Germany was to the west. His decision was strengthened by the reality that all civilian traffic was moving towards the east, while the traffic going west consisted of only a few army vehicles.

When they reached the main highway, the road was jammed with a mass of humanity made up of thousands of refugees fleeing from the front. A caravan several miles long of escaping refugees was heading towards the capital and largest city in Poland, Warsaw. Traffic moved at a snail's pace, and at times not at all.

Shimon was sixty eight years old when the war broke out. He was now long retired. He spent all of his time either studying Torah or praying. One would think that to him the war was just an inconvenience. But in truth, being well-versed in history of the Jews, he knew that the invasion was but the harbinger of a worse catastrophe that would threaten the very existence of the Jewish people.

Shimon sat on the wagon quietly, appearing lost in his thoughts. Family members were worried about him They all had heard stories about German soldiers taking pleasure in harassing *frum* (Orthodox) looking Jews. That included cutting off their beards. One look at Shimon and it was obvious he would be targeted by the anti-Semitic invaders. So, fearing for Shimon's safety, they urged him to change his clothes and shave off his beard. Shimon adamantly refused. He understood that his future and his family's future as well was not dependent on whether he had a beard or not. His refusal, however, did not deter his family to continue to pressure him. They said that if he didn't cut off the beard, it could endanger the younger family members that were with them.

Eventually he agreed to a sort of compromise: he would cover his beard with a handkerchief. Of course, the Naimans knew that this was nothing but a bad joke. They asked themselves, "How could a handkerchief around his face fool the Germans?" But the family was resigned to the fact that further protest would be in vain. So Shimon wore a handkerchief around the lower part of his face covering his beard.

After days of traveling, the Naiman wagon was overtaken by forward elements of a Wehrmacht mechanized unit. This was the Naimans first contact with the German invaders. The soldiers were stern but professional. They didn't seem to care if the Naimans were Jewish. What they did care about was executing their orders. The officer demanded that the Naimans as well as the everyone else in the endless stream of refugees turn around and return to their villages and homes. Having no choice, the Naimans complied with the order and returned to Radziejow.

Radziejow survivor Roman Rogers stated that on this same road he was confronted by a less professional German soldier. For whatever reason, the German was carrying a small bale of hay. The soldier warned Rogers that the Jews of Poland, like the Jews of Germany, would soon be slaughtered.

Radziejow survivor Sally Klingbaum was in Radziejow when Germany invaded Poland. She remembered that everyone was afraid, but no one knew exactly what to expect. Ten days later, like the other Jews, she and her family fled Radziejow. Within two weeks, she and her family had returned. When they arrived, they discovered that all their household belongings had been stolen. She said that all that was left were a few items that had the total of value of seven zloty. At that time in 1939, the exchange rate was about 639 zloty to the dollar.

Radziejow survivor Geroge Gronjnowski was twelve years old when the Wehrmacht occupied Radziejow. Despite the danger, his family was one of the few Jewish families that decided to remain in the town. He remembered the soldiers entered the town riding on motorcycles with attached side cars. Sitting in the side cars were soldiers aiming machine guns at everything that they passed. The soldiers first took up stationary positions in Market Square. They set up machine gun nests at the four corners of the market. One of the machine gun nests was opposite the Naiman building, less than a hundred feet away. He said that the Jews that had remained were in a state of shock, fear, and bewilderment. The had no delusions that all was going to be well. All knew of Hitler's despicable policies toward Jews. Still, some were hopeful that the British and French would quickly come to the aid of Poland.

Radziejow survivor Ann Goldman Kumer said that soon after the German occupation of Radziejow began, the Jews were gathered together and forced to stand in Market Square. They were surrounded by both Wehrmacht soldiers and German police called Gendameries, dressed in their distinctive green uniforms. It soon became clear that the reason for this gathering was to separate the Jews from the Poles in order to degrade and humiliate the Jews. As the Poles watched, they forced one Jew to get down on all fours and howl like a dog. Then the religious Jews were lined up to have their *payos* (sidelocks) cut off. She remembered that in those first days Jewish girls were raped by German soldiers. Her mother, upon learning of this, placed Ann and her sister in a safe-room hidden behind a wall in their cellar.

Geroge Gronjnowski, then a young boy, soon learned the word for Jew in German was Jude. The Jews of Radziejow were dumbstruck when several of their Polish neighbors collaborated with the Nazis by identifying the Jews of the town. The Jews were both disappointed at the unpatriotic behavior and felt personally betrayed. Such cooperation, they felt, was treasonous even for an anti-Semite.

One Jew asked another, "Are not the Germans the enemy of the Poles as well as the Jews?"

The Jews quickly learned that the Poles, for whatever reason, could not be counted on for help. It didn't matter whether the reason that a Pole pointed out Jews was due to anti-Semitism or that they were just looking out for themselves – the results were the same.

Joyce Wagner remembered that on the day that the war broke out she was in the family store. Suddenly the news spread around town like wildfire that Germany had invaded Poland. She said that she cried like a baby, and was overwhelmed with a feeling of dread. She recalled that within a few days, the Germans entered Radziejow. She saw haystacks on the outskirts of the town on fire. The smoke billowed in the air around her as the shouts of panicked townsfolk came from all directions. Joyce remembered that she and her family escaped to a nearby town. This was to no avail, because the Germans soon thereafter occupied that town. Her family too felt that they had run out of options. So they decided to return to Radziejow.

When the Naimans arrived back in Radziejow, they were both physically and mentally drained. As they drove through the town, they immediately noticed that many of the stores and homes owned by Jews had been ransacked. They later learned that when the Jews fled Radziejow, Poles began looting the unguarded properties. Fortunately, the Naimans found that the looters had not completely cleaned out their storeroom. There remained some precious merchandise, mainly because the Naimans were among the first Jews to return.

In the street in front of the Naiman building, German soldiers and police were out in force. The Naimans watched in horror as they saw patrols made up of five or more soldiers parading down the street. This display of power was to make it clear to all the townsfolk that the German Army was now in charge of Radziejow.

Radziejow survivor Roman Rogers stated that at the very beginning of the occupation, the Jews of Radziejow were falsely accused of paying the Poles to kill Germans. This lie was an excuse to round up Jews to murder them. One of these roundups included thirty-seven men and several women. The men were taken ten miles from the city. There they were shot to death in cold blood and buried in a long ditch. The women were sent to prison.

The situation in Poland went from catastrophe to even worse. On August 23, 1939, Russia and Germany signed a nonaggression agreement known as the Molotov-Ribbentrop Pact. Among the non-disclosed terms was an agreement that divided up both Northern Europe and Eastern Europe between the two nations. Russia monitored the success of the German invasion of Poland. Seeing that the Poles were being routed, on September 17, 1939, just sixteen days into the invasion, Russia invaded Poland and claimed its eastern half. The Russians did not cite the secret agreement, rather they claimed that they were reluctantly entering Poland out of responsibility to their neighbor. They proclaimed that the Polish government was near collapse and only Russia could protect the Poles as well as Ukrainians and Belarusians that lived in Eastern Poland.

Poland's Government sent out pleas for assistance to their western allies. They demanded that their allies provide immediate military aid. For the most part, their request went unanswered.

The British and French ambassadors in Berlin met with

Germany's Foreign Minister, Joachim von Ribbentrop. The ambassadors presented a united front and told the Foreign Minister in no uncertain terms that, absent a complete withdrawal of German troops from Poland, both France and England would support Poland.

In Hitler's mind, this ultimatum was similar to the other vacuous warnings given by these two countries when Germany annexed Austria and the Sudetenland. This time, however, France and England had resolved to enter a state of war against Germany if the Germans failed to meet their demand. Unfortunately for Poland, Hitler knew that both France and England were not in any position to come to the aid of Poland.

Radziejow was now completely under German rule. The town's name was officially changed to Radichau. All the village's officials and police were disbanded, and strict martial law was enforced.

A series of devastating edicts were announced to the townspeople. One of the first was the confiscation of all Jewish merchandise. That order requisitioned anything the German Army deemed "vital" to the war effort. The Germans used this order not only to provide provisions for the troops, but also for their own personal benefit.

The Naimans soon learned that the German war effort demanded enormous quantities of leather for the manufacturing and repair of boots and coats. The Naimans possessed a large quantity of valuable leather. These precious materials were kept in their storeroom, secured by a simple lock. The Germans knew that shoe stores in general held leather. Thus, upon their return to the village, they were greeted by a menacing looking German policeman who entered the Naiman store and demanded their cooperation as he placed wax seals both on the front entrance to the store and the storeroom's back door that separated the store and the Naiman's living quarters. A stern warning sign was placed adjacent to the wax seals that declared that anyone tampering or breaking the seals and entering the restricted area was subject to the punishment of death.

The Naimans were now officially out of business. One conciliation for the family was they were permitted to remain in the living quarters located behind and above the store. The Naimans spent the first few days back discussing the war and how they were to cope with the dramatic changes. The family members understood that they were in a life-and-death dilemma. They realized that they would soon run out of food. The only way to get food was either to buy or trade for it. Since the zloty was now worthless, one needed foreign currency to purchase food. However, those who grew the food were simple peasants that were wary of accepting payment in currency they did not recognize. Thus, realistically, the only way to get food was to trade for it. The only items of value that the Naimans had that could be used for barter were the leather and other supplies located in the storeroom. It was clear that their survival depended on removing the merchandise from the storeroom. However, if they were caught, they would be collectively subject to the death penalty.

The family hesitated for a few days. During that time they watched the remainder of their food supplies dwindle. They realized that continued inaction would mean certain starvation. The temptation to remove the leather from the storeroom was great, regardless of the danger. Moreover, time was of the essence. The Germans could at any moment enter the storeroom and confiscate all of the merchandise. Or the Germans simply could do an inventory of the merchandise and leave the items in the storeroom. Either way, the merchandise would no longer be their lifeline for survival.

Once again, the adult members of the family met. They discussed the pros and cons of breaking the law. Shimon did not take part in the discussion. He sat in the other room studying Torah. He divorced himself from the reality of Poland now being controlled by world's biggest anti-Semite, Adolf Hitler.

His response to the events around him was to lose himself completely in his beloved world of Torah. For in his mind, without God's protection, they were all ultimately doomed.

That very night, the brothers made the crucial decision to act. They began to implement a carefully designed ten-step plan that they had formulated over the last few days. Step one: water was boiled in a kettle. Step two: the steaming kettle was brought to the storeroom door. Step three: the steam was released on the wax seal. Step four: the wax seal was carefully removed in a way that would leave the integrity of the symbols on the seal intact.

As my father explained step four, I wondered to myself, "Which brother was responsible for the critical removal of the seal?" Then I remembered that when I was a boy, my father once used steam to reopen a letter that he had accidentally sealed. As he worked on the letter, he told me that he was an expert in these things. So I was not surprised that upon questioning, my father answered with a gleam of pride that he was the one that removed the seal.

Step five: when the seal was removed, all the brothers entered the storeroom and removed the majority of the merchandise. Some merchandise was left behind and distributed throughout the room to give the appearance that nothing was disturbed. After the brothers were satisfied with the room's appearance, they exited. Step six: my father artfully returned the seal in a manner that made it nearly impossible to detect that it was tampered with. Step seven: the merchandise was taken to the small basement underneath the living quarters. Step eight: the merchandise was organized and divided it into several caches, which were placed into metal canisters and sealed. Step nine: the brothers dug deep holes in the basement's dirt floor. Step ten: the canisters were placed into the holes and the removed dirt was used to completely cover the canisters.

Upon finishing, the brothers, as well as the rest of the family, let out a collective sigh of relief. Their success gave the family the feeling that together they could overcome any adversity. In fact, the Germans never discovered the tampered wax seal, nor did they realize that that the Naimans now possessed the majority of the items in the storeroom.

From then on, whenever the Naimans needed to trade for necessities, they simply went down to the basement and dug up one of the caches, exchanging the leather or merchandise contained in the canister for food and other vital items. The brothers developed a rule that, to minimize the danger of being discovered, they restricted all trading to those Polish shoemakers they had done business with for many years and trusted.

The invasion of Poland was complete by October 6, 1939. Poland suffered approximately 200,000 casualties of war, and nearly 700,000 soldiers were captured. On October 8, 1939, Germany officially annexed the western part of Poland where Radziejow was located. This area was now renamed Wartheland. Germany considered the conquered area east of Wartheland as an administrative area under occupation. That area was called the General Government of Poland.

The Naimans, along with the rest of the Jews of Radziejow, understood that they were no longer living in Poland. Rather, they were unwanted inhabitants of Greater Germany. It was no secret to them or anyone else that, given the way Germany treated their own Jewish citizens, Polish Jewry was now in danger of annihilation.

Binem had several cousins that had served in the now-defunct Polish Army. Unfortunately, none survived. Rumors spread that the Jewish soldiers imprisoned by the Germans were either killed immediately or incarcerated in specially designated POW camps for Jewish soldiers. One particular camp, the subject of many rumors, was located outside of Lublin.

The Germans demanded a ransom of gold from the Jewish townspeople living in the city of Lublin. The Jews were told that if the ransom, which was an astronomical amount, was not paid, then the soldiers would be killed. The Jews did not have that much gold to pay the ransom. As a result, the German guards executed forty to fifty prisoners a day.

The Wehrmacht entered Radziejow sometime between September 9 and September 17, 1939. The town was initially occupied by a German infantry division, which was then replaced with a garrison of approximately thirty uniformed soldiers. At the time, many of the occupation forces were made up of members of the Gendarmeries (Rural Police), who were headed by one of Germany's most notorious anti-Semites, Heinrich Himmler.

Assisting in the administration and policing of the Wartheland were the Volksdeutsche, ethnic German citizens of Poland who were now drafted into the Wehrmacht and its auxiliary branches. It is estimated that approximately 6,000 Volksdeutsche were recruited from the regions of Poland and Czechoslovakia that bordered with Germany.

The majority of these draftees were integrated into the Gendarmeries. Their main duty was to supplement regular forces that were occupying the hundreds of towns throughout the Wartheland. The Gendarmeries were eventually replaced by Wehrmacht soldiers, mostly from motorized and transport units.

One of the first laws the Nazis enacted in Radziejow was that whenever someone passed a German soldier, he was required to give the Nazi a one-arm salute and shout "Heil Hitler." In protest, some Jews and Poles would say *pół lidera*. Hearing this, a German soldier would believe that he heard "Heil Hitler," but in fact they were saying in Polish "half a leader." This law lasted only a short period of time. The German occupiers decided that Poles and Jews were not worthy of giving the Nazi salute, so the practice stopped.

Joyce Wagner stated that the Germans would beat Jews in the streets. She remembered that Germans would enter her store and take whatever they wanted without paying. She noted that the Germans especially liked cigarettes.

However bad it was for a Jew to be abused by the Germans, it felt even worse when Poles joined in. Joyce Wagner recalled that soon after the occupation began, she heard an old Pole shouting the old expression, "*nasze ulice wasze kamienice*," meaning, "the streets are ours, and the buildings are yours." The Pole was insinuating: "What value is it that you live in these buildings, when such ownership is only by our permission – which we will now remove." She added that the Poles began looting and openly robbing Jewish stores. She remembered watching a Jewish shoe store burn to the ground after having been set on fire by looting arsonists.

The Naimans learned that bartering with trusted Poles worked most of the time, however, some Poles learned to take advantage of the Jews' predicament. Since the Germans occupied Radziejow, they enforced the law, and Jews had no protections under German law. As time went on, some of the Poles, even those who had been considered friends of the Jews, took advantage of this.

The Naimans learned this the hard way. One day, a Polish shoemaker who had been a loyal customer before the war came to the Naimans to purchase some leather products, saying that he heard the Naimans still had some supplies. The Naimans asked him what he needed, and he produced a list. The Naimans did not hesitate in bringing him all the items he requested. They laid out the merchandise on the kitchen table. The Pole smiled, gathered up all the supplies, put it in his bag, and walked away without paying.

As he left, he turned and said, "If you say one word, I will report you to the Germans for hiding the leather, which, if you hadn't heard, is punishable by death!"

During the first stage of the German occupation, the Naimans were relatively free to travel around Radziejow and the surrounding countryside. After the terrible experience with the crooked Polish shoemaker, Shmeil and the rest of the brothers decided that they should use some of their leather to produce shoes. Once the shoes were produced, they would bring the shoes to the local farmers in the area surrounding Radziejow and barter the shoes for food.

The Naimans employed a skilled Jewish shoemaker. He moved in with the family, and with his expertise and a combined effort of all the family members in the production they soon were able to manufacture men's, women's, and children's shoes. This proved to be highly successful. Notwithstanding the bad experience, they also continued to trade leather and supplies to trusted Polish shoemakers.

Within a few months of the invasion, the Jews in Radziejow were ordered by the Gendarmeries to affix yellow Jewish stars to their clothing, one on their front and one on their back. Any Jew found without the stars prominently displayed was punished, usually by being beaten physically and publicly humiliated. It did not matter if the Jew was young or old, healthy or ill, rich or poor. It did not matter if the Jew was accompanied by his young children. The Nazis took great pride and appeared to even enjoy enforcing this law.

Today, living in free society, it is difficult to understand the implications of living under draconian laws. We can understand how a person who has been wronged can feel when their suffering is inadequately addressed by a government or legal system. What is more difficult to grasp is the result when a government uses laws and their enforcement as a means to perpetuate suffering. Jews under the iron fist of the Nazis were beaten and killed for breaking nonsensical laws enacted by evil men who had been elevated to glorified status as the rulers of the land. This official program to promote Jewish suffering was escalated to the point that it became clear to everyone that the Nazis' ultimate goal was that all Jews must die, period.

Still, despite the danger, some Jews refused to obey the evil men and their nefarious laws. In Radziejow, for the most part, they were elderly Jews. They would avoid confrontation by either remaining at home or staying away from places that the police and soldiers patrolled. Shimon was a prime example. He never wore the yellow Star of David. He made it a point to always stay indoors and study Torah day and night.

During the next few months, the occupiers slowly increased pressure on the Jewish community. Every day a new order intended to harass the community was handed to the head of the Judenrat, or Jewish Council. One cannot comprehend how evil minds could promulgate such oppressive decrees day after day. As a result, Jews suffering increased and the Jews became more and more despondent.

Despite it all, there were a few that remained cautiously optimistic. Some would say, "As bad as things are, they are still bearable." Their goal was to stay alive and hope for a miracle.

With all the danger and chaos, Jewish life continued. Survivor George Gronjnowski remembered that his family celebrated his Bar Mitzvah during this time, on his birthday, January 14, 1940. The religious service was held in a small room attended by relatives. The *Parsha*, or weekly portion of the Torah, was read along with the reciting of traditional prayers. After the service, a spartan reception took place.

In March 1940, Henry Gronow was taken from his POW camp in Germany to Lublin, Poland and released. When he made his way back to Radziejow, he was shocked to find that the beloved mayor had been removed from office and replaced by a German Burgermeister. He remembered his first impression of the town after arriving, describing the town as "dead." He observed that his fellow Jews, many of whom were his relatives, fearfully awaited the unspoken inevitable.

Despite the fact that the practice of Judaism in any form was prohibited and punishable by death, Jewish life went on. In fact, three times a day, Jewish religious services were secretly held in private homes. All holidays were celebrated. Women lit the Shabbos candles Friday before nightfall. Even kosher meat was available. One survivor described how chickens were ritually slaughtered clandestinely at night.

Even more surprising, despite the dangers involved, Jews were still getting married. Survivor Henry Gronow courted Kazin Fox during the occupation. When the traditional courting period was complete, Fox insisted on marriage. So an informal ceremony was performed by Meir Levine, who was a religious Jew, though not an ordained rabbi. Unfortunately their marriage was short-lived, for within four years Kazin Fox was murdered at the extermination camp infamously known as Auschwitz.

Jews suffered new indignities every day. There was an infamous Gendarmerie in Radziejow who the Jews referred to as "the Potcher." He terrorized all the Jews in town.

My father said of the Potcher, "He was a real sadist."

The Potcher was considered to be the cruelest Nazi terrorizing the Jews of Radziejow, which in and of itself was an achievement of sorts. He was infamously called the Potcher (in Yiddish, "The Slapper") because whenever he saw a Jew, young or old, male or female, he would slap him or her across the face, oftentimes repeatedly. When the Potcher walked the streets on his daily patrol, he was constantly on the lookout for a Jew to assault. Any Jew seeing him would, without hesitation, take off in a run and seek the nearest hiding place.

As a result of this Jewish countermeasure, his pool of victims quickly dried up. Not willing to give up his favorite sport, he changed his tactics. He began entering Jewish homes at random, unannounced. He searched room by room until he found a Jew in the home. Then he would proceed with his dirty work. His new tactic was so outlandish that many Jews concluded no place was safe and therefore their situation was hopeless.

One day, the Potcher, on random patrol, entered the living quarters of the Naimans. This was completely unexpected, as Shimon's house was outside of the Potcher's usual hunting grounds. As the Potcher searched the lower level, room by room, he spotted his helpless prey, Shimon. Shimon was sitting in the parlor, oblivious of the imminent danger. Even though the Potcher stood only a few feet away, Shimon was completely unaware, as he was deeply engrossed in his

Talmud study. Shimon, through his devotion to Torah learning, had elevated himself to an existence completely divorced from the grim realities of the outside world. The Potcher approached Shimon and then, for no apparent reason, stopped right at the entrance of the parlor. The Potcher appeared transfixed as he stared at Shimon, whose head was seemingly buried in the oversized book in front of him.

Binem had heard the Potcher's entrance. The Potcher was not shy. His modus operandi was to make loud noises to frighten the inhabitants of whichever house he was entering. Binem had been watching the Potcher from the shadows from the moment he had entered the house. Now, Binem was astonished as he stared at the Potcher from his perch at the top of the stairs. He had a clear view of the downstairs hallway. Binem was frightened, watching helplessly as the Potcher made his way toward the parlor. He knew that his father was in the parlor and that the Potcher was about to attack him.

As Binem watched in dread, the Potcher suddenly stopped and stood frozen at the parlor's entrance. After a long moment, that seemed to Binem an eternity, the Potcher inexplicably turned around and left the building. Binem was greatly relieved as he descended the stairs and looked into the parlor. It was obvious to him that Shimon hadn't even noticed the presence of the Potcher and was completely oblivious of the danger that had just passed.

I asked my father what he would have done if the Potcher had attacked Shimon.

He answered, "What could I do? He had a gun."

I pressed, "Did it cross your mind to do something, anything?"

He replied, "The reason that it didn't cross my mind was that if a Jew would kill a German, then they would kill all the Jews in town. Everybody had a responsibility, not only to his family but to other Jews."

I continued to press for a satisfactory answer. "What if he attacked your father?"

He answered, "I was watching. I didn't make up my mind what to do, I don't know what my reaction would be."

That night, as the brothers were eating a sparse dinner, they discussed the incident with the Potcher. They concluded that only an act of God prevented the Potcher from striking Shimon, tearing up the Talmud, and who knows what else. The Naimans were well aware of the law that banned the possession of Jewish religious books and other items. Anyone caught in possession of these items was to be severely punished. Even knowing of the danger, the Naimans did not have the heart to deprive their father of his most sacred possessions. They loved their father more than they feared the Germans.

When Radziejow was annexed by Germany and incorporated into Wartheland, it was administered by Military District XXI. Its provisional capital was the city of Pozan. Although a military district, the entire Wartheland was now incorporated into Greater Germany. The Polish-occupied territory outside of Wartheland was governed from Poland's largest city, Warsaw.

Radziejow and its surrounding countryside was controlled by Himmler's General SS, known as Allgemeine-SS, specifically regiments 109 and 110. These troops were augmented in Radziejow by a garrison of Wehrmacht soldiers and a police force. For most of the occupation, the administration of Radziejow was controlled by soldiers known as Gendarmeries, or German rural police. My father frequently pointed out that the Gendarmeries were responsible for the daily routine oppression of Radziejow Jews.

In order to implement Nazi plans for Polish Jewry ,the Germans needed collaborators. These collaborators consisted of both the willing and the unwilling. The Nazis preferred using the willing, so they recruited those Jews that were considered by their own *lantzmen* to be criminals and bums and made them overseers of their fellow Jews. Many of these overseers were delighted by their newfound status and power, and did not hesitate to use this opportunity for revenge against their fellow Jews who had shunned them before the war.

In contrast, the Judenrat of Radziejow was controlled by the unwilling. The Nazis forced members of the community to serve on the Board. These members tried their best to ease the suffering of the Jewish community. The President of the Judenrat, known as the Judenkommisser, was a school teacher, Manes Sheiman. Members of the Judenrat board included Jakub Laski and Szmul Burstyn.

Sheiman was a fair-minded family man. His position of authority made his life a daily hell. He had to deal with the complaints and requests from his fellow Jews, and at the same time work under the Nazi scum that constantly harangued him. Each day he was ordered to physically appear in front of the German authorities. There he would receive new inane demands for that day.

With each new directive intended to burden the Jewish community, Manes had to find a way to both comply with the directive and simultaneously mitigate its impact. Sheiman and the Board succeeded in this impossible task for nearly two years. They were able to ease the burden of their fellow Jews as each member of the community tried to survive an additional day.

Binem praised Manes and the Board. "In Radziejow, there were no Jewish criminals. In fact, there was not a single Jew that could even be classified as a bum. Just the opposite, all the Jews were *lantzmen*, like one family. Anyone appointed to the Judenrat would treat their fellow Jews with respect."

Survivor George Gronjnowski believed that Sheiman was chosen to lead the Board because he was a university graduate and had served in the Polish Army as an officer. What made him even further qualified for this thankless job was that he was of German origin, and spoke fluent German. So it was believed by the Jews of Radziejow that he would be the best "go-between" to represent the community in dealings with German occupation authorities.

In one example of Sheiman's unique ability to deal with the Germans, a sixteen year old boy got in trouble with the Germans. It was alleged that the boy called a Polish woman a *kurva*, or prostitute. The woman was known for consorting with a German. The woman was outraged and told her boyfriend. That caused the Gendemaries to go looking for the boy. All knew that if he would be found, he would most likely be executed. When the boy's family were informed, they hid their son and then beseeched Sheiman to intervene with the Germans on their behalf. Sheiman made his way to the German in charge of finding the boy and explained that the boy didn't mean prostitute but rather he actually meant that she was "curved." The two words sound alike in Polish. By adding a bribe to this creative excuse, Sheiman was able to save the boy's life. The boy survived the war and eventually emigrated to the United States, making his home in California.

Likewise, George Gronkowski remembered a serious incident that involved his father. A swastika-wearing Volksdeutsche started a heated argument with his father. George's father lost his cool and called the man a "Hitlerite." The Volksdeutscher was outraged over what he conceived as proof that George's father was impudent and did not respect Hitler or Germans. The Volksdeutscher was so insulted that he sought revenge against the Jew by reporting him to the German authorities. Upon finding out that he was being sought by the Germans, George's father went into hiding. Again, Sheiman was asked to intervene. Sheiman was able to placate the man and the authorities and the charges were dropped.

A new order was issued. Jews were now forced to work as slave labor for the Nazis. In the beginning, work assignments were managed according to a list prepared by the Judenrat. Sheiman and his fellow board members did their best to assign their fellow Jews tasks they were capable of performing. Younger Jews were assigned heavy physical labor, while older Jews were sent to do lighter work. The jobs included cleaning the streets with brooms, working for German farmers in their fields, and cleaning the houses of the Volksdeutsche. The pious Jews understood that the Jews of Radziejow were now experiencing the same misery that their ancestors had endured as slave laborers in Egypt. The secular Jews hoped that their predicament was a temporary political problem that would be solved as the forces of government changed.

Orders issued by the Nazi occupiers required the Jews of Radziejow to submit to a daily routine of abuse. This abuse began early in the morning when all Jews were required to assemble at Market Square for roll call. Many of the town's Poles would gather to watch. Apparently, watching the Germans ridicule their "Jewish brothers" was part of their morning entertainment.

First, the Jews were ordered to line up. Then the *Oberjude*, a senior member of the Judenrat, would call off each name from the official list of Jews living in Radziejow. When the name was called, that person was required to shout out that he was present. Roll call would take place whether the weather was good or bad, sunny or raining, warm or cold, snowing or hailing. After going through the hundreds of names, the *Oberjude* would turn to the German officer in charge and certify to him that all the Jews in the town were present.

The *Oberjude* knew that this certification was a lie. In fact, all the Jews in Radziejow were aware that some of their friends and relatives were not present. A perfect example of the untruthfulness of the certification was my grandfather, Shimon. He never attended, even though everyone knew he lived in the town. In fact, Shimon's name was on the list of Jews living in Radziejow that the Nazis compiled in April of 1940. However the board member would never even contemplate the thought of turning Shimon in, despite the risk. So the Germans never knew that, from day one, Shimon was continuously absent from the daily roll call.

After the certification ceremony was completed, a German soldier or policeman would then order the Jews to form a line. The Jews were now to put through physical denigration called *ein training*. It always started by the Jews being ordered to run the four corners of Market Square in a line. No one was exempt from running. It did not matter if the Jew was very young or very old, sick or healthy. For the older Jews, it was physically difficult. They would slow down the line even with others helping them along.

Next the Jews were told to do random calisthenics such as push-ups, jumping jacks, or running in place. As the Nazi in charge racked his brain to come up with new ways of demeaning the Jews, the Polish spectators watched in fascination. Sometimes they would laugh as they watched the Jews suffer some new form of abuse. After more than an hour of continued debasement, the *ein training* ended. The Jews were then ordered to go to their respective work assignments.

One day, the Poles that had, until then, enjoyed watching the Jews being abused, found that the Nazis were no longer funny. A replacement unit of the Wehrmacht took control of the town. The first act of the new garrison officers was to teach the Poles of Radziejow just who was in charge. They did so by an act that destroyed the town's pride and joy.

A monument stood proudly in Market Square of the legendary Polish war hero Andrzej Kościuszko. In an official ceremony, the Germans tore down the statue as the Poles watched in horror. Then the Nazis mounted on the same marble pedestal a toilet.

I asked my father if he felt a sense of revenge or find humor watching the Poles suffer like the Jews.

He replied, "No, I didn't laugh. I found no pleasure in this insult. Even though I knew it was aimed directly at the Poles, I also felt insulted because I was a citizen of Poland."

Still, a few Jews thought it was good that the Poles now lost something, too. What was clear, even those Poles that were anti-Semitic were now very angry with the Germans.

As bad as conditions were, the Jews of Radziejow understood that they were faring better than most Jews living in the surrounding towns. Ironically, they attributed this to the presence of several Volksdeutsche, Polish citizens of German ethnicity, many of whom owned large estates and farms surrounding the town. The Jews of Radziejow had developed good relations with the Volksdeutsche through years of mutually beneficial commerce.

The Volksdeutsche, like the Jews, were a minority group living in Poland, and sometimes suffered prejudice against them from Poles. During the period leading up to the German invasion, some Poles targeted the Volksdeutsche with malicious acts, justifying their bad behavior as necessary punishment for Volksdeutsche fifth columnists. During the invasion, over five thousand Volksdeutsche were killed as a result of this kind of persecution, with thousands more listed as missing.

When Hitler received the news of the treatment of the Volksdeutsche in Poland, he was infuriated. He ordered the Army to punish the Poles. Units under Himmler's command committed reprisal shootings throughout Poland. This action resulted in the indiscriminate murder of many thousands of Poles.

Approximately 400,000 Volksdeutsche that were "liberated" by the German conquests of Poland and neighboring countries were subsequently recruited into the Wehrmacht, the German Armed Forces. All Volksdeutsche were registered on official Volkslists and given special German status. They were accorded many of the benefits of German citizens. As a result, the Volksdeutsche were catapulted to the top of the socioeconomic ladder with the Nazi invasion.

From the beginning of the occupation, Germans had requisitioned several buildings in town. Beis Rochel, the main shul of Radziejow, was defiled and used as a storehouse. Polish members of Radziejow's main church were expelled and forced to pray in a small wooden church on the outskirts of town. In the newly consecrated main church, German occupiers now worshiped along with the local Volksdeutsche population. Their faith apparently justified their cruelty, especially towards Jews, but also toward anyone that was not of the Aryan race.

The Volksdeutsche of Radziejow now could claim German racial superiority over the Poles. The occupiers considered the Volksdeutsche fellow Germans, while Jews were subhuman vermin. Just slightly above the Jews were the Poles. The perverse Nazi racial stereotyping dictated that, as part of the grand German plan for world domination, the Poles were to be lumped together with the racially inferior Slavs. These two groups were earmarked to be slaves of the master Aryan race. The children of these slaves were to be afforded only a rudimentary education that would be just enough to allow them to serve the German people as productive slave laborers.

Not all the Volksdeutsche were on board with Hitler's ravings. Some Volksdeutsche did not let this newfounded position of privilege to change their character. These good people even tried to alleviate the suffering of the Jews. For example, when they would learn that a new decree was about to be issued against the Jews, they used their connections with the German Police to mitigate the harshness of the implementation.

Survivor Joyce Wagner had mixed feelings concerning the Volksdeutsche. She recalled one incident involving a Volksdeutsche during the occupation in her autobiography, *A Promise Kept.*

"One day we went to pick up some flour for the bakery. I went to a Polish man who owned a mill. Driving back home we passed a German Volksdeutsche, a German national who was living in Poland, who also owned a flour mill. He reported me to the Gestapo because I had conducted business with the Pole instead of him.

In another incident, Wagner writes, "a Volksdeutsche came, selected merchandise, and told us to deliver it to their home without paying for it! The Germans now felt that everything that the Jews of Poland possessed belonged to them."

On the other hand, she tells how a Volksdeutsche couple that were friends of the family before the war hid her when she made her way back to Radziejow soon after the liquidation of the ghetto.

"I went to the home of a former customer of ours a German Volksdeutsche named Lange. She cried with me over the tragedy of what had happened to my family, as well as the sad fate of other Jews from the Radziejow ghetto who had been sent to Chelmno to be gassed. Her husband arrived, and he was so surprised and happy to see me. He openly encouraged his wife to help me."

Each passing day brought new indignities to the Jews of Radziejow. One day, an order was issued from Pozan, the military command center of the Wartheland, to begin an "aktion campaign." Among the earliest aktions was the destruction of all synagogues located within the boundaries of the Wartheland. Jews in town after town watched in horror as their beloved houses of worship went up in flames. German soldiers became arsonists sanctioned by law as they burned synagogues in Piotrkow, Aleksandrów, Zgierz, Bielsko, and Bydgoszcz, all villages and towns near Radziejow.

On the night of August 11, 1939, the Jews of Radziejow awoke to the sound of a terrifying explosion. Since there was a strict curfew in place, no one dared to go outside to investigate. All they could do was wait until morning to find out what new tragedy they would have to deal with. The next morning the townspeople, both Jews and Poles, learned that the Nazis blew up the newly constructed and dedicated Beis Rochel Synagogue and the old shul.

Binem remembered that night and the following day vividly. He said that he learned from friendly Volksdeutsche that the Nazis encountered a problem on their first attempt to destroy the shul. After setting fire to the two synagogues, the older shul burned down, but Beis Rochel remained intact because the structure of the synagogue was made of fireproof materials. This only made the Nazis more determined. So it was decided to use an alternative method. Explosive charges were set throughout the building. The subsequent explosion left only the shell of the original, magnificent structure.

The following morning, during the roll call in Market Square, a Nazi officer asked, "Does anyone have a box of matches?"

A few Jews innocently raised their hands. Those that did were quickly plucked from the line and presented to the German officer. The officer, with a devious grin on his face, proceeded to confiscate the matchboxes from the clueless volunteers. He then triumphantly proclaimed that he had succeeded in apprehending the arsonists that burned down the Jewish houses of worship. He prominently held up the matchboxes and declared that this evidence proved that Jews had burned down their own house of worship.

As this nightmarish event took place, seemingly every Jew present in Market Square fell into a horrible spell of despair. Many thought that it was bad enough that the Germans had destroyed the holy synagogue, the center of Jewish life in Radziejow, but now this Nazi had the *chutzpah* (audacity) to blame the crime on innocent, God-fearing Jews.

Survivor Jack Marcus had a slightly different version of events regarding the destruction of Beis Rochel and its aftermath. He lived on the outer edge of the Jewish ghetto between Marketplace Square and Beis Rochel. In the middle of the night, he woke up. He looked out the window and saw the synagogue on fire. He remembered that several people were standing in the street watching the inferno.

The next day, a German officer shouted out to the Jews, "Which one of you burned the synagogue?"

On hearing this accusation by this Nazi, the personification of evil, many of the Jews standing in the vicinity of Marcus tossed away any matches in their possession so as not to be accused of starting the fire.

It is unclear which version is a more accurate portrayal

of the events on this terrible day. One thing for sure, the Jews listened in terror to the officer's absurd and cynical accusations. The older, pious Jews were most affected. They couldn't bear the pain of such an evil act against God and his chosen people. God had truly hidden his face from the Jewish people. Their spirits were now completely broken. They knew that without God's protection, the Jewish people were now lambs for the slaughter. On that day, many lost their will to live. In relatively short period of time, approximately ten of these righteous, older, pious Jews died.

Among the first to succumb was my grandfather, Shimon. Just a few months later, my great-grandmother, Miria Pocziwy, also died of natural causes. She was buried alongside her husband, Baer. When the Jews of Radziejow discussed this rash of deaths among the pious, no one actually stated what many were thinking: God, in His infinite mercy, had spared the pious from the real horrors that were yet to come.

Shimon's death was shrouded in mystery. A few weeks after the destruction of the Beis Rochel Synagogue, Shimon, without any warning, became very ill. He gathered his sons around his bed and ordered them to bury his most treasured possessions. Those items were his holy books and cherished religious items such as menorahs, spice boxes, his silver Shabbos candelabra and his grand Shabbos kiddush cup. He instructed them to dig a deep hole inside the woodshed in the backyard and place the objects within. The books were part of Shimon's extensive library of Jewish holy books that included a complete set of the Talmud. Shimon's Talmud was comprised of dozens of portfolio-size volumes that were covered with the finest, elaborately embossed leather.

Shimon's sons, having the greatest love and respect for their father, obediently followed his instructions to the letter. While preparing the hidden treasure trove, one brother commented to the others that he was relieved that the Jewish books and religious objects were now being hidden away because the possession of these items was considered a crime by the Germans. Another brother said that he was terribly distraught for Tatte (father). He explained that Tatte would never part with his Gemoras unless he was sure that his end was near. All knew in their heart that the latter was correct. Because if they were sure of anything, it was that Shimon was unflinchingly devoted to God and his commandments. Therefore, if Shimon was ordering such a drastic action, it must be his last request as a dying man.

During the next few days, Shimon's condition deteriorated. His skin turned a sickish pale white, and his breathing was forced and appeared to be painful. Shimon called his sons together again and made the unusual request that they move the recently buried holy items. He wanted them to exhume his treasure from the woodshed and bury the items in the basement where the hidden leather caches were located.

When one of his sons sheepishly asked why, he replied, "I realized that the location was too close to the outhouse."

I asked my father if my grandfather's second request was carried out. My father hesitated and said, "We thought that there would be time later to move them. A little while later we were ordered to relocate to the ghetto. Then there was no time to move the books."

Binem explained that his failure to comply with his dying father's request caused him great anguish. After Shimon died, he was so distraught that he went to the Shammas (assistant rabbi) of the destroyed Beis Rochel Synagogue, who was a scholar and friend of Shimon, and asked him what he should do about the promise he made to his father. The Shammas showed little patience with this *shailah* (question involving Jewish law).

The Shammas answered impatiently, "You're worrying about books! Books can be replaced. You should worry about the Jewish people! The people cannot be replaced."

After Shimon's second request to move the treasure trove, his physical condition went from bad to worse. The family was at a loss as to how to help their father. There wasn't a Jewish doctor to treat him because when the Germans invaded Poland, the town's doctor, Dr. Paniski, fled and never returned. The only doctor in town was a German physician assigned to the German military forces in Radziejow. He treated German soldiers, Volksdeutsche, and, on occasion, Poles. He was under strict orders not to render any medical assistance to Jews.

Despite this fact, one of the brothers had an idea as to how to get medical treatment for Shimon. A few months earlier, Binem, who spoke some German, was assigned by the Judenrat to the task of being the doctor's valet. Binem's primary duty was to guide the doctor around the town for home visits for sick Volksdeutsche. Also, he served as a translator for the doctor when he treated Poles. His other duties included being the doctor's schlepper (valet) and car washer.

The brothers demanded Binem, "Why don't you go ask the German doctor to see Tatte?"

Binem knew that the doctor was forbidden to treat Jews. For a moment, Binem contemplated his brother's demand. Binem thought that from all indications the doctor appeared to be a well-meaning person. He never degraded Binem like the other Germans. So, despite this obvious violation of the doctor's protocols, Binem thought that perhaps the doctor might be open to the idea of making exception.

Binem replied, "I'll give it a try."

The following day, Binem waited for an opportunity to approach the doctor. Near the end of his shift, he requested his assistance. The doctor looked Binem in the eye and agreed. He said to Binem that it would have to be done at night because it was forbidden. Binem's face shined. He was relieved and very grateful. He knew that if the doctor was caught treating a Jew he would be severely punished. That night, despite the curfew, Binem made his way to the German doctor's house. True to his word, the doctor without hesitation accompanied Binem to the Naiman dwelling.

Binem's brothers watched the doctor suspiciously as

he carefully and thoroughly examined Shimon. They were relieved that the doctor conducted himself in a respectful manner towards Shimon. Judging by Shimon's face and body movements, it was obvious that he didn't trust this German doctor. After completing the physical examination, the doctor told the brothers that it was his opinion that Shimon had pneumonia. He explained that Shimon's condition was grave, and the only course of treatment was a certain powerful medication. Having no alternative, the brothers agreed that the doctor proceed.

The doctor then prepared an injection. He first set up his equipment on the nightstand adjacent to Shimon's bed. The doctor then proceeded to sterilize a long needle that was attached to a syringe by passing the needle through a bluish white flame produced by a special alcohol lamp that the doctor had set up on the nightstand. Shimon stared at the blazing flame and the now red-hot needle. He became terrified. His fear grew as the doctor approached him with the syringe. The doctor, in a very professional manner, managed to overcome Shimon's effort to grab his arm in a futile attempt to prevent the injection. The doctor then told the brothers that he had done all that he could do. With that, the brothers thanked the doctor and Binem escorted the Doctor to his home.

When Binem returned, he immediately went to Shimon's bedroom. Shimon was asleep in his bed. Binem was consumed with worry for his beloved father. As he watched his father sleeping peacefully, Binem decided that it would be best to sleep that night just outside of Shimon's bedroom door.

Binem fell into a deep sleep. At around four o'clock in the morning, he awoke suddenly. His first thought was to check on his father. Quietly opening the bedroom door, he approached Shimon's bed. Binem was startled to find that his father was not breathing. He reached out and touched his father's feet, which were still warm. He cried out to his brothers to quickly come. Within seconds, all the brothers entered the bedroom and gathered around their father's bed. They stared at Shimon's body, and concluded that their father had died in his sleep. All that was left to do was send word to the members of the Chevra Kadisha (Jewish Burial Society) to come.

As my father related this story to Spielberg's interviewer, he became quite emotional. Tears streamed down his face as he described the moment he discovered that Shimon had passed away.

I asked my father, "Do you think the German doctor killed your father?"

He replied, "I don't know. I do know that my father was very scared of the needle."

I wasn't satisfied with the response so I asked again, "What does that mean?"

He replied, "My father was scared of the fire and the needle."

I then asked, "What was in the syringe that the doctor injected."

He said, "The doctor told me that it was medicine used in the treatment of pneumonia."

Still not satisfied, I decided to continue to press him. "Do you think that the doctor might have poisoned him?"

My father finally admitted, "I had some suspicions, but those suspicions faded as I watched what was happening to the Jews."

Using their connections with the Volksdeutsche, the Naimans petitioned the German authorities to allow a burial at the town's Jewish cemetery. The friendly Volksdeutsche approached the administering Nazi occupation authorities and successfully procured the necessary burial permits for Shimon. According to Jewish law, the dead must be buried as soon as possible. Thus the Chevra Kadisha, the Jewish burial society, ritually prepared Shimon's body in compliance with the strict rules of Jewish law concerning the burial of the dead.

Just about the entire Jewish population of Radziejow attended Shimon's burial. Many commented that they hoped to be lucky enough to die like Shimon did, in his own house, surrounded by his children, with dignity.

It's hard for us today to understand such a reaction. Perhaps the Jews of Radziejow felt that Shimon had cheated the sadistic Nazis of another murder. Most likely they were just appreciative that Shimon died in such an honorable manner. Whatever the motivation, the comment reveals the impending doom felt by the Jews of Radziejow. They knew that death alone would relieve them of their daily torment. However, they understood that there was little chance they would be given a respectful burial.

Shimon was laid to rest at age 69 surrounded by his sons, daughters, relatives, and the Jewish community. The funeral service concluded with the Mourner's Kaddish. The sons recited the prayer, "May His great Name grow exalted and sanctified." Despite all the suffering of the Jewish community under the Nazis, the entire Jewish community that was standing around Shimon's grave responded "Amen," meaning that is the truth.

As per custom, the family sat the traditional seven days of mourning called Shiva. During the Shiva period visitors were encouraged to visit the Naiman house in order to comfort the mourners. Many visitors came and told the Naimans that while death is generally something to be avoided, in Shimon's case it was a gift from God. Binem, sitting on the traditional low chair for mourners, in his heart had to agree. He was relieved that Tatte no longer had to suffer any further. Binem had long concluded that the only reason why he and his fellow Jews were still alive was that the Germans needed them as slave laborers. As a result of this logic, Binem knew that even if his father had recovered from his illness he would have been too feeble to work. Therefore, he would have served no purpose in the minds of the Nazi murderers. History was to prove Binem's prediction to be correct. Soon thereafter, Binem became a slave laborer for the Germans doing work that his father, in his old age, could never do. After the mourning period ended, the Naimans emerged from the shelter of the Shiva house and returned to the dreaded reality created by the Germans.

The family now had a chance to think about the comments. For the family members themselves now understood that they would not likely die of natural causes. They would not be given a proper burial. There would not be a Shiva house for them. And, most dreadful of all, no one would be left to say Kaddish for them.

Soon after, the Germans accelerated their tightening of the screws on the lives of the Jews. An order was issued requiring all Jews to register with the office of the Burgermeister. Then it became law that they must carry at all times on their person identification documents stamped with the word Juden on it. Failure to present these documents when demanded by any German would result in severe punishment.

THE RADZIEJOW
GHETTO

On November 18, 1939, the Nazis issued a new directive ordering all Jews to leave Radziejow within eight days. After about half the Jewish population left, leaving behind most of their assets, the Germans rescinded the order for some unknown reason. The remaining Jews were ordered to leave their homes and move into the area between Torunska Street and Szewka Street. This designated area was to be the Jewish ghetto. Along with the Jews of Radziejow, additional Jews from outlying towns were also relocated to the ghetto. It is estimated that approximately 800 Jews moved to this area. It was designated an open ghetto, meaning there was no fence or wall enclosing the ghetto. However, it had the same rules as other Nazi-controlled Jewish ghettos, including the rule if one was caught outside the ghetto without written permission, that person was subject to the most severe punishment, death.

The Naiman's building was not inside the perimeters of the ghetto area. Therefore, the family had no alternative but to make arrangements for living quarters inside the ghetto The Naimans were able to bribe a Polish couple that was living within the ghetto to allow them to use their house. It was much smaller than the Naiman building, but that did not matter in the end. According to the Nazi order, Poles living within the area designated as the Jewish ghetto were permitted to take all their belongings with them when relocating. On the other hand, Jews relocating to the ghetto were restricted to bringing only those possessions that they could physically carry on their person. The Naimans could not bring with them even basic furniture and other essential household goods. Therefore there was plenty of room for the entire family and the hired Jewish shoemaker in the small Polish house.

Nazi Barracks in Radziejow

The Naimans' new residence was located on Torunska Street. Living in the house was Binem, Azriel, Shmiel, Macho, Masha her husband and children, and Malka. A Jewish leather cutter also moved into the house with them. He brought with him his precious sewing machine. The Naimans provided the cutter with leather that they periodically smuggled into the Jewish area from their hidden leather stashes. The cutter would then form the leather into shoe uppers. The family would help him attach the uppers to the soles. Then the finished product was traded for food. Although this was illegal, and if caught both the Naimans and the buyers would suffer unspeakable punishment, the trading went on because the Naimans needed food and the buyers needed shoes. There was no choice but to take a chance.

The Naimans continued to sell leather and materials to trusted Polish shoemakers. These shoemakers were always poor but honest. Once the bad ones were weeded out, the remaining shoemakers never took advantage of the weak position that the Jews had found themselves in.

Despite the real threat of severe punishment for being caught outside the ghetto, many Jews decided to take the risk to leave the ghetto and trade for food. The Germans had put the Jews on much less than adequate rations. Eating only the food provided by the Germans meant a long, painful death from starvation.

The Jews of Radziejow were faring better than their *lantzmen* in other nearby towns. Survivor Gabriel Brzustowski-Bross was living in the small town of Bobrowice when the Germans entered on the eve of Rosh HaShanah. The soldiers entered the small synagogue and brutally dragged out the Rabbi during the sacred prayer service. They proceeded to humiliate the rabbi by forcing him to pull a wagon while dressed in his white ceremonial robe called a Kittel. Appropriately, a Kittel symbolizes a burial shroud. The kittel became soiled as the Germans laughed. Soon thereafter some of the local Poles, either for pay or to curry favor, informed the Germans who were the Jews in the community. For Bross, this disgusting act of betrayal both to Poland and as well as their Jewish neighbors remained a sore point. For only with this type of collaboration and treachery were the Germans able to identify the Jews of Poland and succeed in their Holocaust crusade against the Jews.

Bross managed to escape from his town and searched for a better place to live. He made his way to the Kutno ghetto and later the Ghiskin ghetto. During his travels he survived by stealing potatoes and other food from Polish farmers. When he reached the Ghiskin ghetto, he found that the Jews were treated just as cruelly, so he decided to move on. He finally made his way to the Radziejow ghetto.

Bross immediately noted that conditions in the Radziejow ghetto were better than the other two ghettos. He stayed there with his cousins and later his mother and sister arrived. He said that the Germans "...didn't bother us, only they had us go to work every day."

In January of 1940, scores of German civilians arrived in Radziejow. They were mainly businessmen and their workers. These businessmen had procured different contracts with the German government. In order to fulfill these contracts, they needed manpower. So they arrived to enlist Jews to work for them on various projects that were considered part of the German war effort. They hired Jewish men and women from between thirteen and fifty years old. In Radziejow they chose around 450 Jews. The work was done at rural sites throughout Wartheland. Most of these sites were a long distance from Radziejow. As a result, those that were enlisted were relocated from the ghetto to live in *arbeitslager* (work camps).

The workers recruited in Radziejow were divided into three groups of between fifty and one hundred workers. Each group was sent to different *arbeitslagers* located near hamlets and small villages. One work camp was made up of all males. A second was made up of female workers. The third work camp was mixed. All three were within a hundred miles of Radziejow.

Nazi Mounted Officer Leading Jews of Radziejow to Work Detail

My father commented that the administrators of the labor camps were Germans that had avoided being drafted by convincing the German government of the need for slave labor. As per my father, they were not anti-Semitic. In fact, on several occasions Jews were arrested by the Gestapo and would have been sent to their deaths if not for the intervention of administrators that traveled to Gestapo headquarters to request that the Jews be returned.

Survivor George Gronjnowski remembers the morning he was sent to the *arbeitslager* Lojewo. He was then a boy of only thirteen. Still, like the adults, he was ordered by the Germans to report to Market Square so he could "volunteer" for slave labor. Against the advice of his parents, George went to Market Square willingly. His father, who was also ordered to report, had already gone into hiding. When George arrived at Market Square he understood the gravity of the situation. Security was very tight. Armed German soldiers were checking the identity papers of the Jews that reported. Many of the Jews were accompanied by their wives, mothers, fathers, and children. Several of the women and children were crying. The men had the look of impending doom on their faces. After registering, George knew that he had made a huge mistake. So he decided to run away. He went directly to the dwelling of a Polish family that were friends of his family where he hid.

When the Germans finished their paperwork, the Jews were separated into three groups. When the groups were ready for departure, disaster struck. The German police officer assigned to George's group noticed that his group was short one worker. That worker was George. The German swore at the group stating that they would just have to stand in place until the missing Jew was found.

From George's hiding place, he could hear the German police officer ranting at his assigned group. A thought entered George's mind: "What if the German would hurt someone because I ran away?" That fear was bolstered when he heard the German threatening to shoot Jews at random until the missing worker appeared. Binem was likely in this group that the German was threatening to randomly shoot.

George could not withstand the pressure. He decided that he would sneak back into his group's line. In the confusion, he was successful. Soon thereafter, the raging German conducted another count. To his surprise, this time the count was correct. The German concluded that the Jews were playing him a fool. Therefore, he demanded that the Jew who had been missing present himself to him. George was never so scared in his life. He knew that this German was was bent on revenge and that revenge would likely be murder! Still, he found the courage to step forward.

George remembered the confrontation with great clarity. He said that he walked up and faced "this big fat German." The police officer began by denigrating him along with Jews in general. He uttered these ravings in the most vile language that George had ever heard. The German repeated a series of derogatory terms such as *Scheissen* and *Schweinhund*. Then the German physically attacked George by slapping him hard across his face. The slapping continued from side to side. George refused to give in and cry, for he instinctively knew that his mother was watching. Without any apparent reason, the German's temper suddenly cooled and he behaved as if nothing had occurred. He then calmly led the group as they marched out of town. All the workers were singing Jewish and Polish songs.

Binem remembered the day that he became a "volunteer" hired worker. As instructed, he reported to Market Square at 8:00 a.m. His group marched from Radziejow to the *arbeitslager* Lojewo located about fifteen miles away. Binem worked in Lojewo with his older brothers, Shmiel and Azriel. His cousin, Joyce Wagner, was also assigned to the Lojewo work camp. Other family members such as Radziejow survivor Jack Marcus and his father Lieb were sent to an *arbeitslager* named Strakoda that was a three hour train trip from Radziejow.

The USC Shoah Foundation describes Lojewo as a forced labor camp for Jews located in Inowroclaw County, Pozan Voivodeship, Poland. According to survivors, it was opened no later than August of 1941 and closed no earlier than August of 1943. The prisoners did construction work for a civilian contractor known as P. Gratz. The *arbeitslager* was located on a farm that had been confiscated from its Polish owners. The administrative building was located in the family's farmhouse. Jews were housed in one of the barns. and slept in bunks. Binem explained that some time after he arrived, the lager was expanded to allow for female workers. They were boarded in a separated barn.

The Lager was loosely guarded by gendarmeries. Wehrmacht soldiers were not assigned to the lager because both Germans and Jews knew there was nowhere to escape to. More importantly, there was little reason for escape. The camps were liberally administered. The work was back-breaking, but still the overseers were not overly oppressive. Jews were fed regularly. Moreover, the constant degradation of living in the Radziejow ghetto was behind them. Many of the workers felt that the hard labor caused time to pass more quickly.

The Jews were assigned several different types of work. They cleaned the canals surrounding the lager, built barracks for soldiers in nearby camps, repaired railroad tracks, and built roads. During the winter, when outside work was not practical, the Jewish workers made straw doormats for the German army and the German home-front.

The camp environment encouraged camaraderie. Strong friendships were made. Laughter was not uncommon because humor was a way of dealing with the foreboding future.

Binem joked with his friends, "If we live over the war it was a good lesson. We now know how to do things for ourselves. Before the war, we would hire gentiles to do manual labor tasks. Now we can do it ourselves."

Binem always added the caveat, "That is, of course, if we actually live over the war."

In the beginning, the Jews were paid a small wage and provided with room and board. Food rations were adequate, consisting of plenty of bread and potatoes. Moreover, the rations were supplemented by buying and bartering with local Polish farmers. Then, a few months later, without notice, the wages stopped and the food rations were cut back. Life in the lager became progressively worse. However, many workers felt the camp was still the safest place for a Jew in Poland. They reasoned that the Germans need them to do these dirty jobs.

Radziejow survivor Ann Goldman Kumer worked at Lojewo. She commented that meals consisted of bread in the morning and soup when the workers returned from work. They also received a coffee ration. There was no work on Sunday. She also recalled that, in spite of the hardship, Jews in the camp continued to have faith and a strong belief in God. She fondly remembers a Yom Kippur service at the lager that was held by the light of one candle. One of the young men served as cantor and chanted by memory the moving Kol Nidre prayer. She added that despite the terrible conditions, all the Jewish workers who attended the service fasted the following day.

In the beginning, the camp authorities liberally gave out passes to the Jewish workers to return to Radziejow for a day or two during the week. In order to get permission to leave the work camp, a worker would ask the foreman of their work crew for a pass. This open policy did not last for long.

Some Jews did not follow the strict conditions placed on home visits. Binem related that on one dismal day, five Jewish boys returned late to the camp. Upon arrival they were detained by the guards. Binem knew that trouble would soon follow. The guards received orders from the camp administrator. One guard picked out three strong Jewish workers to grab hold of one of the tardy boys.

The German guard then announced, "We will teach you how to obey."

The boy received 25 brutal lashes from the whip. Then, the other four boys were unmercifully whipped in the same manner.

From that day on, Binem no longer trusted the German civilian administrator.

Binem said of the administration, "Their promises didn't live up to their actions."

Another policy that was eventually restricted was home convalescence. When a worker became ill, he was allowed to return home to recuperate. Binem's two brothers, Shmiel and Azriel, took advantage of this policy. They both feigned illness, allowing them to return to Radziejow. The two brothers remained and never returned to the work camp. As more and more workers became suddenly ill, the policy of returning home to rest was later severely restricted.

Binem's work crew was always escorted by a guard that he described as being "a nice German watchman." As the Jews worked, the watchman would lounge around, barely paying attention. The watchman would often talk with Binem who was the only one in the crew that spoke German. He told Binem that before Hitler's rise to power he was a member of a German communist organization. He confessed that he felt very sorry for the Jews. Because of these feelings, he was always civil to the Jews on his work crew, and often even helpful. For example, he would authorize passes for Jews to return to Radziejow for any reason. Binem and the others often took advantage of this nice German's goodwill, so they frequently traveled back and forth to Radziejow to rest and visit their families.

The precious pass allowed Binem to travel both outside the camp and outside the ghetto. So, before entering the Radziejow ghetto, Binem would regularly sneak back into the unoccupied Naiman building and dig up one of the smaller caches of leather goods still hidden under the basement dirt floor. With the leather concealed under his clothes, he would pass through the ghetto's entrance without incident.

He would go directly to the Naiman's assigned house. There he would be greeted by his brothers Shmiel, Azriel, and Macho and his sisters, Malka and Masha. He would remove the leather goods and give them to his brothers so they could barter for food and other needed items. The system worked so well that often Binem was able to bring back extra food to the lager.

At the end of the summer of 1940, Survivor George Gronjnowski and many others were released from forced labor at Lojewo. George returned to Radziejow and moved back in with his mother and father. He described the situation in Radziejow as grim. German soldiers, with no justification or warning, would attack the helpless Jews during authorized missions called *aktions*. During these *aktions*, men were kidnapped from their homes and placed in forced labor battalions. George remembered that before one scheduled *aktion*, a rumor spread that allowed some Jews a chance to hide. George ran to the end of his backyard and jumped a fence. That area was outside the ghetto boundaries. He then made his way deep into the adjacent field where he hid for several hours. He then surreptitiously made his way back to his house. By then, the *aktion* was over.

In spite of German laws prohibiting contact between Poles and Jews, contact was maintained secretly for purposes of trade. Jews were able to purchase and barter for food with the Poles by parting with their precious possessions. So, no matter how severe were the edicts restricting rations, the Jews managed to have enough food and clothing to survive.

The period following the German invasion of Poland could only be described as a nightmarish existence for the Jews of the Radziejow ghetto. Life was literally like living in a house of horrors. Even more bizarre was that the psyche was able to adapt, which protected the sanity of the Jews. The average Jew clung to the hope that, if this is as bad as it gets, then it is possible to survive. So for many of the ghetto Jews these terrible hardships became a passable existence.

German atrocities continued to escalate both in Radziejow and the surrounding area. For example, in one incident, several German soldiers, apparently for their own amusement, escorted a group of defenseless Jews from the Radziejow ghetto to a nearby field. There they forced the Jews to dig deep holes and then buried them up to their necks. The Germans found this quite funny and continued to laugh as they returned to Radziejow, leaving the buried Jews to their fate. Luckily for the Jews, hours later Polish peasants passed by and heard the cries of the buried men. Endangering their own lives, the peasants broke the law and rescued the Jews.

German Military Band in Radziejow Market Square

The year 1942 proved to be the most deadly for the Jews of Poland. Prior to March 1942, about eighty percent of Polish Jewry had managed to survive the inhumanity of the Nazi occupation. The other twenty percent were murdered. But starting in March and ending in February of 1943, close to sixty percent of those remaining Jews were rounded up and transported to the extermination camps of Chelmno, Treblinka and Auschwitz.

The mind-boggling part of this was that the Germans considered the slaughter of innocent men, women, and children a sacred duty. Hitler and his cohorts' dreams of racial purity had reached the level of realization. In the Nazi scheme of things, success was defined as the murder of hundreds of thousands of defenseless Jews. To the vast majority of Nazi fanatics, killing Jews was more important than winning the war. In fact, during this period of catastrophe for the Jews of Poland, the German Army was subject to defeat after defeat in Crimea, the Caucasus, and finally the death blow that took place at Stalingrad.

Jews Lined Up in Radziejow Ghetto

Even before March of 1942, the Jews of Radziejow knew that their doom was soon forthcoming. Starting on January 26, the Germans raided the Radziejow ghetto and plundered any remaining possessions of the Jewish inhabitants. The stolen items were stored at the local firehouse. This heinous act did not end the confiscations. Just to make sure nothing remained, the German Police made periodic inspections. The inspections had the added effect of constantly terrorizing the defenseless Jews who were just barely hanging onto life. During these so-called inspections, the Germans removed any item that caught their fancy. Simultaneously, the Jewish food ration was reduced from a near-starvation diet to a one that guaranteed death. Jews were prohibited from owning any personal hygiene items such as soap or sanitary items. The little electricity that had been provided to the ghetto was shut off. Jews were forced to use whatever fuels that could be found. When lucky, they were able to obtain meager supplies of kerosene for lighting and heating. If these hardships were not enough, the local *Volksdeutsche*, once the neighbors of the Jews, were now regularly entering the ghetto to find and exploit free workers for farm work or other labor. This included forcing Jewish tailors to mend clothing and Jewish craftsmen to make a variety of items such as furniture, shoes, pottery, woodwork, and glassware.

A strict five o'clock curfew was imposed. Collective punishments became the norm for the ghetto residents. The Jews would be assembled in Market Square where the gendarmeries would experiment with new techniques of sadism to dehumanize and degrade the Jews. Oftentimes they invented imaginary crimes to rationalize their attacks on the Jews.

From March 2, 1942 through June 23, 1942, the German occupiers implemented the *aktion* called "Operation Field Worker." During this period of time, the Nazis murdered 171,947 Poles, most of whom were Jews. One of the goals of this operation was the complete liquidation of all Jews still living in Wartheland. This unimaginable crime was to be accomplished by the systematic destruction of all existing Jewish ghettos. Specialized Nazi military units moved from town to town carrying out the goals in *blitzkrieg*-like attacks. The plan was grotesque in its planning and implementation. These specially trained units would liquidate a ghetto within twenty-four hours or less. The actual raids always took place under the cover of darkness.

The first step was to set up an impregnable perimeter around the designated Jewish ghetto so that the Jews would be unable to flee from their impending doom. Then soldiers would be sent into the ghetto to brutally round up the Jews. The would shout at the defenseless Jews *schnell* and *rouse,* meaning "move it!" and "get up!" They would shoot Jews randomly and set vicious dogs upon the defenseless Jews in order to gather them to a collection point. Then special units used trained dogs to search the now-vacant houses and buildings for any Jews that had the audacity to hide. Once the commander was assured that the ghetto was cleared of Jews, the next step, which usually took place the morning after the *aktion*, was to transport the Jews to a designated killing zone.

LIQUIDATION OF
THE GHETTO

N ear the end of May, 1942, a friendly Volksdeutsche man endangered his life by telling the Naiman brothers living in Radziejow that their ghetto was soon to be liquidated. He told the Naimans that they must flee for their lives immediately. So the family, consisting of Azriel, Shmiel, Macho, Masha, and Malka had to escape.

The first question was: how could they leave the ghetto? The second question: if they managed to escape, where would they go?

Shmiel, the oldest son, took charge. All Jews were well aware of the law that a Jew found outside of the ghetto would be subject to immediate and severe punishment, including execution without trial. Luckily, there was a town official, Walter Foretsch, that was susceptible to bribes. So the Naimans, along with several other Jews, bribed this city official to issue them travel papers. Walter Foertsch was eventually caught by the Germans, tried, and found guilty of issuing illegal documents. He was sentenced to four years in prison.

With travel papers in hand, The Naimans fled eastward, away from Germany. They were misled by other Jews who told them that better conditions existed in the territory of the Polish Protectorate of Czestochowa. Little did they know that the Jews of Czestochowa were facing the same life-and-death struggle as the Jews of the Radziejow ghetto.

Upon arriving in Czestochowa, the family was detained by the Polish authorities. Then the Poles turned the Naimans over to the Nazi occupiers who immediately imprisoned them in a walled Jewish ghetto that had been established in April of 1941. The Naimans were aghast when they entered. The ghetto was packed with Jewish refugees from all parts of Poland, and had long ago reached its maximum capacity. Many of the Jews looked famished and half-crazed.

The Nazis had a solution to the crowding problem, which was daily roundups. The Naimans immediately joined their fellow Jews as prey for besieged Judenrat to fill their daily roundup quotas. The Naimans quickly realized there they were now cornered in a death trap where there was no possibility of escape.

In Radziejow, word spread throughout the ghetto that another friendly Volksdeutsche told of an impending final *aktion*. This caused panic among those residing in the ghetto. More and more Jews fled. By the time that the final Radziejow *aktion* took place, most of the of the pre-war Jewish residents of the town had already escaped to other parts of Poland. Those that remained were mostly Jews that did not have the resources or the strength to flee.

The exact number of Jews living in the Radziejow ghetto on the day of the final *aktion* is unclear. One source regarding the transportation of Jews to the Chelmno extermination camp states that "[t]he last known transport, with 630 Jews, arrived from Radziejow Kujawski on June 11." Another source approximates the number of Jews from Radziejow was 600.

Photo Taken Just Prior to Aktion Liquidating Radziejow

The *aktion* took place on either April 1 or June 10, 1942.
Coincidentally, June 10th was my father's birthday - he was 23
years old. The reason for the controversy concerning the date
of the *aktion* is that there are different accounts by Jews and
Poles. Radziejow survivors had difficulty remembering precise dates after the war. The typical Holocaust survivor used
referenced points such as birthdays or holidays to approxi-

mate dates.

Additionally, most accounts of the Radziejow final *aktion* are from second-hand sources, since most of the Jews present at the time of the liquidation of the Radziejow ghetto were sent to Chelmno. Of all the Jews of Poland sent to Chelmno, totaling several hundred thousand, only two or three survived. What remains are the memories of Poles and Jews that escaped prior to the transport, or their retelling of unreliable hearsay.

Survivor Jack Marcus was with Binem at Lojewo starting in June 1941. He returned to Radziejow two months before the liquidation of the ghetto. He remembered that a Volksdeutsche told several Jews just prior to the liquidation of the Radziejow ghetto that "the whole city" was to be "taken away." Later, the Nazi occupiers hinted that something big was about to occur. They told the Jews that the time will soon come when the ghetto will be closed. The Nazis assured the Jews that they will be able to "take with you whatever you want, the best you have, and we will resettle you to a different part of the country."

Upon hearing these pronouncements, Jack's mother knew that the Nazis were planning to kill all of them. She told Jack to run away. He made his way back to Lojewo and was there with Binem until August of 1943.

Joyce Wagner wrote a heart-wrenching account of what happened the day of the Nazi *aktion* in the Radziejow ghetto.

> At daybreak the ghetto was awakened by the voices of the Gestapo screaming, "JUDEN RAUS! JEWS OUT OF YOUR HOUSES NOW!" There were the loud barks of vicious dogs, and there was pounding on doors. With this raid at early dawn the Gestapo caught everyone in the Radziejow ghetto completely by surprise. Whole families were captured. No one was prepared. All were herded by the Gestapo into a church overnight. The conditions

were unbelievable. People received nothing in the way of food or water. People had been evicted from their homes so swiftly by the Gestapo raid that none had time to take along provisions. Some Jews watched as family members who tried to flee were gunned down. People were crying. So the Jews of the Radziejow ghetto stayed locked in that church for a day and a night.

She vividly remembered that the liquidation of the ghetto started with shooting and screaming. Prior to the *aktion* she had devised a plan in the event that the Nazis invaded the ghetto to take her and her family away. The plan was to hide in her neighbor's attic. When the *aktion* began, she and her three siblings ran to the attic. Unfortunately, because of the chaos, her younger brother panicked. After they were well hidden in the attic, her brother got up and ran out, shouting that he was not safe there. He ended up hiding in the building's basement.

That night, at the height of the *aktion*, a German Gestapo agent named Bropkowski discovered Joyce and the her two siblings hiding in the attic. Fortunately, the Gestapo agent was friendly with the neighbor that owned the attic. When the neighbor heard the commotion, the neighbor ran to the agent and pleaded with him. When the neighbor was done, the agent shouted down to the German raiders that there was no one there. Unfortunately, the agent then checked the basement and found Joyce's brother. The brother was forced to join the other Jews that were being marched off to the nearby church.

There the Jews awaited their fate. The conditions inside the church was intolerable. It was hard to breathe, and there was no food and water. The depressing sound of hundreds of people moaning was amplified by the acoustics inside the church. The next day the Jews were forced out of the church and ordered to climb onto trucks. They were then transported to the Chelmno Extermination Camp. There they were processed then murdered by carbon monoxide gas. Joyce Wagner estimated that there were over six hundred victims.

Binem was not in Radziejow when the *aktion* took place. He had procured a pass to go back to Radziejow on the day of the liquidation. During this visit he was planning to retrieve one of the hidden stashes of leather. When he arrived, he found that the ghetto was empty of Jews. Perplexed, he decided that he would ask his Polish neighbors what happened. The Poles told him that armed Germans had entered the ghetto in the middle of the night and rounded up all the Jews. The Jews were marched to the nearby church and held inside overnight. That morning, trucks arrived and the Jews were packed into them. One Pole stated that the truck looked unusual because of the configuration of the exhaust pipe. He remarked that the truck bed itself was covered by a tarp that appeared to be some kind of oil cloth.

I asked my father what did the Poles do when they saw the Nazis violently liquidating the ghetto. He replied, "The Poles didn't do anything." He paused, then added, "they were probably happy that it wasn't them."

Lenny Marcus, son of Holocaust survivor Jack Marcus, visited Radziejow during the 1980s. Armed with a map that his parents had provided him, he rented a car and drove to Radziejow. His car was packed with camera gear, which he used to film a documentary that was shown on PBS Boston.

During Lenny's interview of Gronjnowski, he learned that the Jews in the church, along with Polish criminals incarcerated in the town jail, were loaded onto death trucks. Once they were packed inside the trucks, they were murdered by carbon monoxide poisoning. The bodies were buried between Kolo and Sluko in a large forest. Marcus and Gronjowski later made a kind of pilgrimage to the large Holocaust memorial located in the very forest where the Jews of the Radziejow ghetto were buried. The center of the memorial is a large concrete edifice surrounded by a garden. Buried beneath the garden and the surrounding area are the remains of hundreds of thousands of murdered Jewish victims of the Nazis.

The idea of gas vans originated with SS Brigadeführer Arthur Nebe, commander of Einsatzgruppen B. Since shootings and starvation had been found by the Germans to be inefficient and psychologically difficult on the executioners, the Germans looked for better ways to exterminate "undesirables." They experimented with the use of explosives, however, in their trials, explosives only killed some of the victims, leaving the majority only maimed. So they turned to poison gas.

Nebe was a former leader of the Reich's Criminal Police Department (*Kripo*) where he became familiar with the euthanasia program that utilized poison gas against the mentally handicapped of Germany. Nebe and a Dr. Widman in Mogilev conducted an experiment in which thirty mentally disabled persons were placed into a sealed room. Two cars simultaneously pumped their exhaust fumes into the room. After a few minutes, the thirty were dead.

A proposal was brought before SS Obergruppenführer Reinhard Heydrich to use this method to kill Jews. With Heydrich's approval, Walter Rauff, of the *Reichssicherheitshauptamt* (Reich Security Main Office), designed a vehicle for this purpose which was made to resemble an ambulance or refrigerator truck. The back cabin was sealed, and the vehicle's exhaust pipe was channeled into the sealed cabin. After Heydrich, considered by many historians to be the "architect" of the Holocaust, advocated for the use of poison gas, Hitler gave his authorization.

Interestingly, Hitler had first-hand knowledge of the terrible death that resulted from the inhalation of poison gas. During World War I, he was an infantryman assigned to carry messages between the trenches. During one of these runs, Hitler was subjected to a poison gas attack that killed many of his fellow soldiers and left him severely injured.

Other sources, however, maintain that the Jews liquidated from the Radziejow ghetto were transported to Chelmno to be murdered. The liquidation of the Radziejow ghetto was part of the overall plan for the complete annihilation of Jews in Wartheland known as "Operation Reinhard." Reichsführer SS Heinrich Himmler was directly in charge. Himmler appointed SS-Obergruppenführer Odilo Globocnik to implement the operation. The prototype death camp named Chelmno, named after its location in Poland, was key to the operation's success.

Chelmno was built just a few months before the Wannsee Conference that took place on January 20, 1942. Fifteen high-ranking Germans attended this secret meeting which took place in a large villa in a suburb of Berlin. The topic of the conference was the "final solution" for the Jews. At the conference, a plan of action was drafted for the total destruction of European Jewry.

Chelmno was the first death camp that used carbon monoxide gas to kill Jews in vast numbers. Its isolated location, in the center of a forest, was ideal for a extermination camp. It was also only 50 miles away from the City of Lodz, whose ghetto held approximately 200,000 Jews.

Chelmno itself was completely off limits to all Germans and Poles, save the actual staff. The camp was located in a small park that already had two structures, a manor house and a granary. The Germans added a few wooden huts. The entire area, approximately 5 acres, was enclosed by a high wooden fence. To maximize secrecy, the nearest town to Chelmno underwent a complete evacuation by the Germans.

Less than two hundred Germans participated in the operation of the camp. Supplementing the German staff were selected Jewish slaves gleaned from the Jews shipped there to be murdered. These Jewish slaves were kept under horrendous conditions, and their life expectancy was extremely short. The slaves were forced to remove the dead bodies of the Jews that were gassed. During the removal process, all hidden valuables were removed, and gold dental work was extracted.

Then the bodies were thrown into a mass grave.

The Jewish slaves were so overworked that they had little time to ponder their fate. As they worked, they were constantly terrorized by the guards. For example, it was common for a German guard to torment the Jewish workers by picking one out and shooting him. The other Jews took no solace in the fact that they were spared, for all knew that they would soon meet a similar fate.

According to historian Patrick Montague, there were no more than three survivors of the killing machine known as Chelmno. They managed to escape through the forest. As a result of these breaches of security, Jews at Chelmno were forced to do their backbreaking labor in painful leg irons.

The extermination schedule took place according to a strict timetable. Early each morning, the guards of Chelmno, approximately 80 to 100 members of the *Schutzpolizei*, would receive truck transports. Once the Jews were herded off the trucks they were lined up in the large courtyard of the manor house. After standing there for a few minutes, a camp officer would make a short speech, usually promising them that they were to be sent to Germany as laborers. An alternative speech by the officer would state that they were to be sent to the Eastern front to build fortifications for the German Army. In both versions, the officer closed his speech by stating that, in order to prevent the spread of typhus, they would be first deloused and have their clothes disinfected.

Immediately after the speech ended, the Jews were marched inside the manor building. There a menacing Nazi shouted orders for them to completely undress. Once they were all standing naked, he barked out that they should hand over any valuable items. Then the Nazi shouted that they were to be transported by trucks to the nearby bathhouse. The naked, terrorized Jews were separated into groups of seventy. The first group was led down a set of stairs that led to the lower level. The stairs led to a dark corridor that ended in a loading ramp. The Jews were then forced into the open back of a truck parked at the end of the ramp. The truck was one of the three gas vans used at Chelmno.

After the approximately seventy Jews were packed inside the truck, its back doors were closed and sealed. The mechanic on duty attached a tube to the van's exhaust pipe and then started the engine, pumping carbon monoxide gas into the chamber where the victims were crowded. The gas entered the truck by way of a screen in the floor. The Jews packed into the small confines of the cabin likely didn't even notice the odorless gas seeping into the near pitch-dark van. However, after a short period of exposure, they likely began to experience headaches, nausea and vomiting, confusion, and then lost consciousness."

After several minutes, all the Jews inside the cabin were dead. Then the van was driven to a nearby forest for burial. Upon its departure, a second truck backed up to the loading ramp, for the next group of seventy Jewish victims.

There were three main drivers of the van: Hauptscharführer Gustav Laps, Hauptscharfuhrer Burstinge and a soldier named Gilow.

The extermination camp of Chelmno was a short drive, less than nine miles, to the town of Kolo. The burial forest was between the two locations. The bodies were dumped into prepared mass graves. Any victim that managed to survive the gassing was shot by the SS and the Police stationed in the forest burial area. Jewish slave laborers scavenged the bodies for any remaining valuables and inspected each body's mouth for gold teeth. If a gold tooth was found, the Jewish slave laborer would yank it out and then handed over to his Nazi guards.

A thousand Jews a day were murdered in this manner. In charge of the burial process was a German known as Wachtmeister Lenz. The decaying bodies gave off a stench that was so pungent the Germans temporarily stopped operations to find a solution to the problem of how to hide their hideous crime. It was decided that the bodies should first be cremated and the ashes buried. A crematoria was then constructed in the' forest. The ovens became fully operational by the middle to the end of the summer of 1942. In addition, trees were planted to help mask the smell. The supervisor for the construction of the crematoria was Hauptscharführer Johann Runge. He was assisted by Unterscharführer Kretschmer.

Historian Patrick Montague reviewed eyewitness testimony given by Heinz May, a German civilian employed as a consultant to the Chelmno extermination camp. May was a German forester who worked in the forest where the victims were buried, and was given the task of the concealing the mass graves. During May's time there, he was told by the unit commander, SS Captain Hans Bothmann, that as of May 1942 there were nearly 250,000 corpses buried in the forest where he worked.

Regardless of whether the remaining Jews of the Radziejow ghetto were killed by gas vans and taken directly to burial, or brought first to Chelmno, all evidence is in agreement that after the ghetto was liquidated, the Jews were transported, murdered, and buried close to Kolo.

Survivor Jack Marcus recalled that during his time at Lojewo Lager, two couples secretly arrived at the camp. They had earlier fled Radziejow with their children to Chestokowa, only to have escaped a liquidation *aktion* there. Unfortunately, their presence became known to the regional Gestapo. Within days, the Gestapo raided Lojewo, bringing with them a transport truck. One Gestapo agent announced that they had information that there were children in the camp, which was against the law. He threatened the workers that they must turn over the children within one hour, and if the children were not turned over, ten workers would be shot. The Jews of Lojewo were frightened and at a loss as to what to do. Some of the Jews reflected, "It is bad enough that the Nazi murderers are torturing and killing us - now they want us to help them kill children!" Other Jews pointed out that the Gestapo didn't need a reason to kill any Jew. Some of the Jews searched out the children that were hiding. Marcus stated that the children and their parents were arrested and the Gestapo put the families onto the transport trucks and drove away.

Survivor Sally Klingbaum and her husband, son, and daughter arrived at Czestochowa around the same time that the Naimans were in the same ghetto. She described the dismal conditions of the ghetto that drained the Jews of all hope. When the Klingbaums were processed, they were told that there was no place for them to sleep and there were no rations of food for them to eat. The family left the processing center and searched for a place to rest. They found a crowded corner next to a dilapidated building where hundreds of Jews sought shelter. That night, rats by the thousands ran rampantly around them. The next day they found a space in a building. Again, when night fell, rats were everywhere. They soon concluded that rats were flourishing, while Jews had become an endangered species. Eventually the family found a place in the kitchen of a small apartment. They spent three months in that kitchen.

Klingbaum remembered that during Pesach, the only kosher food available was potatoes. Although the corner of the kitchen that her family occupied was cramped, it was at least livable. Then the Germans forced the Jews out the building and relocated them to a part of the ghetto that Klingbaum described as three times worse.

Soon after, rumors spread that the area of the ghetto where she now lived was to be liquidated. The *aktion* finally occurred a day before Yom Kippur. She and forty-eight others living in her dilapidated building hid in the attic. There they remained for thirty days. Not even the cries of her children pleading for a morsel of bread justified risking one's life to search of food.

Survivor George Gronjnowski described the Czestochowa *aktion* to liquidate the large ghetto as taking place just before dawn, between three and four in the morning. The ghetto was transformed to a living hell on earth that even Dante could not have imagined. The defenseless Jews were

Scott M. Neuman

assaulted in a military fashion by units of the S.S. and Sonderk-
ommandos, along with various "ad hoc" military units. There
were also units of Polish Police along with vicious dogs. Flares
illuminated the sky while the buildings were lit up by powerful spotlights. The ghetto Jews were accosted with a cacophony of menacing sounds that permeated the air. All one could
hear were the screams of people, gunfire, dogs growling and
barking seemingly out of control, and the sounds of children
crying along with their parents.

During all of this chaos, the Nazis in a systematic
method scoured the ghetto rounding up the panic-stricken
Jews. Then the Jews were marched like cattle to a collection
area that was located near the railway station. There the men,
women, elderly, and children were forcibly separated. When
it was over, the men and women went through a selection process. An S.S. officer with his hands on a baton walked down the
line of Jews. When he saw someone that he deemed unfit for
work he would point his baton at him and said "Roust." Everyone in line knew that the person selected was as good as dead.

Those that were "lucky" enough to pass selection were
conscripted as slave labor. These Jews were relocated into a
smaller ghetto located next to the large ghetto that was in the
process of evacuation and liquidation. The small ghetto's living conditions were only slightly more bearable than the hell-
ish conditions of the large ghetto. These Jews were now forced
to do back-breaking labor that included working in the boiler
factory and welding. The food rations for these workers were
still meager. The workers were quite aware that their days
were numbered.

Reinforcing the feeling of inevitable death were the
never-ending selections in which German officers would pick
workers to be sent to an extermination camp. In the beginning, weaker ones were sent to death while stronger ones
earned yet another short reprieve. When there were no longer
any weak ones, able-bodied workers were selected to maintain the daily quota of Jews to be sent to extermination camps

by the insatiable Nazi murderers.

Survivor Sally Klingbaum and her family managed to find their way to the small ghetto where they remained for ten months. Sally and her husband were constantly haunted by the knowledge that it would be impossible for them to save their children. They did their best, keeping them hidden while they worked. One day they returned from work to find out that their daughter had been caught and shot. Some time later, they learned that their son had been caught and sent to the Tschenstochau-Pelzery Concentration Camp.

During these most desperate times, matters went from bad to unimaginably worse. Just after Rosh Hashanah in 1942, Binem received a letter from his older brother Shmiel that contained horrific news. Shmeil wrote that Azriel had been killed by the Germans for a curfew violation. Michal, Azriel, and three of their sisters were now dead. Shmiel appealed to Binem to save him. He emphatically wrote that his only chance for survival was if Binem obtained for him official papers transferring him back to Binem's lager. He emphasized in blood-chilling words that without the transfer papers, it would be only a short time before he would be selected and sent to his death.

Shmiel's desperate cry for help completely devastated Binem, who was still reeling from the news of the liquidation of the Radziejow ghetto. As bad as life was, he had become accustomed to slave labor. Now to learn that all his brothers and sisters, save Shmeil, had been murdered, was too much for him. Over and over he thought that his father, sisters, brothers, cousins, aunts and uncles were all either dead or soon to be murdered. All that was left of his family were his brothers in America and Shmiel.

Binem decided that he must save his older brother, no matter the risk. Shmiel had taken over as the de-facto family leader when Shimon retired. Up until now, Binem had always gone to Shmiel whenever he needed help. Now the roles were reversed - Shmiel was turning to his little brother for salvation. Binem, himself helpless, felt he had to find a solution. He was well aware that he had absolutely no connections with the authorities at Lojewo. He was to them a mere slave. After racking his brain for some time, he developed an plan.

Binem decided to approach his lager supervisor, a German national. Binem had never personally spoken to him. In public, at least from a distance, he did not seem too unreasonable.

With much trepidation, Binem went to the supervisor's office in the farm house. The supervisor was alone behind his desk when Binem entered his office. The supervisor looked mildly surprised to see a Jew approach him.

The supervisor, in a superior tone, inquired, "What do you want?"

Binem stuttered out his answer. "My b-brother is now living in the Jewish ghetto located in Czestochowa. He w-wrote me that he would like to w-work with me at this camp. Could you m-make arrangements for him?"

Binem stared at his supervisor, whose face revealed that he probably knew what was going on in Czestochowa. So, with only a slight hesitation he replied, "Yes, but it would cost."

Binem, after learning from his father and brothers how to deal with the gentile community, understood that this meant that the supervisor would be receptive to a bribe. The problem was that Binem did not have a German mark to his name.

Still, he asked, "How much?"

The supervisor answered, "What do you have?"

Binem thought fast. Again, an idea shot into his mind, "I have no money, but I have first-rate processed leather back in Radziejow."

Binem watched the supervisor's facial expressions. He could see that he was interested. Binem thought to himself, "Good processed leather was a hard commodity to come by."

The supervisor finally said, "I could use some leather so I can have a pair of boots made. Is the leather boot quality?"

Binem knew that the family had stashed excellent boot leather with an honest Polish shoemaker.

Binem said, "Yes, it is. But for me to get the leather I need a travel pass to Radziejow."

The Supervisor reached into a desk drawer and pulled out an official looking pad. It contained a number of blanked passes, known to the workers as "shines."

He pulled one off the pad and wrote out a pass. He then handed it to Binem. The supervisor then returned to his paperwork, not even acknowledging that Binem was still in the room. Binem turned and left the farmhouse, pass in hand. He was on his way to shoemaker.

Binem had no intention of actually going to Radziejow. There was nothing there for him. But he told the supervisor that the leather was in Radziejow just in case the supervisor would turn him over to the Gestapo for having been in possession of the leather illegally. Binem stopped in a small village that was in the same direction as Radziejow. There he went directly to the shoemaker's hut. During his journey, Binem was praying that the shoemaker was as honest as he remembered him. Upon arriving at the shack, which was both his workshop and home, he was greeted by the shoemaker in a most pleasant manner. Binem asked the poor Pole for the leather. The shoemaker without hesitation went to his hiding place and produced the large piece of soft leather.

Binem sat for a while with the shoemaker and talked as they shared a piece of bread and some tea. Then Binem got up, thanked the shoemaker, and wrapped the leather around his body under his shirt. He then walked back to the Lager and went directly to the administration building. The supervisor saw Binem approaching and ushered him into his office. Binem then removed the leather from his body and handed it over to the supervisor. The supervisor examined the leather and stated that he was quite pleased.

True to his word, the supervisor then asked Binem a number of questions concerning Shmiel. As Binem gave him the information he observed that the supervisor was incorporating Binem's answers into a letter. The letter was addressed to the Administrator of the Jewish ghetto of Czestochowa. He requested that Shmiel Naiman, a former skilled worker at the Lager, was now needed back at the Lager. He requested that the Administrator assist him in transferring Shmiel back to the Lojewo Lager. The letter was promptly mailed. A few weeks later, Shmiel had the appropriate transfer papers and a shine to travel to Binem's Lager.

When Shmiel arrived, Binem was overjoyed. After exchanging hugs and kisses, they talked. Binem observed that his brother's speech and appearance was not the same. Shmiel appeared to be a broken man. It was as if he had given up hope on life. Binem had observed this in many other Jews over the past three years. These Jews spoke with no confidence, and displayed on their faces the abandonment of any hope. They seemed to succumb to fear of everyone and everything. Shmiel had clearly joined those ranks and now merely existed as a condemned man awaiting certain death that could come at any time.

I asked my father, "Did you ask Shmiel how your brothers and sisters were killed?"

He answered, "Azriel was out during a curfew and he was arrested. The Germans killed him."

I asked, "What about Michal and your sisters?"

He replied, "Shmiel said that they were seized during the round-ups and transported to, what he feared, to certain death."

After researching the matter, I determined that the majority of Jews that were rounded up in Czestochowa were sent to the Treblinka Extermination Camp. According to the historians at Yad Vashem, Israel's main Holocaust museum, between September 22, 1942 and October 8, 1942 a total of 39,000 Jews from Czestochowa were sent to the Treblinka extermination camp." Estimates reveal that during its operation, around 800,000 Jews were murdered at Treblinka.

According to survivor Jack Marcus, around August of 1943 Binem and his fellow workers were assembled for an important announcement. The supervisor of lager told them that the lager was being closed. All the Jewish workers were to be reassigned to a larger camp called Auschwitz. The Jews were shocked. When the camp supervisor finished his announcement he was followed by a German officer with yet another announcement. The Jews of the camp had never seen this German before. With a devilish smile he declared, "In Auschwitz you will continue the same way as you are living here. They will treat you very nice if you work nice." The Jews were incredulous about the announcement. Most were thinking, "Who are they kidding? We know we are all doomed!"

This was not the first time that Binem and the other Jews had heard about Auschwitz. In fact, all the Jewish workers knew that being sent to Auschwitz meant absolute death. It was no secret. For many months, German guards at Lojewo had threatened the workers with the possibility of being sent to Auschwitz if they did not work as hard as was demanded. Moreover, the Jews of Lojewo used to joke about Auschwitz in the type of black humor coined concentration camp humor. The unfunny joke was that "Jews enter Auschwitz through the door and leave through the chimney."

Despite the ring of armed troops that had encircled the camp, some of the Jewish workers naively believed the pronouncement. Some even deluded themselves into believing that "maybe Auschwitz was bad, but one can still survive there." But for the most part, the majority of Jews knew what was in store for them and were resigned to their fate. Sadly, many Jews had long ago lost the drive to survive as a result of the Nazis constant program of degrading them. Now, these Jewish workers were physically and mentally unable to find the superhuman strength required to defy the Nazi juggernaut by taking their destiny into their own hands. For those few that still had some gumption remaining, they were convinced that because death was at hand they had nothing to lose. "So why not escape the Lager?"

Indeed, several Jews attempted escape. Most of them were almost immediately caught and killed. Observing these failures, the remaining Jews in the Lager awaiting transport to Auschwitz were less inclined to make a mad dash for freedom. Many justified their inaction by saying that even if one successfully escaped, there remained the question: "What comes next?"

In other words, the big question was where to go, hide, flee? How to find food? Which direction to run? Where to seek shelter? The slave laborers of Lojewo knew of no underground or partisan groups. Even assuming there were some Poles out there that might assist, in their hearts they knew that "for every one Pole that might help them, there were two Poles that would turn them in for the reward."

Binem was faced with the most important choice of his life. He had no idea what he should do. He knew that Shmiel had been making decisions for the family since his father retired. Shmiel was a leader. He was older and wiser then Binem. So Binem looked for him and found him lying on his bunk.

Binem approached him and asked, "What should we do?" Then Binem spontaneously blurted out, "Let's run."

Shmiel hesitated to answer. He stared at Binem with wide eyes. "I cannot run anymore, you run."

Binem thought to himself that he couldn't leave his brother. How could he bare the dismal future of being alone, a fugitive on the run. He assumed that just about every Jew that he knew was either dead or would soon be dead. For Binem, life had reached that point of pure panic. He thought to himself, "How can I possibly survive this hell?"

But Shmiel was insistent. He stood up from his bed and physically pushed Binem out of the bunkhouse, all the time assuring Binem, "It's okay. You go. You are going to live over the war."

At this point during the Spielberg interview, Binem's eyes welled with tears. He said, "I told Shmiel, I don't want to go."

My father's tears bore witness that the same emotions still haunted him even into his old age.

Shmiel said to Binem, "If you live over the war, tell what happened." He then added, "We can't put all our eggs in one basket. Maybe I too will live over the war."

Binem parted from Shmiel, thinking to himself, "What's the difference? Either staying or leaving means death, so why not? I will run!"

As Binem made his way to the perimeter of the camp, he kept repeating to himself, "It doesn't matter, I'm going to be killed anyway."

Shmiel returned to the barn, and Binem never saw or heard from him again. After the war, Binem learned from friends that survived Auschwitz that Shmiel was murdered soon after he arrived at the camp.

As incredible as it sounds, Binem's plan for escape was to simply walk out of the main gate! In his heart he knew that this was foolhardy, but he thought, "What's the difference, I'm going to be killed anyway."

He shortened his stride as he approached the main gate. He was very much aware of the danger, but surprisingly at peace as he neared the gate. He reconciled with himself that he was likely to be murdered soon anyway. Trying to find something positive in his actions, he thought, "It makes no difference, why prolong the suffering."

He promised his older brother that he would try to escape, so there was no retreat. He would keep his word. For Binem, it was not a question of success rather, he had to at least try.

Binem's attempt to escape was also a small statement of protest to the Nazis for the indignities he, his family, and the Jewish people have suffered under their evil rule. This walk announced to himself and the Germans, "Despite everything you have done to me and my people, I still have free will."

As he entered the threshold of the gate he found himself walking into the center of a group of German and Polish guards. It looked and felt to him that he had voluntarily placed himself in the middle of a pack of wolves.

Binem, in typical Holocaust humor, weakly smiled to himself after thinking, "These Poles and Germans have at least one thing in common, they all want to kill me!"

As he continued to walk at a snail's pace he passed right through the "heart of a hurricane" continually repeating in his mind, as if he was reciting a mantra, "If they are going to kill me, let them kill me right here."

In seconds, which felt to Binem like a lifetime, he passed the guards and exited by way of the gate. Not one guard said a word to him. It was as if he was invisible. They had been oblivious to his presence.

He thought, "Did they think that no one would be stupid enough to try to escape through the main gate?"

Looking back on the incident, my father commented, "It must have looked to them like I was leaving because someone had ordered me to do so."

My father confessed, "I was praying they would stop me." Then he added, "I couldn't believe it, nobody stopped me."

In the end, there is no logical explanation for why Binem was not stopped. In my mind, a miracle took place. Binem had simply walked past guards whose orders were to kill any Jew trying to escape.

ON THE RUN

Once he was some distance outside of the Lager grounds, Binem, now 24 years old, quickly realized that he had no idea what he should do next.

He thought to himself, "I have nowhere to go."

Binem had second thoughts about his "success." He regretted leaving his brother. He thought, "If I had stayed, we could have met our fate together. Maybe I would have been better off going to Auschwitz – at least I would have a roof over my head. Here, I am like a dog living in the streets."

Since Binem never contemplated that his plan for escape would actually work, he didn't bother taking with him essential items needed to stay alive, such as food, water, and adequate clothing. As he stood in the field within sight of the Lager he suddenly became aware that he was cold. As he shivered, he wondered how could he possibly survive when winter came. In Radziejow, temperatures in the winter were said to be mild, averaging around zero degrees Celsius, which is 32 degrees Fahrenheit.

Still he thought, "I can't survive even a mild winter outside in the cold."

Binem then realized that his prospects for even making it to winter were slim. Binem was well aware that it was forbidden for Poles to aid a Jew on the run. Hans Frank, the German governor of Poland's occupied area had proclaimed on November 10, 1941 that a Pole who helped Jews "in any way by taking them in for the night, giving them a lift in a vehicle of any kind, or feeding runaway Jews or selling them foods, was guilty of a capital offense that the sentence for such a crime was death." Binem knew that proclamation was true for all of Poland. And, in fact, hundreds of Poles were ultimately murdered by the Nazis for aiding Jews.

Binem understood that he had to immediately find a hiding place. Once he was hidden he could decide on what he must do in order to survive. He spotted a small stone culvert only a few hundred yards from the Lager's perimeter. He ran to the opening and saw that there was adequate space for him to hide.

The area was crawling with uniformed soldiers and plainclothes Gestapo agents looking for escapees. He watched with trepidation as the German police and soldiers searched. Binem became extremely frightened when he felt the vibrations of the soldiers' footsteps as they walked above him. His fear turned to complete panic as he overheard the soldiers brag to one another about the number of Jews they caught. Also, Binem cringed as he heard only a short distance away the sounds of shouts, gunfire, and screams.

As twilight set in, Binem decided to evaluate his situation. He took an inventory of what he possessed. He had the clothes on his back, a pair of work shoes, a belt, a bar of soap, and identification papers issued by the Germans in 1942. The papers indicated that he was Jewish, lived in Radziejow, and was a *sheftenmacher* (a maker of the tops of shoes, or uppers). Interestingly, that card remained in my father's possession throughout the war. His retention of the card remains a mystery. Unfortunately, I never asked him why he would keep an item that identified him as a Jew. Perhaps he thought that having proof that he was a skilled worker might help him if he was captured.

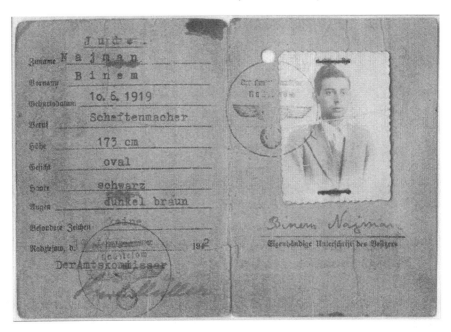

Binem's German ID Papers

Lojewo was not the only labor camp being liquidated. In fact, the Nazis had already initiated a plan to kill all the Jews of Poland. In the seminal book *WWII*, historian Martin Gilbert notes that Richard Korherr, a German statistician for Hitler, attested in a report on March 23, 1943 that 145,301 Jews in Wartheland had already been killed. Gilbert adds that "...the remnants of Jewish communities throughout Poland, most of whom had been deported to their deaths six months or a year earlier were now being searched out, or taken from the labor camps to which they had been sent in 1942, and killed."

Binem quickly learned that darkness was his ally. As soon as darkness set in, the Germans ceased their aggressive searching for Jews. Binem knew he could not stay under the culvert. He felt that it was only by sheer luck that he had not been discovered. Binem assumed that there may be soldiers lying in ambush in the fields surrounding his location. Still, if he was ever going to get away, the time was now.

In the area around Lojewo, like much of Poland, the terrain is mainly flat and consists of villages, fields, farms, and forests. Binem knew that the beautiful landscape of August would soon transform into the lifeless wasteland of winter.

Binem walked for several hours. During that time he saw no one. Binem realized that as long as it remained dark, there was little chance that he would be discovered.

His mind wandered. He thought about his Jewish brethren. "Was there anything I can do?" he asked himself.

Binem had relatives in a women's lager not to far away. He thought that perhaps he could warn them. So, despite the danger, he made up his mind to try. He knew the general direction of their camp and estimated that it was about seven kilometers away. He thought that by warning these helpless Jewish women that they were going to be sent to an extermination camp, his escape would have some value.

As he walked through the fields, he continuously repeated in his mind, "Whoever runs away will have a chance to live over the war."

After a few hours of walking, he was pleased with himself that he actually found the women's lager. He stealthily approached the perimeter and entered the compound. He immediately sensed something was wrong. It was eerily silent. A chill ran down his spine.

Binem quickly came to the conclusion that this camp had already been liquidated. He knew that meant the women were on their way to Auschwitz. And everyone knew that death awaited Jews at Auschwitz.

Binem stood there motionless. His eyes focused on a dim light coming from a building. He crept closer to the light. There was a lamp burning in what appeared to be the administration building. Binem stealthily approached the window. He glanced inside and saw three Poles, presumably guards, sitting around a makeshift wooden table. They were dividing up a number of items laying on the table. It suddenly dawned on him that these must be crooked guards splitting up the possessions of Jewish women that had been shipped to Auschwitz.

One of the guards glanced up and noticed Binem at the window. He quickly alerted the others. In a flash, the group of thieving guards went outside to investigate.

One of the guards spoke up in a very menacing voice, "Yid, What are you doing here?"

Binem answered in a subservient manner, "I came to see some people here." He then quickly added, "By the way, where is everyone?"

One of the other guards answered, "They are not here anymore, and they are already dead."

The apparent leader, thus far silent, spoke up and ordered Binem, "Go over to the barn there and sleep, while we figure out how to show you how to go home."

Binem didn't believe these thieves would go out of their way to help him. He knew that he was in mortal danger. Having no choice, he walked slowly towards the barn. One of the guards was just a few steps behind him. When he finally made his way into the barn, the guard quickly bolted the outside lock of the barn door.

Binem looked around the empty barn. The first thing he noticed was that there were no animals, only straw. The barn had no exits except the door he had entered and a small window located in the rear of the barn. Binem checked the door and concluded that it was locked tight. So he made his way to the back of the barn to examine the window. After staring at the window for a few minutes, he had an idea. It seemed that the window's frame was not securely attached to the wall. Binem figured that he probably could remove the window frame and make his escape.

He had no tools, so he searched the barn and found a piece of metal on the barn's floor. Using the metal as a makeshift crowbar he managed to pry the frame of the window completely off the wall. He did this without making too much noise. When he was done, he calculated that the hole in the wall was just big enough for him to squeeze through. So Binem boosted himself up and made his way through the hole, unnoticed by the guards.

Once outside, he ran as fast as he could. He escaped into a field just outside of the camp. As he was running, he heard noises from the direction of the camp. He turned and saw several armed German soldiers exiting from a truck as motorcycles drove around the compound.

He said to himself, "I can't believe it, they are actually looking for me."

Binem ran and ran between the high standing stalks. He finally stopped when he could run no more. He was now hidden deep within the field. He felt relatively safe being guarded by these plants that stood taller than him. He remembered that a feeling of calm enveloped him. He thought that this sense of peace and well-being was a result of his earlier decision to accept whatever fate had in store for him.

Binem knew that the Nazi murderers would eventually catch him. "When they catch me, they catch me, so what? Am I any better than other Jews?"

Binem kept repeating in his mind an old saying of the Jews of Radziejow, "What will happen to *Klal Yisroel* (the Jewish nation) is what will happen to Reb Yisroel (a simple Jew)."

After thinking long and hard about his next move, Binem decided that his best bet for survival was to make his way back to Radziejow, the only place in Poland he knew well. He figured that there he may find someone who might help him. So the following night, after a long rest, he set off in the general direction of Radziejow.

Around midnight, Binem came upon a very small village named Brinevo, located a little more than four miles from Radziejow. By then, Binem was starving. Surveying the town, he picked out a very poor looking house with a lamp shining through the window. Binem assumed that a Pole lived there. Binem knew that when the Nazis invaded Poland, one of their first acts was to requisition the large houses and estates, leaving the peasants to live in their rickety huts. Binem cautiously approached the hovel. He spied through the dirty window and saw a tall and lanky man, sitting next to a workbench, repairing shoes.

Binem thought to himself, "Perhaps he was a customer of ours."

So he gently knocked on the window. The Polish shoemaker appeared startled. He did not generally entertain customers or visitors at this late hour. Regardless, he cheerfully came to the door and opened it. To Binem's amazement, Binem recognized the elderly Pole. It was none other than Aleso Kaminski, a shoemaker who was a loyal longtime customer of the Naimans. Binem recalled that Kaminski liked to imbibe large quantities of alcohol. He was such a good customer that whenever he came to the Naiman store for supplies, the brothers made sure that they had an ample supply of whiskey on hand.

Kaminski was a strict Catholic and an avid reader of the Bible who read the Old Testament every night. A few years before the outbreak of World War II, on one of his visits, he predicted that the upcoming war with the Germans would be a religious war against the Jews. At first, the Naimans listening to this prophesy thought that it was the alcohol talking. But later, after discussing it among the brothers, they concluded that Kaminski might indeed be predicting the future of the Jewish people.

Binem now looked at the shoemaker and recalled his prediction. "That Kaminski was right, this is a war against the Jews," he told himself.

Kaminski recognized Binem. He even remembered his name. "Binem, what are you doing here," he said. " There are no more Jews around."

Kaminaki invited Binem in, and instructed to sit opposite him on the other side of his workbench. Binem told over his whole story, pouring out his soul to the shoemaker. The shoemaker listened patiently. He said to Binem that he was very sympathetic with the plight of the Jews and would like to help.

Then, after a second thought, he said, "I'm so sorry, but you cannot stay here. I only have one room and an attic. Every day Germans are constantly coming into my house to have their shoes and boots repaired."

The shoemaker lived with his wife and two daughters. On the main floor was the repair shop that also served a kitchen and the main bedroom. His daughters aged, 14 and 18, slept in the attic. The only entrance to the attic was by way of a stepladder located on the outside of the house.

The shoemaker sympathized deeply with Binem's plight. He had an idea. "I can keep you a couple of days, upstairs in the attic."

He warned Binem, "Don't come down, we will bring you your food. And be very quiet. Every movement from above is heard in the room below."

He then added, "We will see how long we can keep you."

Binem was boarded in the attic with Kaminski's daughters. They were very nice and polite. During the day, Binem would hear customers speaking German going in and out of the shoemaker's shop. Binem understood from his broken German that they were either ordering shoes to be made or bringing shoes in to be repaired. He eavesdropped on conversations between German soldiers. More often than not they would discuss the war. By and large the Germans constantly boasted to one another that they were victorious in just about every battle.

As Binem listened to the braggadocio he thought, "German victory is a Jewish defeat.: Based on the way they described the progress in the war, he realized that his chances of surviving were slim to none.

Binem described the living arrangement as tight but tolerable. In the beginning Binem was embarrassed to be sleeping in the room with these young women. He knew, however, that he had no choice. For their part, the teens were very polite but distant. They had little in common with a Jewish young man on the run.

Binem settled in to a daily routine. Every morning he was given sufficient food for his daily needs. The daughters would descend the ladder and eat breakfast with their parents. When they finished, they would dress in the workshop and go to work. Kaminski would remove the ladder to the attic for the day.

After eating breakfast, Binem spent much of the day reading different German newspapers. Kaminski provided these newspapers to him from soldiers that would leave them in his shop. In the evening Kaminski would replace the ladder to the attic for the daughters returning from their jobs. When it was night, Binem could descend the ladder in order to relieve himself.

The fatal flaw in this arrangement was that nature required Binem to leave the attic at night. So, even if the call of nature occurred during the day, Binem had to struggle to hold himself back until it was dark. He did his best to adjust his water intake in order to reduce the urge to urinate. However, just the knowledge that he had to wait until dark in order to relieve himself caused him to constantly think about this basic need.

One day was particularly difficult for Binem. As soon as he thought it was dark enough, he quickly descended from the attic. Unfortunately, while he was urinating, he saw a Polish man approaching him. Binem panicked, ran back to the Kaminski's cottage, and quickly made his way back up the ladder to the attic. When the Pole continued down the road, Binem again descended from his attic hideaway to relieve himself.

The next day the Pole who had seen Binem came to the shoemaker and accused him of hiding someone in the village.

The shoemaker played dumb. "How do you know?" he asked.

The Pole replied, "Every day I walk past a certain area.

Lately, I see piles of human excrement. Nobody from our village would do such a thing."

The shoemaker knew that his neighbor was warning him that he must rid himself of this liability to the village. Kaminski felt pity for Binem. He did not have the heart to throw Binem out.

Other villagers approached the shoemaker giving a similar warning.

One Pole said bluntly, "Because you are hiding a Jew, the entire village will suffer."

Still, Kaminski held out. He knew how helpless Binem was.

Finally, the first Pole came back and told the shoemaker that he had called the German police and told them that there was a Russian prisoner of war hiding in the village. He said that they would be coming the next day to investigate.

The shoemaker was distraught. Knowing that he had no options, in the middle of the day, he ascended the ladder and entered the attic. He told Binem all that had transpired. Binem understood that Kaminski was truly heartbroken. He told Binem that he would like to keep him longer, however, he just couldn't endanger his family and the entire village.

Kaminski continued, "You made a mistake. You shouldn't have run back to my house, you should have run to the fields. Now the townsfolk know about you. I'm sorry, but I have no choice. You must leave. If you stay, the Germans will find you and kill my family."

Binem knew that Kaminski was a good person and would not have told him to leave unless he had no alternative. Binem wanted to stay, but he understood that if he tried to convince Kaminski to allow him to stay, Kaminski, his family, and the whole village would suffer. Moreover, if that evil Pole that warned Kaminski was telling the truth, the Germans would be searching the village tomorrow.

So Binem answered, "Don't worry, I will leave. I don't want to endanger your life. My life is already over, but you should live because you are a nice man."

So Kaminski gave Binem some food and said to him, "God bless you."

He then added, "As bad as things look to you, there are some nice people around. You only need to find them."

During the Spielberg interview, Kaminski's parting words brought tears to my father's eyes.

That night Binem descended from the attic for the last time. He left the village with great uncertainty. He had no idea where to go.

Binem remembered the words of Kaminski and thought to himself, "How do I find nice people?"

It seemed like hours as Binem trudged aimlessly through a deserted field. It was near morning when he saw in the distance what looked like a haystack. He decided that it may be good place to hide. He dug himself deep inside, and covered up the path he made to the center of the haystack. He cleared out some space in the haystack. When he finished, he noticed that the temperature inside was much warmer than outside. Surprisingly, it was easy to breathe in this tomb made of hay. It didn't take more than a few minutes and he was fast asleep.

Binem described sleep as a God given blessing. By sleeping, he had a blissful break from his troubles. Sometimes he had bad dreams, but, for the most part, he dreamed of life without war. He found that time passed quickly when asleep. That was fine because Binem thought that it would take a long time for Hitler to be defeated. So the faster time went by, the better. Time held the key to surviving the war.

On the other hand, when he was asleep, he was vulnerable. He was not on guard for potential danger. The primary danger was that of being discovered. Binem knew that the Germans paid a reward for every Jew that the Poles turned in. So some Poles searched for stray Jews that had escaped the Germans for profit. He also knew that the Germans themselves were constantly patrolling for stray Jews as well as Russian escapees from POW camps.

Binem spent two days inside the haystack. Then his bread and water ran out. Binem had no choice but to leave the relative safety of the haystack and start searching for food. When night fell, he cautiously left behind his haven. Again he walked aimlessly. After several hours, Binem saw in the distance a small remote village.

It took an additional two hours before he arrived. It was still dark. As he entered the village, a dog began to bark. Within seconds, all the dogs of the village were barking. The noise caused the inhabitants of the sleepy village to light lamps and candles and look out their windows. Binem knew that if he was discovered there was a good chance that the townsfolk would turn him over to the Germans.

Having no other options, he ran out of the village and back into the fields. It was nearly dawn when he found another haystack. This time, when Binem dug himself into the center of the haystack, he was extremely hungry and thirsty.

The next night, he left the safety of the haystack. By now, he was suffering hunger pains. He knew that he couldn't return to the village of the previous night because of the tumult he had caused. With that in mind, he had no choice but to wander in a different direction. Within a few hours he found another, even smaller village. He entered the village by stealth but again, a dog began to bark. Soon the entire canine population of that village followed. Within minutes it appeared as if every shack was lit up.

Binem said to himself, "I'm just too hungry, I have to take a chance."

In spite of the danger, Binem decided not to run away. He spied a peasant shack. Without even peeking inside, he knocked on the window. The door opened and an poor man opened the door. Binem immediately asked for food.

The sleepy man answered, "I would like to give you food for the road, but if you get caught, the Germans will beat you. Then the Germans will ask you who gave you the food. So come in, eat as much as you like now, but you can't take any food with you."

Binem's eyes teared up with gratitude. This poor peasant, completely aware of the dangers, had offered him something more precious than gold and jewels: he gave Binem food. While Binem gorged on the simple fare he told the man about his struggle and his most recent problem. "Every time I approach a village, dogs start barking, and that's not good for me because it alerts the entire village and possibly a German going by."

The man contemplated the problem and then offered a simple solution. "From now on, when you approach a village, don't go with the wind, go against the wind. When a dog smells a strange person, it barks and that in turn causes the rest of the dogs in the village to bark. When you approach against the wind, a dog will not smell you."

Binem thought to himself, "That sounds true. Why didn't I think of it?"

Binem thanked the Pole for sharing of his food and his practical advice. Binem then returned to the field and found the same haystack he had slept in the previous day. Binem was satiated. He spend the next two nights in the protection of the haystack.

On the third night, Binem was again hungry, but he decided to stay put and sleep in the safety of his hiding place. He dreamed of his childhood and the delicious foods his sisters would prepare for him. He dreamed of their kugels, cholent, briskets, and their sweet and tasty pastries. He remembered all the dishes he had rejected, but now in his dream they were all delicious. He then dreamed of his cozy bed, the heating stove, the warm boots, and his thick wool coat. He dreamed of good times where he laughed with his friends at the delicatessen and the shul. He dreamed and dreamed to avoid reality. No matter what, he did not want to wake up. All he wanted was to continue to sleep and dream. He knew that when he awoke he would be hungry, thirsty, and in danger. Hunger meant searching for food, and searching for food meant leaving the relative safety of his fortress of straw. Binem knew he would face the countless enemies of the hostile outside world.

The following night, Binem's belly ached from hunger, and with no alternative he approached a small village. It was the first time in his life that he had attempted to determine the direction of the wind. He licked a finger and stuck it in the air. Then he positioned his approach to enter the village against the wind. Binem stealthily entered the village. He managed to make it halfway into the village undetected when suddenly, disaster struck. First, he tripped on an object and fell. As he recovered from his fall, he saw that he was only a few meters away from a rickety doghouse. Alarm bells starting ringing in his head. A doghouse meant there might be a dog. He turned around quickly and saw a dog. Not just any dog, but a giant, vicious-looking dog. It was staring right at him. Binem realized that he had in fact tripped on this very dog. As Binem stared back at the dog in utter terror, he discerned from the dog's expression that the dog, too, was puzzled. Apparently the dog had not been alerted by human smell, and thus, when Binem tripped over him, he became just as startled as Binem. The dog was now deciding what it should do.

A few seconds elapsed before Binem's adrenaline kicked in, demanding that he run like the wind. At the same time, the dog was released from the fog of uncertainty and began to act according to its natural instincts. That being to first bark loudly, then give chase, then catch, and finally bite. So without delay the dog began hot pursuit of the hapless running Jew. Binem thought that any second he would be finished, but, for no apparent reason, the dog abruptly stopped chasing him and and lazily returned to its doghouse.

Binem, realizing that the danger had passed, came to a stop. He evaluated the situation. He was still trembling from fear. Still, he thought to himself with satisfaction, "It worked! I can enter villages without being discovered by dogs."

He continued his train of thought. "I have learned a

valuable lesson. Now all I have to do is be more careful."

However, the reality was that it was getting close to daylight and he had not found any food. He saw an abandoned shack and decided to stay there until the next evening. Binem knew that regardless of his hunger pains, they did not override the life-threatening danger of being seen during the day.

I asked my father, "Couldn't you find food in the fields and forests?"

He replied, "The only thing I saw in the fields was straw and dirt."

I asked, "Why didn't you hunt for some animals?"

"For what animals?," he smiled.

I said, "I don't know, maybe a rabbit or a dog?"

He politely responded as if he was talking to someone that didn't have a clue. "To hunt, you need something to hunt with."

He was probably thinking I would be completely helpless if I was forced to survive in nature.

The pattern of hiding and begging continued for some months. As the winter of 1943 approached, the storage shacks in the field were emptied. Their contents were moved into the barns located next to the farmers' homes. Binem found himself constantly shivering from the cold. His only recourse was to find a haystack and dig himself deep within. Unfortunately, as it got colder, the number of haystacks remaining in the field dwindled to none. When winter began, there were no more haystacks in the fields to dig into, and the empty shacks in the field afforded no relief from the bitter cold.

Left with no choice, Binem decided that in order to survive he must alter his routine and find shelter in the barns located next to the farmers' homes. Only there could he find the warmth of large amounts of straw. Just about all the barns were locked. So, out of necessity, Binem developed methods to open the locks on barn doors undetected. After a while, Binem took pride in his ability to open and close the lock on every barn door.

This essential skill allowed him to access the life-sustaining straw that was stored within the barn. Upon entering a barn and locking it behind him, Binem would hide deep within the piles of straw. There he would sleep as long he could. His greatest solace was dreaming about the delicious food his sisters had pampered him with growing up. When he woke up, he would not only be hungry but also depressed. So he would make every effort to force his body to go back to sleep so he could continue his favorite dream.

It seemed that every day on the run Binem encountered new dangers. In order to face these dangers, he created in his mind a set of rules of survival. The first rule was to avoid being exposed. That meant that he must stay where he was hidden until he could no longer stand the hunger pains. His second rule was that if he had to leave his hiding place to find food, he would leave and return during the night. Binem was acutely aware that each time he begged for food he was vulnerable and in real danger of being caught. Still, darkness was his ally. For even with moonlight, a pursuer could not follow him from a distance, and when it was pitch black, the hunter would not see him even if he was standing right next to him.

I asked my father, "Were you afraid of moving around in the dark?"

He replied, "Just the opposite, darkness was my friend."

I then followed up the question, "Were you afraid of wild animals like wolves?"

He replied, "I didn't care. Whether I was caught by an animal or a human made no difference, it just didn't matter."

Binem employed many tricks in order to minimize his chances of being caught. His favorite was to beg food from the farmer that owned the barn where Binem was hiding. Binem would knock on the door of the farmer, then ask for food. Usually the farmer agreed, on the condition that Binem eat the food in the farmer's presence. When Binem finished, he thanked the farmer and then pretended to walk away from the farm. Without the farmer realizing, Binem would circle back and return to the farmer's barn. He would again sleep in the barn for the next few days, and then return to the unknowing farmer to again beg for food. This method worked, most of the time.

Unfortunately, Binem used this trick one time too many. One day, after a farmer gave Binem food, he became suspicious. The farmer followed Binem leaving the farm. When Binem returned to enter the farmer's barn, the farmer confronted him. "You cannot continue doing this. If you would be caught by the Germans, then my entire family would be killed!"

Binem apologized and immediately left.

Late in January of 1944 the real cold days of winter descended on Poland. Even inside the straw Binem felt as if his body was frozen. His extremities ached. He knew that frostbite was a real danger. His main problem was lack of proper clothing. He had only one thin jacket, one shirt, and a pair of pants that was threadbare. His face was relatively warm because his beard had grown thick and wild.

Binem was surprised that even suffering from the cold did not suppress a growing belief that he would survive. He was proof of the old adage that "what doesn't kill you makes you stronger." Binem reasoned that he would ultimately overcome all obstacles in his path, as there was no alternative.

Like the Jews, Polish peasants feared the Nazi menace. Binem represented to many of them a means of rebellion against the invaders. So, for the most part, they were generous to Binem. Binem slowly learned to admire this simple, downtrodden lower class of Polish society. The fact that many Catholic Churches preached hatred against Jews was for the most part irrelevant. The peasant knew that Binem, the desperate human being standing before them, was begging for assistance. Those who helped him taught Binem that even in the darkest hour of humanity, the powerless possessed the capacity to overcome their own interests and understand and offer a helping hand to the plight of fellow humans that were even worse off.

Not that Binem became a great lover of all Poles. In his mind, the Polish peasants and farmers were a cut above the Poles that remained anti-Semitic during and even after the war. These Polish anti-Semites were in many ways no different to the Jews than the Nazi oppressors. For many believed after the war that Hitler did the Poles a favor by ridding the land of Jews.

On one nightly outing in search of food, Binem fell into some good luck when he knocked on the door of a poor, single woman. Binem immediately sensed that this middle-aged peasant woman had a good soul. As Binem described his plight, it seemed that she honestly felt sorry for him. When he was finished, she not only fed Binem but also invited him into her house. That night he slept in warm surroundings. The next day she allowed him to stay with her. Binem felt that he had finally found a secure place. This arrangement continued for about a week.

The situation changed dramatically when the woman's brother suddenly appeared. He was tall and wide, and would best described as a thug. He spoke as if he hated everyone and everything. On top of it all, he was obviously drunk. One glance at Binem and he demanded from his sister to explain who this "freeloader" was. She patiently and calmly explained Binem's plight to her brother, using the most sympathetic terms possible. He listened with a facial expression that revealed that he did not have a sympathetic bone in his body. When she mentioned that he was a Jew, the brother's pink face turned red like a ripe tomato and he shouted at her to stop talking. He started swinging his arms from side to side as if he was preparing for a brawl.

Binem sat in complete horror as he watched from his seat at the kitchen table less than a dozen feet away. Finally, the brother gained control of himself and told his kindly sister in no uncertain terms "You know we wanted to get rid of the Jews and now you're helping them."

She calmly replied, "Don't be silly, he's a nice guy."

The brother angrily retorted, "I don't care if he is a nice guy, he is a Jew."

He then turned to Binem and shouted, "Why are you trying to live over the war? Even if you live over the war we are going to kill you anyway. And the fact is I don't want to wait so long, so I am going to kill you right now."

The brother's bright red angry face made him look as if he was under an evil spell that was compelling him to kill Binem. Suddenly he pounced on Binem with the full force of his enormous body. Binem was hurled to the floor, with the man sitting on his chest. Within seconds, the Pole was choking the very life out of Binem.

The sister, seeing this, grabbed a hard object. She then attacked her brother with the object, repeatedly pounding him with it against his head using every ounce of her strength. After several stinging blows, he released his death grip around Binem's neck.

She shouted at her brother, "Get out of here!" She then grabbed him by his coat and forcibly led him out the front door.

The brother seemed resigned to the fact that he was not going to be allowed to kill Binem. As he left, the woman, looking obviously distressed, called Binem over and said, with regret, "You better leave before my brother sobers up and comes back with the Germans."

Binem left that night in a state of anxiety. It was a terribly cold winter night. Binem thought to himself that he much preferred the freezing winds and blowing snow to the sting of repeated blows inflicted on him by the kind lady's brother. Binem trudged through the snowstorm, not going anywhere in particular. Eventually he found shelter in a dilapidated barn.

A few days later, Binem mentioned his confrontation with the woman's brother while speaking with a farmer. The farmer told Binem that he knew both the brother and his kindly sister. He then shocked Binem by informing him that the brother had been found dead three days earlier. His body was frozen in the sitting position on a large boulder on the side of the road leading to the village. The farmer said he was told that the brother died of a heart attack. As the farmer talked, Binem calculated that the brother died on the very night of the confrontation.

Binem parted with the farmer and pressed on. A few hours later, he found a barn near a small hamlet. Binem entered the barn using his newfound skills. He got his bearings inside the dark barn and fell asleep in a pile of hay. About a half hour later, he awoke to the sound of someone opening the barn door. Alarm bells went off in Binem's mind, and he was enveloped by fear and trepidation.

Binem's eyes, now accustomed to the dark, were able to track the shadowy figure as he closed the barn door. Binem was surprised that the man was able to close the outside latch of the barn door using a technique that he thought he had developed himself! Binem was overcome by curiosity, and continued to observe the man as he dug himself into the straw right next to him.

To Binem's astonishment, the shadowy figure began to talk to himself in Yiddish. He was mumbling. "In my old age, I am sick, I don't feel good, and I have no home to go to. I don't know what to do."

Binem immediately recognized the voice. It was none other than his favorite neighbor from Radziejow, Moshe Frankenberg. Although Moshe was now in his sixties, Binem remembered him as the toughest and strongest Jew that he had ever known. In fact, Frankenberg was a legend among all the Jews in Radziejow. He was known as a man who never shied away from the use of force when it came to standing up against Polish ruffians.

Binem's mind wandered back to one incident that had made Frankenberg forever a hero in his eyes. One terrible night, a monster of a Pole broke into the living quarters of the Naiman building. He was drunk and brandishing a large carving knife. He waved the menacing blade at the frightened members of the Naiman family. While the brute was busy terrorizing his family, Binem then just a small boy in grammar school, saw an opportunity for escape and managed to slip out the back door. Once outside, he ran as fast as he could to the police station for help. When he arrived, he found that the station was closed.

Binem was taken aback but, knowing his family was in peril, he quickly thought to himself: "Where can I get help?"

Binem remembered the legendary hero of the Jewish community, Moshe Frankenberg. "Surely Mr. Frankenberg will save us."

Binem raced to Frankenberg's house. He was preparing to go to sleep when Binem frantically pounded on the door.

Frankenberg answered the door and looked down at the obviously frightened boy. "Binem, what's the matter?"

Binem replied, "My family is about to be killed!" He then explained the family's dire straits in a shrill voice that one would expect from a small boy who felt the weight of responsibility to save his loved ones.

Frankenberg listened carefully. Then he cut Binem off and responded without a second thought, "Don't worry, I'll take care of it."

Frankenberg left his house and quickly arrived at the back entrance of the Naiman Building. Binem followed, running at full speed trying to keep up with Frankenberg. He noted that when Frankenberg opened the door, he was cool and collected, completely without fear. The Polish assailant saw Frankenberg rushing in his direction. The Pole lifted up the large knife and prepared to stab Frankenberg. Without any fear of being harmed, Frankenberg made a fist and charged the attacker, punching the Pole in the head with great force. The Pole collapsed like a bag of potatoes and appeared to be unconscious. Binem couldn't believe it, Frankenberg had knocked out the thug with one punch. Frankenberg was silent as he dragged the unconscious attacker by his collar out the side door and tossed him into the street like a pile of garbage.

Frankenberg did not return to discuss the events with the Naimans, rather, he started walking home. Binem caught up to him.

Frankenberg said, "Go home and lock the door."

Binem wanted to express his gratitude, but thought it was better to follow Frankenberg's order.

Binem's thoughts about the incident ended and he returned to reality. He said to himself, "I must not burst out and greet Frankenberg, lest he become startled and attack me, or worse yet, he may be shocked and have a heart attack."

So Binem spoke softly with an angelic tone, "Moshe, Moshe."

Upon hearing these words, Frankenberg sat up and looked confused. He later confessed to Binem that for a second he thought that, just as God had said "Moshe, Moshe" from the burning bush, now the Lord Almighty was trying to communicate with him. Frankenberg scanned the barn and confirmed that he was alone. He chalked it up to a mistake and tried again to fall asleep.

A few moments later, Binem repeated, "Moshe, Moshe."

This time Frankenberg recognized Binem's voice. He called out, "Binem, where are you?"

Binem answered with a laugh, "I am right behind you."

Binem and Frankenberg dug themselves out of the straw. They then stood face to face in the middle of the barn. There was a look of joy on both faces. To my father, it was a miracle from God that there was another Jew from Radziejow who was still alive. They proceeded to embrace each other warmly as if they were brothers. Both reacted to this surreal encounter as if this might be the last Jew that they would ever meet.

Frankenberg, the giant, the legend, the hero who feared no anti-Semite, displayed uncharacteristic emotion. Tears of both joy and sadness fell down his cheeks.

In a broken voice he said, "Look at you. You are young, you can take it. I cannot take it anymore."

Frankenberg proceeded to explain his plight from the day he ran away from his Lager. Just like Binem, from the day of his escape he had been wandering aimlessly from one barn to another.

As Binem listened to this person that he admired so much his entire life transformed into a broken shell of his former self, Binem asked himself, "If Frankenberg can't take it, how can I?"

Binem hoped that Frankenberg was just in the midst of the same mental crisis that Binem periodically had. So he tried to comfort his hero.

"Don't worry, maybe not too long from now we'll both be free."

Frankenburg was silent for a long moment, then with a disbelieving look on his face, he replied, "I hope so, God willing."

Frankenburg told Binem that tomorrow he planned on visiting a farmer to whom he had entrusted merchandise before the war. He was hoping that this farmer might give him some food and shelter.

It suddenly dawned on them that they were conversing out loud during the night; when the slightest sound could carry great distances. Perhaps the farmer might hear them. So they gave each other one last hug and then dug themselves back into the hay in separate spots. Minutes later they were both fast asleep.

They slept in their burrows until the next night. They left the barn at different times, not even giving each other a last goodbye. Binem's main goal was to find food. Frankenberg was headed to the farmer holding his merchandise. The reason that they did not travel together was that they both knew it would be impossible to survive together. A peasant might find it in his heart to share his meager rations with one Jew, but not likely with two.

That was the last time Binem ever saw Moshe Frankenberg. Three nights later Binem, was begging food from a Polish farmer. The farmer told him that he had heard the night before a farmer turned a Jew into the German Police.

Binem asked, "Do you recall the name of the Jew?"

The farmer answered, "I believe the name Frankenberg was mentioned."

During that interview I asked my father, "Was Moshe Frankenberg religious?"

My father answered, "That was his downfall. When I used to go into a farmer's house I would talk about the Bible. The farmer thought I was a rabbi, especially because I had a beard."

In contrast, my father explained, Frankenberg had a bad habit of playing cards with the farmers that helped him. The problem was that sometimes Frankenberg would win. "Farmers probably didn't like Jews winning money from them. That must have been the reason the farmer turned him in to the Germans."

Unlike Frankenberg, Binem based his survival on evaluating the mindset of the average Polish peasant. He would approach the peasant in a the manner that he felt was most likely to elicit a sympathetic reaction. The key was to generate enough sympathy to override the peasant's fear of endangering himself and his family.

Most farmers were practicing Catholics who read the Bible on a regular basis. The trick was choosing the right one. In general, the poorer the Pole, the more likely Binem would receive help. Binem learned that religious Poles enjoyed discussing the Old Testament, even with a Jew. Thanks to Binem's father Shimon, Binem had learned many insights in the interpretation of biblical passages found in the Old Testament. Often during these discussions, the farmer or peasant was so pleased with Binem's knowledge of the Holy Scriptures that he would volunteer the name and location of another pious farmer. The farmer would then give Binem permission to tell the other farmer that he had sent him.

One night, Binem was looking for a new barn to hide in when he arrived at a remote village. After surveying the buildings on the perimeter of the village, he picked out a large barn. Based on Binem's experience, larger barns often held deep piles of hay, which provided for him warm insulation from the frosty weather. He entered the barn by expertly picking the lock. Once inside, he skillfully locked the door behind him. Binem then groped his way in pitch-black darkness until he found a straw pile. Then he dug himself deep into the pile, making sure that the tunnel he created behind him collapsed, leaving him undetectable from the outside.

What Binem didn't know was that the farmer had placed tobacco leaves to dry in a neat arrangement on top of the very straw where Binem had dug himself in. Binem couldn't see the leaves in the darkness, and didn't feel them when he burrowed into the pile. In the morning, the farmer entered the barn. As soon as he entered, he saw his tobacco leaves were scattered and damaged. The farmer called out to his wife to come to the barn. He irrationally accused her of having entered the barn and destroying the leaves. Though his wife adamantly denied it, the farmer chose not to believe her. The farmer, known for his violent temper, shouted at her, calling her a liar. He then beat her mercilessly, declaring that he would only stop if she confessed. In anguish, she tearfully maintained her innocence.

The farmer eventually realized that this approach was getting him nowhere. So he shouted, "If it wasn't you, it must have been our lousy kids!"

So he called his young children into the barn and turned his wrath on them. He yelled at the children and chased them, clearly intending to beat them. Luckily the children were able to evade their ranting father.

Binem, buried only a few steps away from the onslaught, remained still. He was at a loss what to do, and in absolute terror of being caught by the farmer. He felt that the only course was not to move. He listened helplessly as the children pleaded for mercy, tearfully repeating that they had not gone into the barn the previous evening.

The farmer eventually grew tired of the chase and stopped. He was silent for a long moment. His next thought was that perhaps some stranger had broken in the barn the previous night. He then realized that it was possible that the same intruder was still in his barn.

The farmer went to the barn door and saw a few of his neighbors walking on the public road only a few meters from his barn.

He shouted out, "Someone broke into my shed!"

One of the men replied, "What happened?"

The farmer ran to the road, leaving his family behind in the barn. He explained the situation to his neighbors.

After listening to the farmer's story, his neighbor said, "It was probably one of those Russian P.O.W.s. I heard a number of them escaped from a camp a few days ago and have been caught hiding in barns. I bet you there are a few hiding in your barn."

The farmer agreed. He told his neighbors, "Gather everyone and bring them here."

In less than a half hour, over two dozen villagers were assembled in front of the barn. The majority were armed with axes and machetes. These Poles had no sympathy for the POWs. In fact, they had a long history of hating Russians. Moreover, some of the farmers that showed up were seeking revenge against the P.O.W.s that had stolen their chickens and crops.

The farmer shouted in the direction of the straw pile in which Binem had buried himself: "Come out with your hands up, otherwise we will call the Germans."

Binem understood the situation had deteriorated from terribly bad to completely hopeless. The last thing Binem wanted to hear was that the Germans would come. While Binem was considering what he should do, a neighbor riding a bicycle rode up to the farmer and shouted to the mob that he had already informed the Germans that there were escaped Russian P.O.W.s in the barn.

Binem felt he had run out of options. With no alternative, he decided to pull himself out of the straw and surrender.

When he stood up before the angry mob, he noticed that all the Poles including the farmer looked puzzled.

Binem thought to himself, "They must have been ready to do battle with five or six dangerous Russians, and instead, out of the pile came one skinny, dried up Jew."

The excitement of the mob had completely dissipated like air released from a balloon. No one knew what to say or do. Binem saw that it was not in the hearts of these kindly peasants to get involved in the killing of a poor, defenseless Jew.

The village leader told his fellow farmers, "Go home, I'll handle it."

The Poles let out a sigh of relief. They were only too happy to leave. They quickly returned to their daily routine.

When the village leader was finally alone with Binem he told him, "I know you are Jewish. The Germans will soon be here, you must run away, right away."

The man then pointed to a bridge that spanned a small creek. "Hide yourself under the bridge, and I will come to you later and tell you where you should go."

Binem followed his instructions. From Binem's hiding place, he watched a truck arrive and saw several German soldiers descend from its rear. They scattered and searched the farm and the surrounding area. After a few hours, the Germans gave up their search.

True to his word, the village leader came to the bridge after the Germans had left. He told Binem that blackmailers were common throughout Poland. "One Pole could literally blackmail an entire village for helping a Jew."

Of this the famous Nazi hunter, Simon Wiesenthal, stated, "It is in times like these that the lowest elements in society surface. The szantażysta (blackmailers) would betray Jews for a bottle of vodka or a pair of shoes."[40]

The village leader continued, "I would like to hide you, but my farm is too close to the highway."

He then handed Binem a piece of paper with a name on it. He said that Binem should go to this woman. He told Binem that the woman's husband was in jail for selling chickens on the black market, and that she hates the Germans.

The mayor then added the magic words, "Tell her I sent you."

He walked alongside Binem, assuring him, "This woman is like me, she returned to Poland from America." He added, "She was able to save enough money to buy a small farm. I'm sure she will hide you for a couple of days."

He gave him directions on how to reach the woman by way of back roads. When he was finished, he wished Binem good luck. Binem walked that evening with the thought that God must have intervened on his behalf. He thought to himself that even in this crazy, evil world, there were some people that remained true to their moral compass.

It was quite a distance to walk, but eventually Binem located the woman's farm. He knocked on her door. When she opened the door she looked at Binem, saying, "Look what the cat brought in." She was polite and asked him what he wanted. Without even answering he handed her the note of introduction written by the village leader.

After she appeared to have read it, Binem explained, "The man said you were his friend and that you would help me."

She stared at Binem. She looked him up and down. Suddenly she spoke up. "O.K., you can stay a couple of days."

The woman showed Binem around her house. Binem, now a sort of expert in evaluating hideouts, quickly determined that there was a problem with this arrangement. The woman lived in a small farmhouse with her three school-age children. As a result of the cramped conditions, Binem thought there was no place he could hide. The woman led him to the kitchen door. She opened it and pointed to an area that was adjacent to the outside wall of the kitchen. It was a fenced-in area that was being used as a pigpen.

She said to Binem, "Here you can stay."

Binem thought it almost laughable that she had proposed he live with these *treif* (unkosher) pigs. He thought of what his father might have said if he was still alive. Still, it was something. So, having no other recourse, Binem gratefully accepted the accommodations.

Binem entered the sty, and found himself up to his ankles in mud. The woman instructed Binem to wait for her in the corner of the pen. Binem was relieved to find that this area was elevated and therefore dry. He stood there, staring at the pigs. Moments later, the woman returned and handed him a blanket and some fresh straw.

She said, "While you stay here I will bring you some food every morning."

She must have felt sorry for Binem for instead of just bringing him food, each night she would call Binem into the house and feed him at the kitchen table. Binem soon became quite satisfied with the arrangement. He thought to himself, "I have a good place." The farm's location was relatively safe, being a good distance from the main road. Moreover, he would jest to himself, "It would take a pretty sharp Nazi to look for a Jew in a pigpen!"

Still, Binem had reservations. The women's children would stand next to the pigpen and stare at him, as if they were observing animals in a zoo. They would take turns pointing at him and saying, "There's a Jew in the pigpen!" The pointer would chuckle, followed by a chorus of laughter from the other two children.

Binem didn't mind the ridicule. Rather, he was more concerned about the danger inherent in the fact that these children knew he was a Jew. He thought to himself that such knowledge could lead to a catastrophe if one of the children would tell a friend or relative.

The mother was also concerned. However, despite acknowledging this problem to Binem, she didn't have the heart to tell him to leave.

Four nights later, when Binem entered the house for dinner, he saw a large Polish man sitting at the kitchen table. Binem had a premonition that this was going to be a bad evening. As Binem looked at the Pole, he immediately felt a chill. The man's face emanated a familiar anti-Semitic hatred.

The Pole turned to the woman and growled, "You are hiding a Jew here?"

She replied, "Leave him alone, he is O.K."

The meal was served in icy silence. Binem knew trouble was brewing and tried to figure out a way to stop it. So after eating, Binem tried to placate the man by telling him interesting stories from the Bible.

Suddenly the man spoke up. "You ate, now go. Get the hell out of here."

Binem knew that there was no reasoning with this man. He didn't want to have a recurrence of the physical confrontation that he had experienced not long ago. So Binem politely thanked the kind woman and promptly left the house by way of the kitchen door.

Binem was apprehensive about the encounter. Perhaps the man would turn him in. So, after walking in one direction for some time, he turned to walk in a different direction. It was getting close to sunrise and he still hadn't found shelter. Luckily he spotted a dilapidated farmhouse in the distance. He rushed there and made it just before sunrise.

There was a small barn next to the farmhouse and Binem entered it undetected. He spent the day sleeping under some straw.

When evening arrived, Binem left the barn and knocked on the flimsy farmhouse door. After a short delay, a disheveled peasant opened it.

He stared at Binem. The peasant focused on Binem's beard. After a moment of staring, the peasant stated, "You must be a Rabbi."

Binem, as a trained salesman knew that the customer is always right. So if the farmer thought he was a Rabbi, he was a Rabbi. He declared without reservations, "Yes, I am a Rabbi."

Upon hearing that Binem was a "holy man," the peasant was delighted. He immediately indicated to Binem that he would help him.

He said to Binem, "I have a great deal of respect for Jewish Rabbis. Still, with Germans around you cannot walk around looking the way you look. Anyone with eyes can see that you are Jewish."

Before Binem could respond, the poor but good-hearted Pole sat Binem down in his own chair. He took from a drawer in the kitchen a pair of scissors and a razor. The peasant proceeded to shave off Binem's beard and even gave Binem a haircut. When he was done ,the peasant took a step back to evaluate his work. By the look on the peasant's face, Binem surmised that the results were satisfactory.

The peasant then searched through his meager belongings and found a warm pair of black pants and a thick wool jacket. He said, "Put them on, it is cold outside."

He then went to the stove and cooked a hearty meal. The two sat and talked about religion and the dreadful state of affairs in Poland. That night Binem felt like a human being, something that he had not not experienced in a long time. The following night, after dinner, Binem said his final goodbye. As Binem walked towards the open field, the Pole stood by his door and watched. Binem heard the Pole say, "God bless you."

The man's selfless humanity lifted Binem's spirit. As he walked, he felt refreshed. He reviewed his experiences over the past few days. He thought to himself, "I guess for every bad one, there is a saint."

Along the way he passed a large, prosperous farm. One of Binem's rules of survival was to steer clear of the larger farms, because there was a good chance it was owned by either a Volksdeutsche or a German settler. Binem decided that after some bad experiences with his *farkakte* (useless or broken) rules, he would take a chance. Unfortunately, this was one time when he should have followed his rules. For, unbeknownst to Binem, the owner of the farm had set up an ambush in the field. He was armed with a powerful shotgun. and was primed to use it.

The farm's German owner was on the hunt. Not for Jews, but for thieves that had been regularly stealing his pigs. He waited for Binem to pass his hunter's blind and then silently came up behind Binem. Binem felt the barrel of the gun in his back. He stopped and waited for instructions. The German then told Binem to turn around. Binem saw a large man with an Aryan looking face. Judging by the menacing expression on the man's face, he meant business.

The German ordered Binem, "Hands up!" Then he announced, "Finally, I got you!"

Binem thought to himself, "This guy was looking for me? Well then, I guess he got me."

The German then grabbed Binem by the neck and started to shake him. During the assault, Binem's hat fell off.

When the German finally stopped, Binem meekly asked in broken German, "Can I pick up my hat?"

The German replied, "Where you're going, you won't need a hat anymore."

In almost military fashion, the German marched Binem to the front of his large farmhouse. He then called out to one of his workers, "Hitch up the horses, and take this guy to the *Asandalamilita*."

Binem knew exactly what that meant - the farmer was going to turn him over to the Gestapo. Binem knew he had to try something or he was doomed. Binem couldn't comprehend why this German farmer was hunting for Jews. With that question in mind, he boldly spoke up.

Binem inquired, "Exactly who were you waiting for?"

The German replied with a tone of disgust. "I was waiting for the guy who has been stealing my pigs."

With that answer, Binem understood that he might have some hope. Binem said in stern voice, "If you were waiting for a thief, you got the wrong man."

He asked, "If you are not a thief, then who are you?"

Binem told him, "I am a Jew."

The German looked dumbfounded. Binem assumed the German probably was thinking that Jews could not be pig thieves!

The German then responded, "You can't be a Jew, that's impossible. I heard that for a long time there were no Jews around here."

The German was trying to convince himself that Binem was probably just a Polish thief trying to weasel his way out of this predicament. However, Binem continued to protest, insisting that he was a Jew.

Binem knew that he was admitting a status that could condemn him to death. But Binem had a plan. As the German farmer decided what to do, Binem sprang a bluff.

Binem spoke in a commanding voice. "I'm no ordinary Jew, I'm a partisan. We are more than fifty fighters. We have made camp near here. My comrades know exactly where I am. So I'm warning you that if I don't return within fifteen minutes, then they will come looking for me here and they most assuredly will kill you and your whole family."

This German was among the first settlers to set up a farm in the Russian territories. Later, the German government transferred him to Poland. The Nazis had confiscated this farm from Poles and put it under his control. The farmer knew from personal experience in Russia what partisans were capable of doing. So he became frightened. Not knowing what to do, he asked Binem to wait for him while he went into his house. Binem watched him as he conversed with his wife near an open window.

Binem overheard him saying, "I was waiting to catch the

thief that was stealing our pigs, and now I am in big trouble. I caught a Jew that is with the partisans. What should I do?"

She quickly answered, "Well, you better let him go."

After hearing those words, the German rushed outside. He said to Binem, "Go, and don't look back."

Binem figured that this German was no better than a Nazi. Not only that, he was armed with a shotgun. He hesitated to turn his back to the German, knowing that he could at any moment shoot him in the back. Binem took a chance. He walked slowly, pretending that he did not fear the farmer. After walking a few hundred meters, Binem thanked God that he was not shot. Binem chalked it up to nothing less than a miracle.

Binem thought to himself, "Why would this German believe he was partisan when there was no partisan activity in this annexed area of Poland?"

Binem knew that he was extremely lucky to get away. This incident was a stark reminder that he must be more vigilant when moving about. He continued to walk, deep in thought, contemplating what he could do better to remain alive.

Binem spotted a small hamlet and positioned himself to enter the small town against the direction of the wind. He surveyed the area and noted that there were about a dozen ramshackle dwellings. Since no particular dwelling looked more or less promising than any other, Binem knocked on the first door he came upon. To Binem's surprise the woman that answered was an old neighbor from Radziejow.

She immediately recognized him, and bursted out with a glowing smile, "Binem, you're alive!"

She continued, "Don't worry about a thing, I'm going to take care of you. Nothing will happen to you any more."

Binem thought to himself, "Good, if it will be so."

He stayed with her for two weeks. The woman told all her neighbors about the nice young man from Radziejow who was now staying with her. She did not hide the fact that he was a Jew. The neighbors were likewise very hospitable and all wanted to help him out. So each night Binem was invited by a different neighbor for dinner. Binem could not believe his *mazel* (luck) had changed so quickly and completely. He truly felt that this small village was a safe place to stay.

One particular neighbor, a widow, was extremely nice to him. She served him the best food out of all the neighbors. Her son earned his living as a shepherd. Unfortunately, he supplemented his earnings through theft.

The farmers in the area had been plagued by thieves stealing their livestock. One local farmer had recently reported to the Gendarmeries that several sheep were stolen from his flock. A few days later, a different neighbor told Binem that the farmer suspected the widow's son. Binem had a feeling that this was going to cause him trouble.

Three days went by and nothing happened. Binem began to think that the danger was over. That evening it was Binem's turn to have dinner at the widow's house. No word was mentioned by the widow concerning the rumor. So Binem didn't think it was appropriate to bring up the subject. In the middle of the main course, there was a knock on the door. Binem stood up, and from a hidden position glanced out the window. He spotted three men in uniforms. He promptly fled out the back door and found a hiding place near the side of the house. The widow then opened the front door. Binem could hear shouting as the police overpowered the widow's son and placed him under arrest. Binem watched in terror as the Gendarmeries dragged him out the front door, beating him senseless while his mother watched, mortified.

When the police left, Binem returned to the house of his neighbor from Radziejow. He told her all that transpired. The next night, Binem went to eat at a different neighbor's house. When he arrived, he was told by the kindly woman that the shepherd that was arrested the night before was scheduled to be executed for stealing sheep. However, his mother had proposed a deal with the police: "Give me back my son and I will give you a Jew." As far as she understood, the police agreed. The kindly woman then advised, "You better not go back to that woman's house."

Binem was distraught. He thought to himself, "Just my luck, I have to run from this great village because a woman's son was stealing sheep! How sad."

Binem returned to his neighbor from Radziejow's house. He explained to her the situation and told her that he must go. She understood and sadly said goodbye.

Binem did not have the mental resolve to take to the road again. It was now much harder for him to live a life on the run after the pampering he had received. He tried to think of ways to return himself to the proper mindset.

He would repeat to himself optimistically, "I'm still alive. I just have to keep it up."

As he was walking, he found himself returning to the distressful thought that no matter what he would do, he could never find a better arrangement than he had in that small village. Eventually, he came upon another hamlet. He found a barn just outside the town, jimmied the lock, and set up temporary residence in a pile of hay.

The next evening, he set out to beg for food. He approached the village against the direction of the wind. He spotted a modest house and knocked on the flimsy window. Upon hearing the knock, a young woman opened the front door. "Who are you?" she said.

Binem replied, "I want something to eat."

She invited Binem in and gave him some food. While Binem was eating, the young woman stared at Binem.

Finally it dawned on her, "I know you."

Binem was taken by surprise. He made eye contact with the young woman.

Binem scrutinized her face and then replied, "I know you, too. We went to the same school."

Binem remembered that more than ten years ago the two were classmates in the Radziejow Public School. The girl would constantly follow Binem around. In fact, she always made sure that she would sit next to him in the classroom. Binem recalled that he regularly assisted her with class projects. He fondly recalled the time they spent together creating a topographical relief map using flour and water. Binem prided himself that their map was recognized as the best map in the class. From then on he had a reputation as being the best at creating these types of maps.

I questioned my father about his relationship with his former schoolmate. He confessed that he always believed that she had a crush on him. Of course, nothing could ever come of it. She was Polish and he was Jewish. So, after the two graduated from public school, they never saw each other again.

The young woman was flushed as she suddenly blurted out, "I'm going to help you."

Binem was both shocked and pleasantly surprised that she would say these words, knowing that such an act would put her and her family in danger. He respectfully asked, "You are going to help me? How are you going to help me? How can you help me?"

The young woman answered as if she had a plan in mind. "My brother works for a rich German that owns an estate. The German's wife happens to be Polish. He will talk with the German's wife to see whether she can do something for you."

It seemed to Binem that his former classmate's answer was too specific for someone to just blurt out. He thought that perhaps her family had once discussed the theoretical situation of how they would respond to a Jew asking for help.

Binem was skeptical but hopeful. "O.K." he said.

She replied, "Now eat as much as you want, then go hide somewhere and come back tomorrow night."

As Binem ate, the two, now in their twenties, discussed their experiences in Radziejow Grammar School as if they occurred only yesterday. As they talked, it dawned on him that now not only religion made it impossible for the two to ever contemplate a relationship, but with the Nazis in power there

196

was a threat of death to any Pole who even attempted to assist a Jew.

After dinner, Binem searched for a hiding place. He concluded that his school friend's offer was probably just words. Still, he had a sliver of hope. He thought to himself, why would she say such a thing if she didn't think it was possible. Since he had no better option, he decided that he would return to her house the following evening and hope for the best. He eventually found a barn some distance from the hamlet.

The next evening, he tried to find his way back to the young woman's house. For some inexplicable reason, he failed. He ended up wandering into a nearby field. He was caught by a giant Pole that happened be the manager of the large German-owned farm where Binem was trespassing.

The Polish manager asked, "Who are you?"

Binem answered, "I am a Jew and I have no place to go."

The manager stared at Binem as he decided how to handle the situation.

Fortunately for Binem, the manager proved to be a decent person.

He said, "You can stay in the barn with the horses. Every night I will bring you something to eat." Binem thought this was a good arrangement, much more practical than his former classmate's proposal.

My father remembered thinking, "This offer was concrete, not pie-in-the- sky."

The arrangement proved to be satisfactory in all aspects save one. Staying in the barn proved to be a living hell. The problem centered on the barn being infested with lice. The lice crawled everywhere, including onto Binem. Binem described the lice as being "the size of a finger." The parasites were all over Binem's body and clothes. At night they would incessantly bite him. The bites were deep and painful. Binem tried to alleviate the constant pain by smashing them as they did their dirty deed. His usual method was slamming the lice with his open hand. At times he would study the dead louse lying in his palm. He was always aghast to see that the act of smashing them released blood. Binem wasn't sure if it was his blood or a horse's blood. Binem concluded that where it came from really didn't matter. What did matter was that "the pain was terrible, beyond description."

Binem lasted a week in the horse barn. On the eighth day, the manager came to Binem and stated "There is something wrong with the horses."

He accused Binem of being the source of the lice into the barn. The manager concluded, "I'm sorry, but you must go."

I asked my father, "Was that an excuse to get rid of you?"

My father conceded, "There were lice." His answer seemed to imply that he did have lice prior to entering the barn.

My father saw the look on my face, so he then added, "It's hard to believe that I could infect the horses."

Binem remembered telling the manager, "Sure, I had a few lice, but in the horse barn there are millions of them."

The manager felt bad. He told Binem, "Look, I am a nice man. I used to hide Jews during the First War. But the Jews left for America. Not one ever wrote me a letter. Still, I don't bear you Jews any hard feelings. In fact, I'm still helping out you Jews."

As an aside, there is a documentary released in 2004 entitled *Hiding and Seeking* about the son of a Holocaust survivor who decided to travel to Poland to find the people who rescued his father. After making arrangements to travel to Poland, he told his father, who was by then a very old man. Though the father told his son not to go, the son didn't listen. Not only did he go to Poland, but he dragged his teenage children with him. Against all odds, he actually found his father's rescuers, who were still alive and living on the same farm where they had hid his father. When he introduced himself, the Polish rescuers proved to be very gracious. They then told him that his father had assured them that he was extremely wealthy and promised that if they would hide and feed him, he would give them a very large reward after the war.

When the war was over, he left and never even sent a postcard. When the son of the survivor returned to the United States, he asked his father if the story told by his rescuers was true. The father remorsefully admitted that it was. He then explained that he would have promised anything in order to survive. Still, there was a happy ending for the Polish rescuers. The survivor's son and family returned to Poland and made good on his father's promise by setting up a college fund for the rescuers' grandchildren.

THE PRINCESS

As Binem began searching for a new hiding place, he remembered his former classmate's offer. He was now determined to find her house to see if she had indeed made arrangements. So he again set out for the remote village. After some time he was able to locate the young woman's house.

He approached the house with a great deal of trepidation. It just didn't make any sense that a Polish woman would go out of her way and personally contact other Poles to help him. By doing so, she would be breaking a law whose punishment, if discovered by the Nazis, would be execution. Still, Binem had no other options, so he decided to take a chance. He knocked on the door.

After a pause, the young woman opened the door. She looked at Binem with beaming eyes and said, "What happened to you?" Her tone was admonishing, but caring.

Binem didn't want to go into the details, so he avoided the question. "Listen, you promised me you were going to do something for me."

She answered, "Yes I'll help. Stay overnight somewhere and tomorrow the wife of the German farm owner will come here and talk to you."

After the young woman fed Binem, they parted. Binem found a hiding place close to her house. He bedded down for the remainder of the night and the next day. Binem was encouraged. She seemed truly concerned about his welfare.

The next night, Binem returned in a hopeful mood. However, upon seeing his former classmate's crestfallen face, he realized something had gone wrong. After explaining to him that there were some problems that needed to resolved, she told him to come back in a few days.

Binem was devastated. He told her that he was "completely beat," and that "The only choice I have is to give myself up."

The young woman was taken aback by Binem's response. She responded, "Don't do it. If you come tomorrow night, she will come to take you and save you."

Binem left dejected. He was so depressed that he didn't have the strength to return to his hiding place from the previous night. Instead, he looked around and saw a patch of dense overgrowth consisting of trees, shrubs, and high grass. He decided that he would hide there. He made his way to the center and quickly went to sleep. He forced himself not to open his eyes until the following night. When he awoke he actually remembered the name of his former classmate: Wanda. He had forgotten her name from the time of their first encounter at her house when she mentioned it. Since then, he had been embarrassed to ask, as he didn't want to insult her!

Binem stood up and brushed himself off. He walked directly to Wanda's house and knocked on the door. Wanda answered and told him to go directly to the living room. Binem looked into the room and saw a woman dressed in a full-length mink coat. She wore a diamond necklace. On her wrist was a matching diamond bracelet. Binem thought, "She must be a Polish Princess!"

The Princess looked at Binem with a penetrating gaze. Noticing that Binem was hesitant, she invited him to join her. She was about forty years old, and dressed in a black velvet dress. She spoke in a very refined Polish.

Binem learned that the woman was not actually a princess, but was married to a wealthy Volksdeutsche who owned the largest estate in the county where Radziejow was located.

She assured Binem that she was 100% Polish. She explained that she met her husband just after World War I. Her last name was Osten-Sacken. My father could not remember her first name. She and husband had two sons, one of whom was serving as an officer in the German army. She nearly broke into tears as she explained that her younger son had died in a drowning accident in the Vistula River just days before Germany invaded Poland in 1939. Judging by her voice and her facial expression, Binem understood that she had not recovered from this tragic loss.

When she was done telling about herself, Binem told her a brief version of his entire life story leading up to this meeting. She patiently listened, looking sincerely interested.

Binem's mind began to race. He had never spoken to an aristocratic woman in his life. The Polish aristocracy had virtually no contact with the Jewish community. But what baffled him was why she would go out of her way to save him. "When I saw her, I couldn't believe my eyes. I couldn't believe that she was going to save me. For what reason would she want to save me?"

So when Binem was finished speaking, he couldn't help himself. He said, "I've read in books about noble people that tried to save people, but I never believed it would happen to me. Why are you doing this?"

She answered in a kind voice. "The reason I want to do this is because I have two sons close to your age. Sadly, one is dead. His room is now empty and I feel it would be only right to use it to do some good."

Binem concluded that she was sincere. Still, he wondered why a privileged woman who was married to German and probably had benefited from the Nazi occupation would put her life and the life of her family in danger for the sake of an ordinary. flea-ridden Jew. As incredulous as it sounded, Binem decided to take a chance.

As he agreed to the offer he thought to herself, "Her German husband would either shoot me or turn me in to the

Nazis."

Binem heard the sound of a carriage approaching Wanda's house. It sounded as if it had stopped near the front door. He glanced out the window and saw a magnificent, ornately decorated coach. When Wanda opened the front door, she pointed to the driver and told Binem that he was her brother. She explained that her brother the watchman of the Osten-Sacken estate.

Binem was told to enter the carriage. He sat very still on a velvet cushion. Next, the Princess gracefully boarded the carriage and sat next to Binem. They were silent as the carriage drove to her estate. During the ride, Binem could not dismiss from his thoughts that it was just too suspicious that both the Princess and her driver would risk their lives to help him. Even if they were sincere, there was a possibility that the carriage might be stopped at roadblock. The Nazi occupation army would frequently erect such roadblocks as a security measure. If that were to happen, they would be doomed. All Poles knew that the punishment for assisting Jews was harsh, and could include summary execution. Luckily, they were not stopped.

A short time later, they arrived at the entrance of a sprawling estate. During the ride, Binem was struck by the staggering size of the estate. He thought that the Princess and husband must be the wealthiest people in Poland. The mansion was enormous. Binem observed what appeared to be several gardens along with buildings that included servant's quarters, granaries, and barns.

Binem thought that it would take nothing less than an army of workers to maintain such an estate. As he glanced out the carriage window with amazement, it dawned on him that there was not a single worker to be seen. Even more peculiar, there was not even a sound of any kind to be heard. It was as if the estate had been abandoned. Binem later learned that the Princess had made arrangements that all workers on the estate were given the night off.

When the carriage finally came to stop, the Princess pointed to a window located near the massive wooden front door of the mansion. She said that the window was unlatched, and he should use it to enter the house. She then gave him instructions on where to go after entering.

Binem exited the carriage and made his way to the window. He opened it and climbed inside, finding himself in a three-story high foyer.

As his eyes adjusted, he had the feeling that he was standing in an opulent palace. Never in his life had he witnessed such luxury. The lighting in the room was relaxing to the eyes. Even the temperature of the room was perfect. He could see that each room connected to the foyer had at least one magnificent crystal chandelier and a giant fireplace. He thought to himself that one could set up a room inside the fireplace.

He next noticed that the furniture was not like the regular furniture he was accustomed to, but rather each piece looked like a piece of art of remarkable craftsmanship. His eyes then focused on the rich wooden floors. The wood was of kind he had never seen. The floors were polished to such a shine that the light from the fireplaces reflected off the floor. Parts of the floor were adorned with handmade wool carpets. Each of these carpets was in and of itself a work of art, magnificent in size with intricate color patterns. Binem thought that the carpets had been individually woven to match the room. Binem was so overwhelmed by the mansion that he felt that he was transitioning from the bleakness of Hell to the Garden of Eden.

Binem proceeded cautiously in the mansion, making sure to follow the instructions of the princess precisely. He made his way to a large foyer that contained a magnificent staircase. The walls encompassing the staircase were covered with dozens of paintings, several of which were large oil paintings in ornate gilded frames. It dawned on Binem that the mansion must contain at least twenty rooms, each room meticulously decorated to meet what could only be described as a royal standard of opulence.

Binem felt completely out of his environment as he ascended the grand staircase. He thought to himself that, prior to entering the mansion, the most impressive staircase he had ever ascended was that of the Naiman building in Radziejow. Eventually he made it to the top floor where the stairs ended. There he had been told he would find the attic.

His first impression was the word attic did not describe this floor. First, the "attic" floor could hardly be distinguished from the other floors of this mansion. It was similarly decorated with paintings on the walls and handmade carpets on rich grain wood floors. He proceeded until he reached a set of double doors. The Princess had told him that these were the doors to her deceased son's bedroom where he would live. When he opened the doors, he was astonished to see that this "bedroom" looked like a museum, and was as spacious as the largest house in Radziejow. He fondly remembered, "The room was so fixed up it was like in a fairy tale."

Binem sat on a wooden chair next to the canopy bed and waited. He was flabbergasted by his plush surroundings. He rattled off in his mind the items around him: a life-size wooden horse, an army of lead soldiers, enough stuffed animals to make a zoo, and every kind of ball imaginable, neatly displayed on shelves. Every item seemed to blend with the next, as if to create a timeline of the history of a child growing up to be a man. Binem thought to himself that the Princess must have loved her son very much to preserve the room as it was. Then he cringed, "Now the princess wants to honor his memory by saving a Jew her son's age. One can never understand how people think."

An hour later, the Princess and the driver entered the room. The Princess graciously handed Binem the key to the room. She then asked him if the accommodations were acceptable. Binem nodded in the affirmative. She instructed Binem that under no circumstances should he open the door for anyone, "unless you hear my signal of three raps in a row."

To make it absolutely clear, she stated the rule again, "When you hear three knocks, then you may open the door. Otherwise, don't open the door for anyone."

She then exited the room, leaving Binem alone with his thoughts. Binem could not believe this amazing stroke of luck. After all the tragedies that had befallen him in the last few years he was now in a position to live out the war like a king.

He said to himself, "Impossible! Too good to be true. Either I am dreaming, or this won't last very long!"

He glanced at the magnificent bed and his eyes focused on the arrangement of clothes and pajamas. He assumed that these were left for him. Since he was sleepy, he decided to bathe and then don one exceptionally luxurious pair of pajamas. He literally had to peel the clothing he had been wearing for so long off of his body. His tattered clothes were so impregnated with dirt that he could not distinguish the material from the filth.

When he was done undressing, he placed his clothes on a large cushioned chair next to the bed. He then entered the bathroom to take a bath. All the grime, dirt, and lice he had been carrying for the past few months literally floated away. When he was done, he carefully put on the pajamas. He joked with himself, "With these pajamas, I am truly a Naiman!" which means "new man" in Yiddish.

He then stretched out on the bed, which was the size of a boat. He observed that the bed was not only ornate, but, more importantly, it was extremely comfortable. Binem had been sleeping on the ground or on top of hay for a long time. Prior to that, he had slept in a bunk with a thin mattress. Of course, before the German invasion of Poland, he and his brother Azriel, now murdered by the Nazis, had shared a bed with a straw mattress.

Binem said to himself, "What fun Azriel and I could have had playing games in this bed. Why, it is big enough to play football in it."

He glanced around the room, absorbing a room that had an almost mystical aura of peace and tranquility, having been carefully designed for this purpose by loving parents. He watched the crackle of the burning logs in the large fireplace near the bed. The warmth it gave off was a true pleasure. Finally, he took account of the extensive library only a few feet from the stool of the bed. He saw books of all kinds, fiction and nonfiction, science and math books, and many others. The books were exquisitely bound, appearing to be in pristine condition.

Binem again thought that this could not possibly be real. He thought it must be a dream he was having in one of his forsaken haystacks. He just couldn't accept the reality that, after all he had experienced in the last three years, such a situation could possibly exist in Poland.

Binem reflected on the situation, asking himself, "Why am I so lucky when my fellow Jews are literally living like dogs?"

Lost in his thoughts, he fell asleep.

The next day he awoke to three raps on the door. When he opened the door, he saw the Princess holding a tray. She had personally brought Binem a hot meal. She watched as he started to eat. Based on her facial expressions, Binem assumed that she had never seen a Jew eat before. She politely waited as Binem gorged himself on several delicacies set before him. When he finished, she asked him if he needed anything. Binem thought for a moment and requested a newspaper.

The next day, when the Princess brought him his meal, there was a German newspaper on the tray. As soon as she left, he began to peruse the paper, scrutinizing each article. When he was done, he chuckled to himself. "At least I now know what news the Germans were being told about the war."

Despite all this luxury, Binem continued to feel depressed. He thought about his dead and missing brothers and sisters. He knew that even if he survived the war, he would remain completely alone. Trying to put aside his feelings, he began planning how he could avoid becoming completely bored. Binem decided to immerse himself in the books on the shelves scattered throughout the room. For breaks, he would gaze out of the window at the picturesque estate and daydream. He watched the gentle snow falling onto the magnificent trees. He tried to imagine what the trees might look like when spring arrived. Another pastime was to observe the servants cheerfully scurrying from one place to another and try to determine what was each servant's job.

Sometimes he would marvel that he was watching a world which, from all appearances, was oblivious to the hatred and fighting of World War II. For brief moments he felt that he was in a safe zone, and the war for him was now over. He envisioned that one day he would be able to step out of the confines of this safe haven when the forces of good would finally subdue the Nazis and their allies.

Then his depression would return. He knew none of his machinations mattered. For no matter what happened, everyone he knew was now probably dead or about to be murdered. Radziejow and the beautiful community that he grew up in would never return. He was truly alone. He also knew that no matter what his future might bring, he would always be haunted by the terrible memories.

He would say to himself, "How can I think that I could survive, when both Nazis and some Poles have looked me in the face and said that, because I am a Jew, I am an evil that needs to be destroyed for the sake of mankind."

Sometimes Binem's thoughts would drift into the realm of curiosity. He was puzzled that he never saw the husband of the Princess. "Why hasn't anyone but the Princess even approached the door? It is too good here. It couldn't be that all the Jews are suffering and I am safe, living in luxury." These questions were red flags for Binem.

Unfortunately, Binem's utopian setup didn't even last a full week. On his fourth day in the palace, disaster struck. That morning, the Princess went to the kitchen to pick out Binem's food for the day. She was now familiar with what types of food Binem preferred. As she went about her selection, one maid became overly curious regarding the Princess's new routine. She couldn't understand why the Princess was now coming into the kitchen every day. In the past, she was never seen in the kitchen. If the Princess wanted something to eat between meals, she would always send one of her servants to the kitchen. Now the Princess was actually walking around the prep table, picking out different foods and putting them on a tray. Even more disturbing, she carried the tray out of the kitchen without the help of a servant.

That day, when the Princess left the kitchen, this bold member of the kitchen staff decided to stealthily follow her. The Princess was oblivious of her "tail." She casually made her way to the attic. The maid observed as the Princess approached the room of her deceased son and knocked on the door, precisely three times. Then she watched as the door opened. The maid couldn't see who had opened the door. The Princess then entered the room and remained there for a brief moment before exiting the room and descending the stairs.

Less than an hour later, Binem surprisingly heard the code being rapped on the door again. Binem, assuming it was the Princess, opened the door without any suspicion. When he looked out in the hallway, he saw a strange woman standing in front of him. A feeling of dread crept over his entire being as the woman stared at Binem, not saying a word. Binem looked back at her for about five seconds. Then the woman abruptly turned around and walked down the stairs. Binem wasn't sure what to make of this strange encounter. He had no idea who the woman could possibly be.

In less than an hour, Binem heard the code of the three knocks yet again. This time Binem hesitated. He thought to himself, "What's going on?" Having no option, he cautiously opened the door. He saw the Princess, with tears in her eyes. The anguished look on her face seemed to exclaim, "all is lost!"

Binem asked, "What happened?"

The Princess answered in a whimper, "One of my servants told my entire staff that I am hiding someone in the attic." She went on to explain that the servant wasn't sure who the person was that was hiding. She then told Binem, "This will leak out and soon the Gestapo will here."

She stared at Binem as she continued to sob. Binem assumed that she didn't have the heart to tell him that he must leave immediately for his sake as well as hers. When he subtly inquired, the most she would say was that the situation "constituted a great deal of danger."

Binem comforted her. "I don't want to endanger your family, so as soon as it dark I will leave."

Binem saw by the Princess's facial expression that this was exactly what she had hoped to hear. He understood that she had been afraid he would refuse to leave voluntarily. Binem then thanked her for all her help.

The Princess quickly arranged that the entire staff have the night off. As soon as it was dark, Binem left the palace, following the same route he had entered just a few evenings ago. This time there was no carriage.

As he entered the barren fields, Binem understood that he was now literally out in the cold. He was alone without any support. As he trudged along, his feet sank deep into the snow. Binem's short stay in the mansion had accustomed him to a life of relative normalcy. He was not mentally prepared to go back to his previous life as prey for the Nazi hunters. He no longer had the willpower to withstand starvation or the freezing cold of winter.

Binem said to himself, "The past few days spoiled me too much. I can't go back to a life hiding in the fields. There is no hope for me."

Due to Binem's growing despondency, he ceased to follow the rules that had kept him alive for so long. Instead, not caring about life, he became reckless. He started by returning to his home village of Radziejow during the daytime. His purpose was to find a means of ending his misery. He decided that he would not voluntarily surrender to the Nazis, instead, he would put himself into a situation in which he would inevitably be caught.

He walked the streets of Radziejow passing Pole after Pole. They themselves looked miserable. Not one approached him. Even familiar faces either did not see him or pretended to not see him. To Binem's utter astonishment, no matter what he did to reveal himself, not a single Pole approached him, let alone made any effort to turn him in. It appeared to Binem that the more he tried to get caught, the more the Poles of Radziejow ignored him. Even while walking down the main business street in broad daylight, not one Pole even acknowledged that he existed. Binem came to the surreal conclusion that he must be invisible. He even contemplated walking into the Nazi Barracks. However, he quickly dismissed this thought. For even though he wanted to be caught, in his heart he knew that it would be a sin to actually turn himself in.

Night had fallen. The streets of Radziejow were dark and empty. Binem stood on a gravel street in a neighborhood that he had long since forgotten. Frustrated by his failure to be caught, Binem now faced the most critical decision of his life. He believed that it was not meant to be that the Poles of Radziejow would have him arrested. On the other hand, he had completely lost his will to survive.

Feeling he was trapped, without any solution to relieve him from his misery, the taboo thought of suicide entered his mind. Binem knew that according to Jewish law, under no circumstances does a person have God's permission to kill himself. Still, he remembered a few stories in the Talmud in which, while not endorsing the act of suicide explicitly, the Rabbis showed a great deal of understanding for those that killed themselves rather then desecrate God's commandments. Complicating Binem's decision was the fact that he was so distraught he couldn't think straight. He was on the verge of a complete mental collapse. After a few hours, he made up his mind. He would commit suicide. But still the question remained as to where. He immediately found the answer. In the still of the night, Binem found his way to the Jewish cemetery located on the outskirts of Radziejow.

Binem entered the cemetery in a trance-like state. It was surreal that, he, possibly the last Jew alive from the town of Radziejow, was standing in a place where the only remnants of the Jewish community lay beneath his feet. He noticed that some of the headstones had been removed. He inwardly laughed as he remembered that in Jewish law, walking alone in a cemetery at night is the definition of crazy. He said to himself that the demons that roamed a cemetery at night would welcome him to the neighborhood of deceased Jews that were buried beneath his feet.

He proceeded to make his way to the graves of his mother and father by the light of the moon. The magnificent grave marker that had stood over his mother's grave was no longer there. Binem remembered being told that it was requisitioned by the Nazis for their unholy war effort. Still, Binem seemed as if he was being guided to the graves.

The first thing Binem did was prostrate himself over his parents' graves. Binem proceeded to talk aloud to his deceased parents, explaining his entire ordeal from the time of his father's death to this very night. He informed them that he believed that he had no choice but to join them by ending his life in this very place.

He said, "I'm going to finish myself here. Better to end it this way then get caught by the Germans and be tortured. This is the end."

Binem suddenly realized that he had no idea how to commit suicide. Binem's mind raced, trying to come up with a method. He searched his pockets. All he found was an alum block that he used after shaving. There was not even a razor.

With no other alternative, Binem decided to crush the block into a powder and swallow it. He conjectured that the chemicals in the alum block were deadly. After swallowing the powder, Binem waited. Nothing happened. A few minutes later, Binem vomited out the powder. While he felt nauseous, he was still very much alive.

After realizing his failure, Binem became even more determined to commit suicide. Binem removed the flimsy piece of leather that he used as a belt to hold up his tattered trousers. He wrapped the leather strap around his neck several times, pulling it as tight as his strength allowed. As he gasped for air, he prostrated himself on top of his parents' graves. He then closed his eyes, recited the prayer *Shema Yisrael* and awaited death. But nothing happened. He noticed that the belt had loosened on its own accord. He tried wrapping the belt around his neck once more, but again nothing happened.

Binem said to himself, incredulously, "What's happening? I cannot not even achieve one simple thing such as killing myself!"

Now he was not only suffering from a near complete mental breakdown, he was disgusted with himself for not being able to even take his own life. He shouted at the top of his lungs repeatedly, "My God, I can't even kill myself."

Binem stood up in this lonely cemetery and realized that he was no different than the dozens of tombstones. He was like a gravestone marker serving as a reminder of the dead. In his case, it was the murdered Jews of Radziejow.

When my father described this event on the Spielberg video, his facial expression and the tears in his eyes revealed that even decades later, he had still not come to terms with that night.

He was confused as to what he should do next. As he thought about his options, either attempting again to kill himself or to turn himself into the Nazis, he heard voices that seemed to be coming from the trees in the forest next to the cemetery. He could clearly make out the sounds that formed the Yiddish words, "*Gay avek, gay avek* (Go away, go away)!"

Binem wasn't sure if the voices were his imagination

forming words from the wind rustling the leaves, or, as illogical as it may seem, a person or even a spirit ordering him to leave this place of death.

As Binem stood motionless, contemplating the meaning of this eerie message, he realized that the sun was about to rise. He decided to leave the cemetery and find a hiding place. As he began to walk, he determined that suicide was not the solution. He became resolute in his belief that God clearly had other plans for him, having taken the trouble to send him a *Bas Kol* (heavenly voice) ordering him to leave the cemetery. So he would not disappoint God. He was determined to let fate decide his future.

Binem left the cemetery by way of the front gate. It was nearly daytime when he found a dense thicket in the nearby woods. He sat himself down on the cold ground and covered himself with branches. He then closed his eyes and was soon fast asleep. Come evening, Binem awoke somewhat refreshed both spiritually and physically. He decided that he would make his way to a nearby village where he remembered that there lived a friendly Pole, a shoemaker. This shoemaker was a valued customer before the war who would regularly buy materials from the Naimans.

The Polish shoemaker immediately recognized him. Unfortunately, the shoemaker's' children, who were sitting at a table finishing dinner, saw Binem in the doorway. Binem's disheveled appearance frightened the children. To them, he looked like a wild man. The children in unison became audibly hysterical. Seeing his children's reaction, the shoemaker approached Binem menacingly, so Binem was forced to turn around and run away.

Binem was already accustomed to such reactions from previous hostile encounters with Poles. He was not flustered. He spotted a small patch of woods near the shoemaker's house and hid himself in the thicket.

His physical and mental exhaustion returned. He felt that he was enveloped in a dark shadow. He couldn't understand why this particular Pole acted in such a violent manner.

Binem thought to himself, "How could that man behave that way towards me? Has he too changed as a result of the war, and became selfish and cold-hearted like so many others?"

He sat leaning against a tree and watched the snow fall. As he watched, he became drowsy and eventually fell into a deep sleep.

A few hours later, Binem suddenly felt that he was in danger. As he opened his eyes, he could distinctly hear sounds moving towards him. He thought that perhaps the shoemaker had informed on him to the Nazis. But instead of Germans approaching, he saw the shoemaker along with his wife. As they came closer, he could see that they were both smiling. In the wife's hands was a tray supporting a steamy hot meal.

The shoemaker spoke in a soft voice. He earnestly apologized for his earlier behavior. He said that he was forced to act in such a uncivilized manner because of his children.

He said, "If I would have invited you in, then for sure at least one of my children would have told someone about you."

Binem thought to himself, "I couldn't have asked God for a better miracle. I was down and out and God sent me these two kind Poles to comfort me."

As Binem devoured his food, he discussed his plight with the shoemaker and his wife. When Binem finished eating, the shoemaker was truly saddened by the pain Binem expressed.

He told Binem, "You can't stay in these woods, there is too much activity taking place here." He suggested that Binem go see a woman that lived not too far away, in a small house surrounded by fields.

"The police never go there. Perhaps she can hide you."

So Binem sought out and found the woman. When he arrived at her small house, he told the woman that answered the door that the shoemaker sent him to her. She smiled and replied in a friendly manner. She apologized to Binem that he could only stay a few days because she was scheduled to return to work and then nobody would be in the house. Binem wasn't sure exactly why that would be a problem, but he was happy to have found food and shelter. "A short time is better than no time," he said to himself.

Those two days refreshed Binem's spirit. He was hoping that she would tell him that he could stay even longer, but she didn't. So Binem thanked her on the third night and left.

Binem searched for a new hiding place without success. When it was almost sunrise, he became worried. He saw in the distance a barn a few hundred meters beyond the main road.

Binem realized that he was facing a life-threatening quandary. He was well aware that police and military vehicles often used this particular road, having passed it several times in his wanderings. In fact, several months prior Binem had made a rule that under no circumstances would he ever attempt to cross this road.

Now it was getting light. He knew that if he stayed out in the open field he would surely be seen. On the other hand, if he successfully crossed the road and hid in that nearby barn, he would be safe. Binem hesitated. He realized that time would soon determine his fate if he didn't take matters into his own hands. His mind raced trying to solve the life-threatening dilemma he faced. With sunrise too close to avoid, he finally made up his mind. With much trepidation, he decided to risk the crossing.

Binem looked in both directions and it appeared safe to cross. He started across the dirt road that was approximately ten meters wide. As he traversed to the halfway point, he was overcome by a feeling of dread. He described it as a dull pain over his entire body foretelling impending doom. This caused Binem to panic. He broke into a sprint and nearly reached the other side of the road when disaster struck. Suddenly, he saw several spotlights shining on him. Binem knew this was the end. He was finally caught.

Binem thought to himself, "I'm trapped by the Germans.

What is there left for me to do?"

Binem realized that it was futile to try and escape. He saw many menacing soldiers and policemen. All were heavily armed. Some of them pointed their rifles at him. Others did not seem to be overly concerned. Still, there were several on motorcycles that were obviously positioned to run him down if he tried to make a break for it. Binem evaluated his predicament and concluded that it was all over. He had been anticipating this moment for several months. However, when it finally arrived, he was totally unprepared to face the consequences.

Then, out of nowhere, he had an inspiration. A glimmer of hope entered his mind. He remembered his escape from the Lager. There, he escaped by simply walking through the well-guarded gate. Could it be that simple? He stopped running and instead acted oblivious to the dire situation by continuing to walk forward, at a snail's pace, towards the field next to the road.

The soldiers quickly surrounded him. Binem kept his gaze down, though he knew he was now surrounded by several of the menacing soldiers. There were guns pointed at him from all directions. They shouted at him in German to stop. Binem came to a stop but stood silent. He listened to their discussions and came to understand that they were not looking for Jews, rather, the soldiers had set up a roadblock to capture escaped Russian POWs that were hiding in the area.

One of the soldiers appeared to be in charge. He had a menacing appearance. Speaking in German, with a deep, frightening voice, he demanded of Binem, "What are you doing here?"

Binem evaluated this hopeless situation. After months of being on the run, he was caught. Thinking fast, he had one last card to draw. He decided to pretend that he was a simple Polish peasant.

In order to convinced the Germans that he was a Polish peasant, he mimicked the accent of a simple Polish farmer. He told the German in Polish that he didn't understand. Still, the soldier continued to repeat in German, more emphatically, "What are you doing here?"

Binem understood every word the soldier had said in German. Still, he continued to protest in Polish that he did not understand. Since the Jews in Poland spoke Yiddish, which is similar to German, Binem knew that if he showed his understanding the soldier might suspect he was a Jew.

Frustrated, the soldier called to a *Gendarmerie* policeman who was sitting on a motorcycle about a hundred meters away. When the officer drew closer, Binem's face turned pale and his entire body began to shake. Binem recognized the policeman. It was none other than the sadistic "Potcher of Radziejow." Being all too familiar with the Potcher's delight in physically abusing Jews, Binem fervently prayed to the Almighty that he would not recognize him.

The Potcher shined his flashlight in Binem's face. He stared at Binem. Then with a seemingly knowing smile on his face, he asked Binem in Polish, "What are you doing here?"

Binem answered, "I work on a farm."

The Potcher gave him an incredulous look. "A farm? It's too early to go to work on a farm."

Binem knew that the Potcher was correct. It was around four o'clock in the morning. He knew from his time on the run that peasants never appeared in the fields or roads to walk to their farm jobs before six in the morning.

Still, Binem persisted in his peasant accent. "I go to milk the cows."

The Potcher again flashed an incredulous smile. To Binem's utter astonishment, the Potcher replied, "O.K., go ahead."

Binem started to walk, but as he took his first few steps the Potcher gave Binem a firm kick in the rear. Binem thought for a moment that this was the prelude to a severe beating. But, in fact, it was more of a friendly kick telling him to hurry along his way.

As Binem entered the field on the other side of the road, he was sure that the Potcher had in fact recognized him.

Binem thought, "Of all the Germans he had met during the war, he was the one I was most afraid of. But he was the one that let me go."

I asked my father, "Were you ever beaten up by the Germans?" His answer sounded almost mystical. "I remember that once I was slapped by a Nazi while I stood in line. After he slapped me, I watched the Nazi's face turned white as if he received an electric shock."

As Binem scurried away from the Potcher and the throng of German soldiers, he heard a German shout, "Look that way, I see three POWs!" With that, all the soldiers and police hurried off in the opposite direction.

Binem continued across the field until he made his way to the barn. He spent the day hidden deep in the hay. That evening, he felt hunger pains and set off to find food. After a few hours, he entered a small village and knocked on the window.

An elderly man answered the door. Binem was in luck, it was a friendly shoemaker named Antoine Claus. The Naimans had known Claus as a *Goyishe Mench* (a stand-up gentile). He was honest and humble. After exchanging a few pleasantries, he invited Binem into his house without hesitation. The shoemaker gathered some food and set it on his workbench where Binem was sitting on one of the two stools. Binem wolfed down a sizable portion of food. Then the two began to talk.

The small house, actually a shack, consisted of one large room. The room was essentially a workshop that had a small area in the back sectioned off by a floor-to-ceiling curtain. Behind the curtain was just enough room for Claus's bed.

Claus was most hospitable. He talked as if there was no war. He surprised Binem by telling him that he could stay with him as long as he wants. But he cautioned Binem that he must remain quiet during the day, because German soldiers would be coming in to have their shoes repaired. This situation didn't seem to concern Claus at all. He simply instructed Binem to remain hidden behind the curtain. Binem was skeptical that this arrangement would work. Still, with no better prospects, he decided to to take the chance.

The two slept in the same bed. At the crack of dawn, Claus arose and immediately went to work at his cobbler's bench. Binem continued to sleep behind the curtain. An hour later, Binem heard the footsteps of people entering the house. They were speaking German. From the conversation Binem understood that these two Germans were soldiers that had come to have their boots repaired. As Claus worked on their boots, the soldiers conversed with one another. Binem listened intently. At first it was all small talk. Suddenly the word "Juden" echoed in the workshop.

One German said, "I killed hundreds of Jews."

The other German scoffed and mocked him. Then he said, "Well, I killed more than a thousand."

The two laughed and began trading war stories about the methods they used to kill Jews.

Binem continued to be a "fly on the wall," knowing that the two would kill him if they only knew that they were but a few steps away from a Jew.

Binem spent the next three days in terror, knowing that at any moment he could be discovered. He couldn't believe how calm Claus remained. Not once did he mention a word about the danger. He was completely fearless. Binem, on the other hand, was fearful that at any moment a German would for whatever reason part the drapes and discover him. Binem was doubly troubled, knowing that if he was caught, then Claus would most likely also be killed.

I asked my father, "Why was Claus so nice?"

He answered, "Because he knew my family before the war. So he didn't have the heart to tell me to leave."

As important it was for Binem to have food and shelter, he knew that this arrangement was fraught with danger. No matter how hard he tried to think of a way to make it work, he was forced to conclude that it was impossible that he could safely hide in this one room workshop that was frequented by German soldiers.

So on the fourth evening of his stay Binem told Claus, ""I cannot endanger you." He added, "If I get caught, you will suffer."

Claus gave a one ord reply: "Nonsense."

Claus's incredible display of humanity gave Binem hope that someday things could return to normal. Nevertheless, Binem told him that he must leave. He thanked Claus for his hospitality.

As Binem left the shack he said, "I hope that one day I will be able to repay you for your kindness."

Binem's level of despondency had reached a new low. He had lost his will to endure the frigid temperatures, hunger pains, the constant fear of being caught by the Nazis, the sorrow in his heart, and his loneliness.

Suddenly, a thought popped into his mind. "What about Wanda? She might be able to help. What do I have to lose if I impose on her a second time?"

So that night he set off for her village. This time, he miraculously found both her village and her cottage after only a few hours of walking.

Binem hesitantly rapped on the door of her cottage. After a short period, Wanda answered the door. To Binem's surprise, Wanda's appeared to be genuinely pleased to see him again.

Binem didn't mince words. "I can't take anymore. It's no use. Tomorrow I plan to give myself up to the Germans."

Wanda's face turned pale. "Don't do it! I can fix this. Come back tomorrow night and we will find a solution," she said.

Wanda told Binem to wait while she prepared some food. After eating his fill, Binem told her about the circumstances that had forced him to leave the Princess's house. A few hours later, he left Wanda's house and found his way to the hiding place he used the previous time he had come for help. He settled in to wait for the coming evening.

Binem returned the following evening, as soon as darkness had descended on the village. He cautiously approached the front door of Wanda's cottage. Wanda answered and invited him in. As he took the few steps from the tiny foyer to the adjacent parlor, to his utter surprise sitting in the room was the Princess. Standing beside her was Wanda's brother.

The Princess remained silent. Wanda's brother told Binem to go outside and enter the waiting carriage. Binem was excited. There was hope. He anticipated the good life he experienced the time before. His mind's eye envisioned the beautiful mansion, the piping hot food, the wonderful view and the soft, luxurious bed. Binem waited inside the carriage. Then the door opened and the Princess entered. Just as the first time, he sat next to the Princess. As the carriage departed Wanda's house, the Princess and Binem exchanged a few words. To Binem, she seemed apprehensive at best. The rest of the way she remained silent.

When the carriage stopped, Binem looked around. He did not see the mansion. Instead, the carriage had stopped in front of a barn. Binem noticed that this was no ordinary barn, rather, it was the largest barn that he had ever seen. Binem thought that the barn was at least two hundred meters long and almost a hundred meters wide. Binem understood that this would be his new home and sadly not the luxurious mansion.

The Princess stayed in the carriage, and Wanda's brother led Binem to the giant barn door. Wanda's brother explained that this was a very special barn. This barn, which was located far from the mansion, was in an area of the estate that was off limits to the workers. The barn's sole content was a sea of straw that was earmarked as an emergency reserve for the thousands of horses of the German Army. From the beginning of the war, the standing rule for workers on the estate was, "If you are caught entering the barn, you will be shot." Therefore, none of the workers would even go anywhere near to this barn.

The Princess exited the carriage and caught up with Wanda's brother and Binem. The three entered through a small door adjacent to barn's giant double doors. Binem was shocked by the abundance of straw, as far as the eye could see. He thought that there was enough straw in the barn to feed an army of horses for a hundred years.

Wanda's brother told Binem that every time he would come by he would use the earlier code of three raps on the door. He said that he would return every night and bring enough food to last until the following evening.

The Princess then told Binem that he could order whatever food he wanted. She showed Binem where a set of clothes, a warm coat, a small lantern, and several blankets had been prepared for him.

Wanda's brother directed Binem to a short barrel with a removable lid that was located about ten meters from the entrance to the barn. The barrel was half filled with straw. Wanda's brother told him that he was to use it to evacuate his bowels. Once a week it would be removed and replaced with a new barrel. Then, without any parting words, the Princess and Wanda's brother exited by way of the small door.

In the Spielberg Holocaust interview that was conducted ten years after my own interview, my father, then in his seventies, recalled that he was initially taken to a cow barn and was led to a loft. There he stayed for 2 months. His main problem was dealing with the rats that were constantly crawling over him, whether he was asleep or awake, and stealing his food. Still, Binem maintained it was better than being on the run. As the rat population grew, Wanda's brother was concerned that the workers would suspect someone was feeding them. As a result of the rats, Binem was moved to the giant barn where the straw was stored.

One additional inconsistency between the interviews regards Wanda's brother. In the Spielberg interview, my father recalled Wanda's brother being an anti-Semite, who had said, "I don't know why I have to put up with this kind of shit." However, in my interview, my father recalled it was actually Wanda's brother who had convinced the Princess to try again to save him.

Now alone, Binem contemplated his fate. He had shelter, plenty of space, warm clothes, straw to protect him from the cold, and his choice of food. Most important, he was in an area that was off limits to the world. Barring any emergency or surprise inspection, he was safe until the conclusion of the war, which he prayed would end with the total destruction of Nazi Germany.

The first thing Binem did was to remove his clothes, which had become no more than dirty rags, and put on the new clothes that had been provided him. They consisted of a flannel shirt, wool pants, wool socks, and a pair of quality fur-lined winter boots. He then put on the heavy wool coat, the warm leather gloves, and the winter hat lined with soft fur. Binem was surprised that all the items fit him perfectly.

Now fully dressed and warm, Binem began to walk. He walked the length of the barn and back. He thought to himself that this arrangement was even better than being in the mansion. Here he had plenty of room and did not have to worry that someone would discover him. He returned to the front of the barn picked up a blanket, and then burrowed himself into the nearest straw pile. Within minutes he fell into a deep and restful sleep.

In the following days, Binem developed a routine. When he woke up, he would wash his face and relieve himself. Then Binem would exercise by walking the length of the barn back and forth several times. When he got tired, he would sit down to eat the breakfast that had been provided the previous night. He then would read the materials that had been delivered along with his meal. As he read, he realized that the world outside the barn continued to be filled with death and destruction. Binem, on the other hand, was living in a seemingly impenetrable fortress, isolating him from the evil and violence that was all around him. One day lapsed into another and time passed quickly.

One night, Binem made a special request. He told Wanda's brother that he was afraid that he would be susceptible to catching colds because there was no direct sunlight entering the barn. Binem reasoned that to remain healthy, he needed to supplement his diet with large quantities of garlic and onions. This home remedy was well known among the peasants of Europe. The next night, and every night thereafter, he received along with his meals an ample quantity of onions and garlic.

Binem's reading material included a German propaganda paper. He became an expert at reading "between the lines" in order to understand what was really happening. Binem understood that when the newspaper reported that there were temporary setbacks for the Wehrmacht on the Russian front, it meant that the Germans were suffering severe setbacks. He learned that there were other fronts in France and Italy where Germany was being assailed by the American and British armies. All this led Binem to conclude that the Nazis' days were indeed numbered. Binem prayed to God to assist all those who were standing up to the Nazi regime. He added in his prayers a personal request to help him survive the war.

Germany's war efforts took a turn for the worse at the battle for Stalingrad that began in August of 1942. The Russians staged a two-prong attack that destroyed the troops protecting the flanks of the German Sixth Army, enabling the Russians to surround the German forces. In December, the extreme Russian winter set in, further weakening the morale of the Germans. Hundreds of thousands of German troops were killed or wounded. Even more demoralizing for the Nazis, about 100,000 German soldiers surrendered. After Stalingrad, the Russians continued a broad advance, pushing back the German line closer and closer to Germany. By December 1944, it became obvious that the German "strategic retreats" were no longer strategic; rather, they were being routed by the Russian forces.

With each delivery of a German newspaper, Binem would take great pleasure thinking to himself, "It appears that things are going bad for the Germans."

Binem noticed that the more the German war effort deteriorated, the better quality and quantity of food he was provided by his benefactors. It appeared to Binem that it was only a matter of time before the so-called invincible Germans would be defeated. Unfortunately, the Germans didn't surrender as fast as Binem wanted. The days and nights of anticipation seemed endless.

I asked my father, "You had all this time in the barn for several months, what did you think about all day while you did nothing?"

He answered, "I thought about living over the war. I read the German papers. I knew all I could do was patiently wait."

This arrangement continued for a period of approximately eight months.

THE NAZI

O ne night, in the month of December, some time after Wanda's brother had already brought him food, Binem again heard the code of three knocks on the door. Binem was suspicious. He walked over to the door and peered through a small crack between the door and the barn wall. Binem thought he was having a nightmare. Standing on the other side of the door was no less than a high ranking German soldier in full uniform. Binem thought he was in the Gestapo. This vision caused Binem's hopes of surviving the war to suddenly fade before his eyes.

The officer, however, was smiling pleasantly. After a moment, he spoke in the direction of the door, saying, "Open up, don't worry about it, I'm your friend."

Binem tried to grasp the meaning of the word "friend." He thought to himself with fatalistic humor, "That's a new one. I never had an opportunity to have a friend wearing a German uniform."

Binem knew what would be the probable consequences of opening the door. But the latch that locked the door would in any case do little to stop a determined Nazi. So, after a moment of hesitation, he realized he had no alternative but to unlatch the door.

The rusty hinges on the door creaked as the German officer pushed the door open. Binem thought the Gestapo had come for him. With an aura of military authority, the German officer marched right into the barn. Binem looked him over. He fixated on the insignia on the officer's uniform of an eagle standing on a swastika, known as the *Reichsadler*, which reflected the light of a small lantern he was carrying in one arm. To Binem, the swastika symbolized the epitome of all that was evil in the world. In the other arm the officer held a wicker basket. The regal uniform he wore was much fancier than those that Binem had encountered during the course of the war.

Binem's eyes then focused on the officer's sidearm. He saw a black holster attached to a belt with a silver buckle. Binem knew that inside the holster was a Luger, the preferred handgun of Nazi Germany. He thought to himself that it really didn't matter if the German was an officer or an enlisted man. As far as Binem was concerned, anyone who wore a German uniform was out to kill him.

The German officer spoke slowly, trying to calm Binem. He explained that he was the son of Osten-Sacken, the owner of the estate.

Despite his fear, Binem was curious. For the first time he had an opportunity to find out why the owner of this barn was willing to feed and protect him. Still, Binem was very much on guard. He asked himself, "If this Nazi really wanted to assure me that he had no ill intentions, then why didn't he come here with his mother, the Princess."

The German officer explained that he was serving in the German army, and was home on furlough from the Russian front. During dinner, he was surprised when his parents revealed to him that they were hiding a Jew in the barn. He told his parents that he wanted to meet the Jew.

The officer removed a cloth that covered the basket. Binem looked at the contents of the basket. It contained a bottle of whiskey, two glasses, and assorted cookies.

The German then said to Binem, "Come over, don't worry about it, I'm your friend."

Binem, who up until now had kept a safe distance from the German, moved just a little closer.

He then offered, "How about a drink."

This triggered a frightening thought in Binem's mind. "This Nazi is going to poison me."

The German understood Binem's concern. So he poured out a drink and downed it in one gulp.

He said, "See, it's not poison."

The Nazi poured Binem a double portion of whiskey. Binem hesitated for a moment, then began to drink.

He told Binem, "I just came back from the front. We are in very bad shape. It won't take long, maybe three weeks, and the Russians are going to be here."

Binem thought to himself, "I'm glad that the word 'we' doesn't include me. Soon I will be free." Then Binem caught himself and added, "Well, as free as a Jew can be in Poland."

The German officer continued. "You have to make a promise. You must promise that you will save my father's life. You will do so because he is saving your life. So make a vow to me that you will save him, and, if you do, I vow to you that you will live over the war."

Binem was taken aback. He thought to himself, "I am supposed to save someone? Only by the grace of the Almighty have I lived this long!" Binem continued to ponder the German's demand. "I am being told to save the father of a German officer? That is out of the question!"

Still, Binem felt he owed a great debt to the Nazi's mother, the Princess. He didn't want to say anything that might upset her. Moreover, he didn't want to say anything to his new "friend," the Nazi, because, he thought, "at any moment I might end up with a bullet in my head."

So Binem decided that he would answer the German in a reasonable matter. "I'm not sure that I can make such a promise. I am nothing! I have no power. I don't even speak Russian. Even if I vowed to save your father, how could I? I don't even know how to talk to them."

The son replied with a smile. "Don't worry about it. There are plenty of Jews in the Russian Army. They will help you."

Binem replied, "If this is true, then I can only promise you that I will do whatever I can."

The officer seemed to accept this response as if he had succeeded. He stopped talking about the matter, and instead focused on drinking with Binem until the bottle was empty. The empty bottle was the excuse the German officer was waiting for to leave.

Binem accompanied him to the small barn door. As the German crossed the threshold, he looked Binem in the eye. "Remember, my father risked his life for you, so now it is your turn. I know that the majority of Russian officers are Jews. It won't be long. They will be here. You tell them that my father protected you. You have vowed to do so. You have an obligation to protect him."

I asked my father, "Did Osten-Sacken really protect you, or was it only the mother?"

My father answered, "He knew that she was hiding me, but he acted as if didn't know. I suppose he did so because even under torture he could honestly say that he never saw the Jew."

I asked, "Did you discuss with the German officer the plight of the Jews?"

He answered. "I did. But the German said that he was in the army so he wasn't involved in what others were doing to the Jews."

The German officer's final statement to Binem was, "Good luck, I have to return to the front tomorrow. I don't know if I will ever see my parents again."

That was the first and last time that Binem ever saw Osten-Sacken's son. My father told me that he never returned home.

Binem had mixed emotions about the German officer. On the one hand, he was the first German soldier who had actually treated him as a human being. Also, he was not exactly a German, rather, he was Volksdeutsche. On the other hand, anyone who wore a German uniform was a Nazi in his eyes. Now that the Germans were losing the war, he would probably do or say anything to protect his parents. Including, in essence, begging a Jew for help.

Binem was at the very least encouraged by the Nazi's predictions regarding the war. He took heart from the fact that his days of hiding were numbered. As far as protecting the Nazi's parents, Binem thought to himself that he would honor his commitment to a point. That point being that Binem would not let his promise compromise his own ability to survive.

In the following weeks, Binem continued his daily routine of eating, sleeping, walking back and forth in the barn, and, most of all, thinking. He thought about his life before the war, how the Nazis had destroyed everything, how he managed to stay alive, and how things would be once he was liberated.

After a few long weeks, there were actual signs that the Russians were approaching. He watched the sky through a crack near the top of the barn wall. During the day he could see air battles raging between Russian and German planes.

About a month after Binem's meeting with the German officer, the Princess came to the barn in broad daylight and told Binem that he could come back to the mansion and stay in her son's bedroom. As Binem walked with her, they did not exchange a word. He could hear the sounds of battle in the distance. He knew that this day was significant. He understood that he would not have been allowed to walk in the open where all the workers could see him unless the Germans were at the very brink of losing the war in Poland.

This time Binem entered the mansion, not through the window in darkness, but rather in the light of day by way of the front door. He felt that he was a guest. The servants saw him but did not say a word. The Princess escorted him up the royal staircase to her son's bedroom. He settled in as he had once before. The Princess came to the room to deliver him food. Everything was the same except that his presence was no longer a secret. The entire staff knew that the Princess was hiding a Jew.

Three days later, the Princess came to Binem's room. Her face was pale and distant. Binem could sense that there was something wrong.

She began by asking Binem, "What should we do? My husband just received orders from the Germans to retreat with the Army towards Germany."

Binem took this as a good sign. The Germans were now being pushed out of Poland. Still, Binem couldn't comprehend why the Princess would seek advice from a poor, dried-up Jew. Until that moment, his opinion had been worthless to any Pole, let alone the wife of a wealthy German. Now she was asking him what she and her husband should do? That was incredible.

Still, he did promise her son to help, so he said to himself that he would give it his best shot. He gathered his thoughts. He knew that it would soon be very dangerous for a German and the wife of a German to remain in Poland, as they could be the target of both Poles and the Russians. He then tried to imagine what would happen if they joined the retreat. Binem remembered the first weeks of the war when Germany invaded Poland. He remembered the chaos that ensued when he and his family set forth as a refugees.

After weighing the two alternatives, Binem replied, "I really can't advise you if you should comply with the order. What I do know is that if you go back with the German Army, I will not be able to keep my promise to your son to try and protect your life as well as your husband's life. So if you go with the German Army, I am free from my promise. But if you stay, then perhaps I can try to do something."

At first, the Princess just stared at Binem with an incredulous look. Suddenly, her countenance changed. She looked as if Binem's answer contained the key to her future. She then thanked Binem and gracefully exited. Binem thought about how ironic it was that the Princess would likely be explaining to her husband the opinion of the young Jew.

Over the next few days, the Princess continued to bring him his food. Binem concluded that the Osten-Sackens must have been swayed to stay. Now he felt a great deal of pressure and responsibility.

Binem thought to himself, "How can I possibly protect my protectors? I cannot even protect myself!" He now spent the majority of his waking hours contemplating this problem. No matter how hard he tried, he found no answers. Finally, he decided to stop thinking about it and just wait and see what would happen.

I asked my father in a probing way to see if he had an ulterior motive. "It was good for you that they decided to stay, because if they left you would have to fend for yourself."

He answered, "No, that wasn't important. At this point it really didn't matter. We all were equally in danger. The mansion was now situated in a no-man's-land between the German and Russian lines."

After a few days, the Princess told Binem that the German civilian retreat was "successfully" completed, so they were now on their own. Which meant that there no longer remained any German soldiers or police in the district.

From his bedroom window, Binem strained his eyes trying to observe the air battles taking place far in the horizon. Binem assumed that these dogfights were being fought between German and Russian fighter planes. Each day these dogfights became clearer, signaling to Binem that the Russian offensive was closing in on the estate.

I asked my father, "Did you ever think about making a run towards the Russian lines?"

He answered, "I understood that the front was constantly shifting. Also, the Russian line wasn't a straight line. If I ran, I wouldn't be capable of determining where the Germans were located or where was the exact location of the Russian line."

Binem came to realize that without a doubt the Russians were winning. He said to himself, "Every Russian victory was a victory for himself and the Jewish people."

He had a wonderful thought that kept popping into his head. "The impossible had occurred. I lived over the war."

Binem couldn't believe his good fortune. He noticed that he no longer suffered from fear. Any time that doubts would creep into his head, he would just repeat to himself that "the Russians were now here."

Only one thing nagged at Binem's conscience. "I have an impossible responsibility to my hosts that I feel obligated to fulfill. I am not fluent in Russian. Just the opposite, I know only a few words and phrases. What was I thinking when I promised that I was going to try and save the Osten-Sackens' lives?"

Now that the Germans had abandoned their positions near the estate, Binem was no longer restricted to the attic bedroom. He had complete freedom to roam the entire house. The servants viewed him as an honored guest of the Osten-Sackens and behaved accordingly. This new freedom and restoration of his dignity slowly removed the constant fear that he had suffered for the past five years.

I doubted that the servants would look at a Jew on the level of the important people that the Osten-Sackens regularly entertained, so I asked directly, "Truthfully, how did the servants treat you?"

He responded with understanding. "They all knew I was Jewish. Still, they treated me with respect. But I was careful. I didn't order them around."

Binem would spend much of the day sitting in the main parlor reading. The Osten-Sacken library was extensive. It included hundreds of books, including classics translated into Polish. At least once a day the Princess would ask Binem whether it would bother him if she turned on the radio to listen to the latest developments. Of course, Binem never refused. He took note that the Princess would avoid listening to the German broadcasts and instead listened only to broadcasts in Polish. Binem too would listen intently. He felt that the Polish broadcasts were probably more truthful and accurate than the news in German that continued to spew forth Nazi propaganda. In contrast, the Polish radio broadcast focused mostly on the military progress of the Russian Army.

Everyone living or working on the Osten-Sacken estate was aware that the entire German Army, in just about all sectors of the Eastern Front, was making a desperate retreat back to the 1939 German border. When the Germans stood and fought, as per the orders of Hitler, they were obliterated by the sheer mass of Russia's overwhelming manpower and devastating firepower.

Binem soon found that the war was approaching the Osten-Sacken estate. News was received that there were skirmishes with German Army stragglers being fought near Radziejow. Binem understood that he was still in a great deal of danger. "No matter what, the Germans still had time to kill Jews!" he told himself.

A few days later, on a bright winter day, Osten-Sacken himself, the owner of the estate, introduced himself to Binem for the first time. Up until that day Binem wasn't even sure if he was in the mansion. Osten-Sacken, sounding like one of the many Germans that had ordered Binem around for the last four years, announced, "I am the man that saved your life."

Binem wasn't sure how to reply to such a statement. He knew that the Princess had saved him, Wanda had saved him, even Wanda's brother could honestly say that he had saved him. So too, Osten-Sacken might be correct in making such a statement. Still, none of the others had ever used such direct language. So Binem decided the best way to answer was by thanking him.

Osten-Sacken then asked Binem a few questions. Binem meekly answered, not knowing how to talk to a man who was so wealthy. After exchanging a few words, the two walked towards the dining area where the Princess was waiting. All three sat at the magnificent dining room table. As they ate a sumptuous meal, the three listened intently to the radio. Osten-Sacken had the radio placed right next to him so he could switch back and forth between his two preferred channels. One station was broadcasted from England in both English and Polish, and the other station was a Russian station that broadcasted exclusively in Polish. Binem was surprised that Osten-Sacken, a German, never listened, at least in his presence, to any German broadcasts.

Historically, the war was coming to a climax in Poland. During the night of January 11, 1945, the Russians launched a massive, all-consuming barrage of artillery against the German forces that lasted for several hours. It was one of the heaviest barrages of artillery thus far in the war. The devastating hail of death was followed by an equally enormous Russian armored attack. The Russian forces penetrated the bloodied and disintegrated German front.

Endless columns of Russian motorized infantry followed in the wake of these attacks. By the evening of January 16, Soviet tank columns were already approaching Krakow, which was only a few hours drive from Radziejow.

After four days of seemingly nonstop assault, the Russians finally arrived at the outskirts of the Osten-Sacken estate. Everyone working on the estate knew that the Germans were no longer a factor in their survival.

The Princess declared to Binem, "Now you are free, you can do whatever you want. If you wish to stay with us, you are welcome. If you desire to return to your town, then please do."

I asked my father, "Why was she so nice?"

Binem answered, "It was her way of stating that she successfully completed a noble act."

Not satisfied with his answer, I persisted. "Do you think that the Osten-Sackens only saved your life as a kind of insurance policy against the prospect of Germany losing the war?"

My father answered, "This is a subject for debate. Why did they save me? Did they save me only to help themselves, or was the wife doing a noble act in memory of her son that drowned in the Vistula River? I just don't know."

My father's answer indicated that he had never come to a conclusion about this question, which may never be answered.

THE LIBERATION

R adziejow was liberated by the Soviet Army on January 20, 1945. Binem described the first Russian soldier he spotted as someone that looked more like a peasant than a triumphant soldier. The man was so dirty that it was hard to see if he was wearing a uniform. He carried a rifle without a belt attached to it. Instead, the gun was supported by a makeshift rope lazily slung over the soldier's shoulder. The rifle itself was caked in a layer of mud. His personal equipment included a knapsack, canteen, and shovel. He carried two sacks of sugar and what appeared to be a loaf of bread.

Binem thought, "This is my rescuer? This is an example of the kind of soldier that was able to defeat the invincible Germans?"

Still, no matter how he looked to Binem, he was most welcome as his liberator. Binem approached the Russian in awe and introduced himself. He knew a few words in Russian, and was able to explain that he was Jewish. The Russian didn't seem to care one way or another about Binem or his religious status. In fact, he looked at Binem as if he did not exist. Binem was at first upset by the soldier's indifference. But on second thought, Binem realized that this soldier might not have any idea what a Jew was.

Binem slowly processed this though. If being Jewish was of no account to the Russians, than what possible chance did he have to fulfill his promise to Osten-Sacken's son? Binem recalled the words of Osten-Sacken's son who advised him to look for a Jewish soldier.

Binem decided that the best place to wait for the Russians was on the road outside of Radziejow that led towards Germany. Approaching the road on foot, he saw a small column of vehicles and soldiers in the distance. The first column was followed by ever increasing numbers of soldiers, tanks, trucks and artillery. It began as a trickle and gradually increased to a raging flood of men and machines of war.

Binem had made up his mind that the only way to find a Jewish soldier was to try to spot a Jewish face among the troops. When he arrived at the road, he positioned himself at a bend in the road that allowed him to look directly into the faces of the passing soldiers.

Binem asked himself, "I know what Polish Jews looked and dressed like, but how was I to recognize a Russian Jew that did not dress as a Jew but rather like a soldier?"

He decided to follow his instincts to search for a Jewish face among the soldiers. Binem at once noticed a tall skinny Russian with a long nose.

Binem thought to himself, "The only chance of recognizing a Jew in uniform was by scrutinizing his nose."

Binem submissively went up to the soldier and asked him in Russian, "Evrietchik?"

The Russian answered, "Nyet, Kyrgyz."

Binem was not discouraged. He continued to focus on the noses of soldiers that passed him.

He soon identified a different soldier that fit the same criteria. This soldier not only was blessed with having a Jewish-looking nose, he also had a beard.

Binem shouted to him, "Evrietchik?"

The Russian stared at Binem for moment, then replied, "Nyet, Uzbek."

Binem was still not dissuaded. He queried a third Russian who answered, "Kazakh." A fourth replied, "Tatar."

Binem started to get frustrated. He thought to himself that perhaps there were no Jews in this long line of soldiers. It seemed to him that there must be at least one. Then he had a flash of inspiration. If he couldn't spot a Jewish soldier maybe a Russian could point one out to him.

So this time he ran up to a soldier and tried a new line in his broken Russian: "Show me an Evrietchik soldier!"

The Russian responded, "No soldiers, Officers, only officers."

Those words were music to Binem's ears. Officers meant the power to do something. So he asked, "Show me Evrietchik officer!"

The Russian pointed lazily at an officer in a parked staff car a short distance up the road. The officer he pointed to was handsome and tall, wearing a crisp looking uniform full of medals.

The Russian said, "There. Evrietchik."

Binem couldn't believe his good fortune. He thought, "A Jewish officer? How could there be such a thing?"

Caught up in the moment, he audaciously ran up to the staff car and was immediately stopped by a menacing-looking Russian soldier. Binem, not to be dissuaded, shouted in the direction of the officer, whose back was now towards Binem, "*Shalom Aleichem*, a Yid!"

The officer heard the words and quickly turned around. He stared back at this skinny young man. The proud officer's face changed to that of a person who thought had just seen a ghost. The strapping officer gathered his thoughts, and then, with great big smile and genuine sound of pleasure in his voice, answered, "Ya, a Yid?"

The Jewish officer followed his words with the enthusiastic behavior of a man that just found his long lost brother. He grabbed Binem, kissed him on both cheeks and gave him a giant Russian bear hug.

Releasing Binem, he spoke in Yiddish. "I have fought the Nazis from Moscow to Radziejow, but you are the first Jew I have seen. How is it possible you lived over the war?"

Binem was astounded that a Russian officer of apparently high rank spoke fluent Yiddish and with such a passionate tone.

Binem evaluated his fellow Yid. He said to himself. "Impossible, such an impressive Jew. He looks strong, fit, a real commander. The world has truly changed since the beginning of this war."

Binem, who had spoken very little Yiddish over the past few years, exploded with a torrent of words trying to articulate his experience over the course of the war.

The officer listened with a look of wonderment on his face. After about five minutes of Binem's non-stop soliloquy, the officer interrupted him. "You must stop for now. My friends woldn't believe me if I repeat ed to them what you just told me. Come tonight to our headquarters and there you will tell everyone."

Binem agreed. As Binem backed away, he watched as junior officers approached the Jewish officer to ask him for orders. He then turned and departed with a renewed vitality to his soul. "A Jew and an officer, wow! And he spoke Yiddish!"

He thought to himself, "With Jews like him, no harm will ever again come to the Jewish people."

Although the weather was extremely cold, Binem spent the rest of the day watching in amazement as the powerful Russian military column passed before him. He was enthralled with the prospect that the Germans were now going to get what was coming to them. As the sun began to set, Binem spotted a smartly dressed Russian soldier. He ran up to him and asked where he could find their headquarters. Without hesitation, the Russian gave him directions. When he was finished, Binem was perplexed. The directions he had given to the Russian Command led to none other than the Osten-Sacken mansion!

Binem laughed to himself, "I didn't have to go to the trouble of searching for a Jew, God planned on bringing many Jews to me!"

So Binem returned to the estate. He told one of the Russian guards that he was asked to come there by an officer. The soldier, appearing completely disinterested, directed Binem to of all places, the Osten-Sacken ballroom.

When Binem opened the heavy, polished wooden doors he was amazed by the sight before him. Sitting around a grand table were more than a dozen high-ranking Russian officers dressed as if attending a party. On the table were cakes and desserts, meats of all kinds, and liquor in abundance. There was even music being played by several soldiers. The officers seemed to all be friends talking and laughing like Binem used to do before the war. But when Binem entered the room and was noticed by one of the officers, a hush fell over the crowd. Then a spontaneous burst of greeting gushed forth as Binem was surrounded by giants of men who greeted him with hugs and kisses.

There smiles remained as Binem was escorted to the seat of honor. Binem felt that he was in the middle of a dream.

Binem asked himself, "How can it be that such a gathering of heroes found time in their holy mission to destroy the evil Hitler *yemach shemo* (may his name be forever erased), to honor me, a skinny Jew from Poland?"

As impossible as it was for Binem to understand, Binem felt a sense of pride looking at these *lantzmen* (fellow Jews) that were doing God's work to avenge the Jewish people.

As the party continued, Binem saw that the Osten-Sackens' servants were now serving their sworn enemy, the Russians, with the very best food and liquor available from the Osten-Sacken reserves.

After several courses of the finest foods, accompanied by large quantities of vodka, whiskey, and wine, the officer that Binem had met on the road stood up and gave a short speech in fluent Yiddish. He boasted that he had won the wager he had made with his fellow Jewish officers as to who would find the first Jew.

As Binem listened to the words of this distinguished officer, who was not much older than himself, Binem suddenly realized that he symbolized to the Russian Jewish officers something very precious. For these men, the war against Germany was revenge against the Nazis for crimes against their Jewish brethren. This gathering of Jewish warriors was about proving to themselves that they were simultaneously fighting both for Mother Russia and the Jewish people.

The officer concluded his remarks with a solemn statement. "Where are the millions of Polish Jews?" Binem was proud to be the representative of Polish Jewry for these gallant warriors.

The officer then turned to Binem and asked him to speak about his long struggle for survival. Binem rose from his chair and began. The room was dead silent as he spoke. Binem, needing no notes, gave a detailed description of his ordeal from beginning to end. The officers were transfixed on his voice and listened so intently that not once did they interrupt. When he finished, many of these battle-hardened soldiers were struggling to hold back tears. After a brief pause, the Russian officers began to ask questions, which Binem answered as best as he could. The officers were especially interested about Binem last eight months at the Osten-Sacken estate. They could not believe that he was saved by the very same German that owned the mansion. He closed the questioning by requesting that they help him save the Osten-Sackens.

Binem then sat down. He reflected on his speech. He felt that God had blessed him with a true miracle by allowing him to speak to a group of high-ranking Jewish officers in their common language of Yiddish. He also saw the irony of the setting. "All this is taking place in Osten-Sacken's mansion where I was saved. This is truly incredible," he told himself.

After a long applause, the officers began a heated argument about Osten-Sacken, the "Savior of the Jew." Passionate pleas were presented in both Russian and Yiddish. The Jewish officers laughed, shouted, argued and drank more and more vodka. Binem tried his best to follow the arguments. He understood that meeting the first Jew they had encountered since leaving Moscow was the catalyst for their soul-searching opinions.

In the end, the officers were split in two camps concerning Binem's request to help him save the life of Osten-Sacken. One side felt they should "take a picture of the German and frame it in gold" for risking his life to save a Jew. Their reasoning was that if Osten-Sacken was caught, he probably would have been hanged by the Nazis for the crime.

The other side was even more passionate. They argued that Osten-Sacken "must have been one of the biggest killers," who only saved Binem to save his own skin. "He wanted an alibi that proved that he wasn't a killer, so he saved one Jew!"

Finally, the officers agreed that they would decide the fate of Osten-Sacken by majority vote. The floor was opened and each officer argued their point. Many spoke in Yiddish. Binem listened intently. It seemed to him that Osten-Sacken didn't stand a chance.

Binem himself was torn by the arguments. Personally, he hardly knew Osten-Sacken. However, he had made a vow to Osten-Sacken's son. So, even though he felt out of place, Binem felt obligated to voice his position. His first words were weak in volume and crackling in sound. "Please, can I participate in the discussion?"

The officers looked at him kindly and nodded in the affirmative, seemingly saying "Why not, he is one of us!" Binem was surprised that he was being treated as an equal among such important high-ranking officers. These brave men genuinely appeared just as interested in his opinion as they were with each other's opinions.

As Binem began to speak, he noticed in the background Osten-Sacken walking around in another room. He was oblivious of the fact that Binem had returned to the mansion, and had no inkling that his very fate was being deliberated at that moment.

Binem gathered his thoughts and began. "I see you are

not sure what to do with the German. Some of you say that he should be honored, the others say that he should be killed. I must in fact admit that I don't know anything about the German's background. In fact, I just met the German a few weeks before you arrived. So I cannot say which side is right. But I do know one thing, the fact remains that he saved me. The proof is that I am alive today to tell you my story. So if he deserved to be killed then let him be killed, but not by Jews."

Binem's simple pronouncement caused these powerful men to take a moment and reflect. As Binem stared at their faces, he could tell that his words struck a weak nerve in these men toughened by war. They then began to murmur to one another. Finally, the officer that invited Binem to this party spoke up. "We will let the Polish Government that is a few days behind us decide his fate."

The party, especially the drinking, continued until the next day. Binem decided to remain in the house. Partly to make sure that the Jewish officers didn't change their minds, but mostly because he liked staying in the Osten-Sacken mansion. A few days later, the Russian divisional command moved on. The house was occupied by civilians made up of both Polish communist officials from the Polish Committee for National Liberation and their enforcement police which was the early elements of the Polish NKVD.

Binem was incognizant to the possible dangers in this changing of the guard. The very day the communists took over the Osten-Sacken mansion, Binem found himself in mortal danger. When a few Russian counterintelligence officers saw Binem talking in a mixture of Polish and German to Osten-Sacken, the officers assumed that Binem was also German.

One of the officers walked over to Binem. Binem could tell from his smell and slurred speech that he was completely inebriated. He yelled, then in a flash was behind Binem squeezing Binem's neck. He then slammed Binem into the wall face-first. Binem was completely stunned as the officer tied

Binem's hands and made him face the wall. Next to him was Osten-Sacken, also tied up. Apparently one of the other officers had did the same to Osten-Sacken.

Binem thought, "How stupid could I be. What have I done? By trying to save this German, I'm now going to die! I lived over all the trouble of this war only to die because I tried to save a German. I don't even have the honor of dying because I am a Jew!"

Binem was completely clueless of what to do next. He didn't speak Russian, and these Russians, who were not Jewish, didn't speak Yiddish.

Binem thought, "I have to try something, but what?"

Binem evaluated the situation and came to the conclusion that his only chance was to try and take advantage of the fact that the three Russians were completely intoxicated. Therefore, they may be susceptible to a bluff.

Binem decided to take a chance. He turned around and faced the Russians as they sat around the small table. All three had the look of surprise on their faces that this German piece of scum had the audacity to actually look at them.

Binem starting lecturing them in Polish, making sure to mix in the few Russian words that he knew. "This man that you tied up isn't a German. He saved me. I am a Communist. I am not German. I was a Communist before the war!"

The three Russian officers stared at the spectacle, trying to decide what to make of it. They tried to sober up to comprehend why the German was claiming to be a Communist. But they were so drunk they simply didn't have the strength to reason it out.

One of the Russian officers responded, "Well, if you are not a German and you say you are a Communist, then come over and drink with us."

With those words one of the officers, a large brute of a man, got up and pulled out a menacing-looking knife. But instead of stabbing Binem, he used it to cut Binem's bonds.

Binem sat down at the table. The officer in charge who

invited Binem over placed a large glass of whiskey in front of their new drinking buddy. Binem knew that he had a serious problem. He knew that with one drink he would be twice as drunk as the Russians. On the other hand, he knew that he would be writing his death sentence if he refused. In the minds of these officers, all communists loved to drink heavily. Binem decided he would take the chance and drink because it was imperative to show the Russians that he could drink whiskey like a loyal Russian communist.

By the time Binem had drank half the glass, the room was spinning. When he finished it, he couldn't tell whether he was sitting down or standing up. Despite his high level of intoxication, he did remember that he was in mortal danger and therefore had to do whatever it took to save himself and Osten-Sacken.

Now completely drunk, Binem spoke again using all the languages he knew, Yiddish, Polish, German, and Russian. Before starting, Binem banged on the table several times employing a common attention-getting technique that he had seen used by communist agitators.

Binem started by repeating his initial statement, "I am a good Communist. This man that you have over there is not a German. He saved me and he knew I was Jewish. He saved me! And I was a communist before the war. I got special orders from Stalin. And I was the head of the Communist Party in my town. You want to kill this man? If you do you will suffer for killing a man that was working with me before the war and during the war against the German Army. And he was working under my command. He knew I was a communist. You have no right to kill him!"

Binem was sure that they didn't understand what he was saying. "I myself didn't understand it. They were drunk, and I was drunk."

So the three Soviet security officers stood up in unison. The head officer spoke. "If it is the way you said we will not kill him. We will leave this matter to the Polish Government which will follow us. And let them judge."

Then they turned to Binem and each shook his hand. The three staggered out of the room toting a bottle of whiskey.

Binem quickly approached Osten-Sacken and untied him.

Binem said to Osten-Sacken, "You are free, they will not kill you."

Osten-Sacken, his face white with fear, suddenly burst out in a hysterical, emotional sob. Tears flowed down his face. Eventually he stopped and thanked Binem over and over again. When the two found the Princess, Osten-Sacken, with a shaky voice, told his wife what transpired. She too broke down sobbing but in a more dignified manner. After a few minutes of the couple clinging to each other, they both turned to Binem and thanked him for saving them.

Binem graciously accepted their thanks. He then said to Osten-Sacken, "From now on you are a free man. But I suggest that you don't stay on the estate. Try to live between the peasants. That way no one will have big eyes on you that you are a rich man. You can be sure that the communists will be coming more and more."

Binem decided that it was time to return to Radziejow. The Osten-Sackens accompanied Binem to the front entrance of the mansion. They said their goodbyes. As Binem left, he told the Osten-Sackens that he would look in on them from time to time.

Binem said, "I have to go back to town, because I can't believe from all the Jews that lived in Radziejow, I am the only lucky man to live over the war. There must be some other people."

Osten-Sacken and his wife immediately took Binem's advice. They abandoned their estate and went to live with Wanda and her family.

I asked my father, "Did they give you any money?"

He answered, "There was no money, neither German or

Polish."

I continued, "What about something of value?"

My father responded, "Nothing."

After a few hours of trudging through the snow, Binem arrived in Radziejow. He decided that he would call on a shoemaker that used to buy leather goods from the Naimans before the war. Binem thought the shoemaker, who had been very friendly to the family, would be glad to see that one of the Naimans lived over the war.

Instead, when the shoemaker saw Binem walk into his shop, he apparently thought that Binem was coming to get back the leather that the family entrusted to him to hide during the war. In reality, Binem did not remember that the shoemaker was holding leather for them. He smiled and walked up to the shoemaker. The shoemaker's face turned red and, without any provocation, ran out of his shop screaming. Binem stood speechless, having no idea why the shoemaker reacted in such a way.

The shoemaker stood in the middle of the street shouting that a German came into his store and is trying to kill him. When the townspeople heard this, they along with a few Russian soldiers rushed to investigate. The Russians entered the store and grabbed Binem.

Binem then said to the Russian soldiers, "I'm not a German, I'm Jewish." Luckily, the townspeople recognized Binem and told the Russians that it was true, he was a Jew.

I asked my father, "When you were later a member of the Police, did you get back at that shoemaker?"

My father answered, "No. He was ashamed for what he did. He apologized, using the excuse that he hadn't recognized me."

Binem searched in vain to find another Jew that had returned. When evening approached, Binem decided that he would walk back to the Osten-Sackens' mansion. When he arrived, he learned from a servant that they the Osten-Sackens had hurriedly packed up and left. Binem was amused that the servant viewed Binem as the replacement master of the estate. Binem didn't discourage this thought. Instead, he decided that for the time being he would remain at the estate and walk daily to Radziejow in search for his fellow Jews. He reasoned that after the incident with the shoemaker, it was safer at the mansion where the servants knew him than living on his own in Radziejow.

Binem ate a large breakfast every morning before he set out on the long walk to Radziejow. The servants were more than glad to serve him since Binem represented the last vestige of the old order. One day, Binem was walking in Radziejow's Market Square when he recognized a Jewish friend at the other end. His name was Aaron Frankenberg. Aaron had been one of Binem's best friends.

Seeing his childhood friend, Binem's was overcome with a euphoric nostalgia for his lost youth. He was now twenty-five years old and hardened from his experiences during Poland's occupation.

Binem thought it would be fun to sneak up on his old friend. With the stealth of a child playing hide and seek, he managed to come upon his friend from behind undetected. Binem then ran up and grabbed Frankenburg with one arm around his friend's chest and his other hand over Frankenburg's eyes.

Binem cried out, "Guess who's here?"

The friend immediately recognized Binem's voice and responded, "It must be you, Binem."

The friend turned and the two embraced, with tears of joy running down their faces. Then Frankenburg and Binem walked together for some time, sharing their experiences of the last few years.

Frankenburg asked Binem if he had been back to the Naiman building. Upon hearing those words, Binem wondered why he did not think of that. He realized that he had been so focused on searching for other Jewish survivors that the thought never entered his mind. He answered, "No." So, with really nothing better to do, they decided to check it out.

The Naimans' building on 5 Rynek, located in the corner of Market Square, stood seemingly undamaged from the years of war. The building looked abandoned. The display window was covered with the same heavy brown paper that he and his brothers had put up at the beginning of the war. After rattling the front door and determining that it was securely locked, they walked to the rear of the building and tried the back door. There the lock felt loose. With a little bit of force they managed to open the back door without damaging the lock or door.

When the two entered, they were surprised that the building was empty. All of its contents were gone. Binem and his friend decided that since it was unoccupied, and it was, in fact, owned by Binem and his brothers, it would be a good place for them to live. So that night they slept on the floor of the room that had once been the parlor. Even though it was now empty, Binem imagined how it had appeared when he was growing up. Most vivid in his imagination was the image of his father Shimon faithfully studying a volume of the Talmud at the head of the table.

Within days, Binem and his friend, Aaron Frankenberg, were joined by Frankenburg's three sisters, Sala, Yetka, and Ganya Frankenberg. Soon thereafter another lifelong chum showed up, the infamous Arthur Lubinski, who was the tough guy of the group. His presence gave the group a sense of security. The friends decided to make their home in the Naiman building. They lived as brothers and sisters. The survivors were of similar age, all in their twenties.

The group moved up to the second floor of the building where there were several bedrooms. The men occupied one of the bedrooms and the women took up residence in a second bedroom. There was no furniture, so they slept on blankets that they spread on the floor. Of course, this arrangement was not only uncomfortable, but also gave the feeling of transiency. So the group elected Binem to approach the mayor of

Radziejow.

The mayor was very busy man trying to bring back a semblance of normalcy to the town, and at the same time comply with the hundreds of directives being issued by the occupation forces of the Soviet Union. These included both civil and military authorities.

Binem found the mayor at City Hall. He walked up to the mayor and said bluntly that the Jewish returnees needed some beds.

The mayor was unsure of his responsibilities regarding the Jews that returned to their town. He was a fair man, so he took a moment to give this new issue on his plate some thought. After a long pause he responded, "We simply don't have extra beds because the Germans took away all the furniture that was confiscated from the Jews."

The mayor, seeing Binem's reaction, realized that he would have to address the issue. So he agreed to find them some beds. A few hours later, he was able to requisition three beds for the survivors. Binem, Arthur, and Aaron dragged the beds across town and up the stairs to the second floor of the Naiman building.

I asked my father, was anyone living in your building during the war?"

He answered, "I imagine Germans lived there but they ran away."

My father described the returning Jews' living arrangements as a kind of "kibbutz." They all shared in doing chores. The Frankenberg sisters did the cooking while the men canvassed the nearby countryside, calling on Polish farmers and explaining their situation. Then they would ask the farmers if they could spare them some food. For the most part, the Polish farmers were friendly and sympathetic.

I asked my father, "Why were the farmers so friendly?"

He answered that the farmers were good people that no longer had to worry about being punished by the Germans.

The good-natured local farmers competed for bragging

rights as to which of them was able to provide the best assortment of foodstuffs to the Jews. Binem and his friends benefited from the competition. The Jews ended up being supplied with an excellent variety of chickens, grains, and vegetables in more than adequate quantities.

A few weeks after Binem moved back into his family's building, he decided to determine what were his rights as the sole survivor. He discussed the matter with a clerk at City Hall who referred him to the civilian civil court that was established by the Russian occupation authorities. There he was instructed to fill out several documents. When he finished, he was assigned a court date.

Arriving at the court for the scheduled hearing, Binem was instructed to stand before a judge. The judge reviewed documents that a clerk had prepared based on research from the town archives. The court then issued a ruling that Binem Naiman was the sole survivor and therefore the rightful owner of the building. The court issued Binem an official certification and deed to the building.

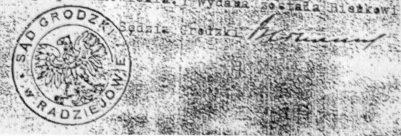

N.Co 316/45r. P o s t a n o w i e n i e. Dnia
1945r. Sąd Grodzki w Radziejowie , w osobie Sędr
Z. Berkana , po rozpoznaniu wdniu 21 sierpnia 19
sprawy z wniosku Bieńka Nejmana o wprowadzenie
siadanie nieruchomego majątku, na zasadzie art.
§1 i 2 Ustawy z dnia 6 maja 1945r. /Dz.U.N.17
o majątkach opuszczonych i porzuconych, postanawia
Bieńka Nejmana wprowadzić w posiadanie północne
Yowy domu mieszkalnego z cegły palonej i placu,
Yeterych w Radziejowie przy ul. Rynek Nr. 7, sta
więcych własność ojca jego.

/-/ Sędzia Grodzki Z. Berkan

Za zgodność świadczy:
Sekretarz Sądu

W IMIENIU RZECZYPOSPOLITEJ POLSKIEJ
Dnia 14 września 1945r. Sąd Grodzki w Radziejowie
polesa i nakecuje wszyntim urzędem i osobom, któ
te dotyczyć może, aby postanowienia tytułu niniej
wykonały oraz , gdy o to prawnie wezwane będą udz
pomocy.
   Klazula niniejsza jest podstawą do wykonania p.
wyższego postanowienia i wydana została Bieńkowi

Sędzia Grodzki

Court Order Awarding Building to Binem

Binem and his roommates felt that the townsfolk of Radziejow and the farmers in the surrounding area had been most hospitable to them. They were all impressed that the Poles, who had their own problems, made such an effort to ease their return and absorption back into society. However, this experience was not true when it came to many other Jews that returned to Radziejow.

Survivor George Gronjnowski chillingly recalled that after his liberation he decided to return to Radziejow. He traveled by train. Since Radziejow did not have a station, he disembarked at the next stop which was Chelm. At the station, Gronjnowski found several transport wagons available to take riders to the nearby towns. George located the wagon designated to transport passengers and their luggage to Radziejow. As he boarded the open wagon, he couldn't help but stare at the familiar face of the large Polish driver who sported a tremendous mustache.

The driver recognized George immediately. His first words to Gronjnowski were, "You survived, but be careful, the partisans are shooting Jews around here!"

Survivor Ann Goldman Kumer told of an even more perilous return. Shortly after being liberated by the Russians, she returned to Radziejow accompanied by her friend, Fella Feldman. Taking the transport from Chelm, she was dropped off near Radziejow's Market Square. From there she walked directly to her family's house. As she walked the familiar path, she hoped that despite the war there might be pictures or mementos from her family there. When she arrived, she tried the front door, which was locked. When she knocked, a Pole that she recognized answered the door. That Pole was none other than a well-known criminal of the town. As the Pole looked at Ann, the criminal's equally infamous wife joined him at the entrance.

Ann could not help but be afraid of the angry faces of the notorious couple. The two immediately verbally assaulted Ann and her friend, repeatedly shouting diatribes against not only them but all Jews. As if possessed by an evil spell, the husband then produced a weathered knife. He waved it ominously at Ann.

He shouted wildly. "What do you want here? This is my house!"

Ann had only one desire, which was escape before the anti-Semite attacked. Meanwhile, the wife of this criminal was instigating her husband to escalate his menacing behavior.

Ann made one last plea. "I only want some pictures of the family."

The man answered angrily, "Out you go from here, if you know what's good for you. You dirty Jews, out!"

From first-hand experience over the past five years, Ann knew that there was no reasoning with anti-Semites. Both she and her friend turned and fled from the doorstep, walking at a brisk pace. When they were about a block away from her house, the two slowed down. As they discussed the surreal encounter, they were confronted by a mob of Poles. Ann recognized one of them. She calmed down, remembering that this Pole had a reputation of being friendly to the Jews before the war.

That reassurance quickly dissipated when the same Pole menacingly pointed a pitchfork at her and barked, "Where are those Jews?"

Ann and her friend broke into a desperate run with the bloodthirsty mob following just a short distance behind. Ann remembered that just around the corner was a house owned by a Polish woman that long ago was the family's seamstress. She had always been very friendly.

Ann and her friend turned the corner with the mob just a few seconds behind them. She banged on the seamstress's door. The Polish seamstress opened the door and looked into Ann's panic-stricken eyes. She correctly assessed the situation.

She told Ann, "Come in, quickly!"

Ann with tears in her eyes, cried, "Thank you! Please save us!"

The seamstress led the two young women into her bedroom. She told them to lay perfectly still on her bed. She then covered both women with a thick goose down comforter.

Almost immediately, there was a loud series of raps on the door. Then the mob forced the seamstress's door open. They spotted the seamstress as she left the bedroom.

One giant Pole demanded, "Did you hear someone running?"

The seamstress replied, "No, why?"

The man shouted out "Those whore Jews came back to the city and we want them."

The bloodthirsty mob turned and exited the house.

After waiting a few moments, the seamstress returned to her bedroom and uncovered the two women. She invited them into her kitchen and they sat and ate some food.

As they talked, the seamstress's son, Bartak, a farmer, entered the kitchen. The seamstress told her son that he must help the two young ladies. Without hesitation, Bartak exited the house and drove his wagon around the back. After making sure that no one was watching, he instructed the two Jewish woman to sit in the bed of his wagon. Then Bartak covered them with straw. He drove the wagon for a long time until they arrived at his farm. There he hid the two in the barn. The next day, Bartak drove Ann and her friend to the train station.

Survivor Roman Rogers recalled returning to Radziejow and staying for a few weeks at a cousin's house, which most probably referred to the Naiman building. He said that the group had no plans and seemed to live life day by day. Rogers was successful in bartering clothes that he had received when he was liberated in Germany for food.

Rogers described an incident in which a Jewish returnee bought a horse and buggy from a Russian soldier. The soldier used the money to purchase a large amount of vodka at a local tavern. The soldier became very drunk and began to verbally abuse the other patrons. When a Polish policeman heard the commotion at the tavern and entered to investigate, the Russian soldier shot at him. After the soldier was restrained, the populace incredibly blamed the Jews because a Jew had given him the money to purchase the vodka! As a result, the Jews had no choice but to flee Radziejow. And flee they did.

Soon thereafter, a delegation of Poles from Radziejow set out and found the Jews. They beseeched the Jews to return to the village, stating that they needed their assistance in dealing with the communist regime that now effectively controlled Radziejow.

A short time after Binem and the other survivors had set up living quarters in the Naiman building, a Polish farmer came to Radziejow and informed the townspeople that the militia had found a destroyed Russian tank. Several Poles followed the peasant to investigate. When they arrived, they found the remains of a body inside the tank. The men brought the body to Radziejow for burial.

When the news spread of the funeral, Binem felt that he must do something. He discussed the matter with his fellow Jews. "This Russian died to set us free. We Jews must be present at the funeral to show our thankfulness to him."

It was agreed that the least they could do was attend the soldier's funeral service. This was no small matter. The service was to be held at the same church that was used by the Nazis to house the Jews the night before they were transported to Chelmno to be murdered. For the first time in Binem's life, he entered the Radziejow Catholic Church.

When the service was finally over, all the Jewish survivors agreed that attending was a giant mistake. The Jews had felt very uncomfortable sitting in a pew surrounded by Catholic imagery and the smell of incense. Although the purpose was noble, the results were not.

A few days later, a Russian tank became stuck in a trench on the outskirts of Radziejow. The tank crew came to the town to enlist help to extract the tank. Binem and two of his friends were among the volunteers. The tank was stuck in mud that was several feet deep. While the Poles had no problem with the digging, Binem his friends were still weak from years of starvation and horrendous living conditions. Within the first hour of work, they were exhausted.

Binem approached the Russian soldier in charge. He explained that he and his two friends were Jews who had barely survived the war. He explained, "We are feeble. We Jews can't work as hard as the other Poles."

The Russian officer frowned and replied with a tone of disgust, "If you could work so many years for the Germans, you can work two days for the Russian Army."

Binem and his friends were ashamed. Deep down, they thought the Russian officer was right. However, they were in fact physically weak. My father recalled that, despite their best efforts, the Jewish contribution to the task was ultimately insubstantial. In fact, when the job was completed, Binem and his friends joked that "with or without our help, the Poles were able to extract the tank!"

For a short while, Binem and his friends had little interaction with the Poles of Radziejow, who generally ignored them. Then officials from the new Polish government arrived. One of their first undertaking was a draft to assist the Russian Army. A selective service board began processing the young men in the town. There were no exceptions.

Binem and his two friends received an order to present themselves before the Board. Standing before the panel, Binem and his friends explained that they were still not physically capable to perform the duties of a soldier. The board members were sympathetic, so they gave the Jewish men a choice.

"You can be drafted and sent to the German front, or if you prefer, you can remain in Radziejow and serve as policemen."

One of the board members explained what their duties would be. "As policemen you would be responsible to maintain order in the town and also you would be sent out of Radziejow to search out and take into custody Germans still remaining in the area."

I asked my father, "Weren't you excited to have the opportunity to go directly to the front and fight the Germans, so you could revenge your family and the Jews of Poland?"

He answered, "I was still too weak to go fight. And I wasn't trained. To live over the war only to be killed in the Russian Army made no sense."

The three Jewish survivors asked permission to discuss their options. First, they discussed the possibility of joining the Russian Army. On the one hand, it would give them the opportunity to help and watch the destruction of the Nazi murderers. On the other hand, they knew that they were not in the necessary physical condition to fight. They also understood that they would be thrown into the fight without any combat training.

Binem and his two friends then discussed becoming police officers. They felt a responsibility to stay and protect the females of their "kibbutz." Also, once the war ended, they would be able to determine whether it was feasible to reestablish their lives in Radziejow. The three unanimously agreed to join the police force.

Binem in Police Uniform

Binem and Arthur Lubinski were drafted into a special section of the Polish Police. Binem's unit was assigned to keep law and order in Radziejow. He became a competent peace officer. That mainly meant making his rounds around Radziejow in his uniform to show a police presence. On occasion, it required him to arrest Poles that became rowdy after consuming too much alcohol. Another duty that he had was to go on patrols to search out remaining Germans in and around Radziejow.

Binem found that his fellow police officers initially treated him with respect. But as time went on, Binem found that the atmosphere changed.

I asked my father, "Why didn't you use your new position to get vengeance on those Poles and particularly those remaining Germans that helped the Nazis."

He answered, "I probably should have. But I didn't have the heart to take vengeance on a German old woman, or for that matter, even a young one."

During Binem's service, the war against Germany continued. Hitler, from the safety of his concrete bunker in Berlin, continued to bark out incomprehensible orders to attack the enemy. In reality, his troops were being decimated on all fronts.

Binem and his fellow Jews didn't feel as if the war was over. In fact, the sounds of artillery shells exploding could still be faintly heard in the distance. Also, there were rumors that military reversal could happen at any time, which would result in the Nazi regime returning to Radziejow.

This fear proved to be unwarranted. Binem and his friends rejoiced as they watched seemingly endless columns of Russian troops, tanks and artillery advancing towards Germany. At the same time, it was said that just as many trucks were heading back with confiscated German property which was now war booty for the Soviet Army.

German radio was still broadcasting reports that Hitler had a secret plan that would snatch victory out of seemingly inevitable defeat. Their hope was in what the Nazis called "wonder weapons." However, by 1945 it became clear that Hitler did not have the promised miracle weapons, at least not in sufficient quantities to change the course of the war. V2 supersonic rockets and jet airplanes were being produced in quantities that were too little and too late to turn the tide of the war. Hitler and his evil regime were heading towards a catastrophe of their own making. The more the Germans fought, the more they were slaughtered.

The Russian army successfully crossed the western Polish border, raining artillery fire on the citizens of Germany. Russian troops entered towns and villages and wiped out the remnants of the German units. The first days of the Russian occupation of Germany were filled with raping and pillaging. There was no end to the suffering. Those Germans who still had a sense of divine justice grudgingly acknowledged that they were deserving of this catastrophe.

In February 1945, Poland was completely liberated, and the Russian Army began crossing into East Germany. By March 1945, the massive Russian offensive was already approaching Berlin. At the same time, the Allies were mercilessly fighting the Germans on the Western front. The Russians, however, were determined to win the race to capture Berlin. The Soviet quest to conquer Berlin was driven by a thirst for vengeance against Hitler and Germany for their crimes against the Russian people, and the strategic goal of controlling and dominating post-war Germany.

Across Germany, the Nazis were conscripting boys under sixteen years old and men over sixty to help defend the home front. These "new recruits" were a joke to the battle-hardened Russian soldiers. Hitler challenged the German people, saying that if the Germans lose, the Slavic race would prove superior to the German race. The Germans were incapable of fulfilling the wild dreams of their insane leader.

Despite the change of fortunes on the war front, Binem in many ways remained a victim. He was constantly recalling the dangers he faced when he was on the run. Sometimes, without provocation, he experienced overwhelming feelings of dread. Even in sleep, he suffered from nightmares that the Germans would retake control of Radziejow. Other times he would dream that the Poles were attacking Jews.

On April 30, 1945, under siege by Russian forces in his underground bunker in Berlin, Adolf Hitler committed suicide. On May 8th, 1945, representatives of the German army signed the first instrument of unconditional surrender, recognizing their total defeat by Allied forces.

With Germany defeated, the Polish people showed little mercy to the Volksdeutsche among them. Binem instinctively understood that the Jews that survived would soon be a target. His fear of the Poles attacking Jews was based on reality. While most Poles were not interested in harming the Jews that survived, there were still many Polish anti-Semites that had been emboldened by Hitler's program to make Europe "Judenfrei."

Binem did not forget the Osten-Sackens. He would visit them at Wanda's house, where they were living. Binem would discuss the progress of the war with them. In Binem's opinion, Osten-Sacken had a great deal to fear from the new communist government. Osten-Sacken was in denial, and preferred to avoid even thinking about the threat.

In June of 1945, Binem was on a routine patrol when he saw a group of police officers from his station dragging a man. Even from a distance, Binem could tell that this man was badly injured. As he drew closer, Binem observed that the man's body was soaked in blood, and his clothes had been literally shredded to pieces. The man, whose face was bloody and swollen, looked somewhat familiar. Binem suddenly realized that it was Osten-Sacken. He asked a fellow officer how he had gotten into such a condition. The officer answered that most of the way back to the station they had dragged him behind a wagon.

Binem's initial reaction was to try and help Osten-Sacken. In the back of his mind, he remembered that the last time he tried to save Osten-Sacken he almost got killed for his efforts. This time, he knew to proceed cautiously. He collected his thoughts, trying to form a plan of action. Finally he decided to act.

Binem went up to one of the arresting officers who he was friendly with and asked, "What did this guy do?"

The officer responded as if he was making an announcement to everyone in the station. "This son of a bitch? We have been looking for him, and finally we caught him. He was hiding himself with a Polish family."

Binem asked, "What is he charged with?"

The officer replied with a sadistic smile. "The son of a bitch is charged with treason. He was a spy for the Germans before the war broke out. Then he worked with the Germans throughout the occupation."

Binem knew that such charges were punishable by death. After an initial inquiry, Binem learned that there appeared to be a great deal of evidence implicating Osten-Sacken as a German spy. Osten-Sacken had taken photographs of Polish towns and army installations, ammunition dumps, and other military targets, and delivered those photographs to the Germans prior to the invasion of September 1939. There were also photos and information regarding vital Polish industrial factories. According to the allegations, Osten-Sacken's materials were used by the Luftwaffe to plan a devastating aerial bombing in which hundreds of Poles were killed.

There was also evidence purporting that Osten-Sacken either worked with the Gestapo or was a Gestapo agent during the Nazi reign of terror. If that wasn't enough, he was charged with mistreating Polish peasants during the war.

When my father told me this, I couldn't believe it. How could my father even think of protecting a Gestapo agent?

I wanted to make sure I understood what he was saying. "Was he in fact a Gestapo agent?" I asked.

My father answered, "He was in the Gestapo." I assumed my father made this statement based on evidence he had been shown.

I asked my father, "Were all the allegations against him true?"

My father chose to avoid the question. "I didn't know this man before I came to live in his house."

I wasn't going to allow my father off the hook so easily.

I pressed on in an indirect, lawyer-like way. "Did your unit always make false allegations against German nationals?"

My father continued to avoid answering directly. "I wasn't interested in other Volksdeutsche. When I saw those arrested for similar crimes, I figured maybe yes. But I was only interested in him because he saved my life, and I promised to save his life."

Not satisfied with my father's answer, I tried another approach. "Didn't you want to take vengeance on these Germans for what they did?"

He smirked and said. "I could leave it to the Pollacks. They were much better killers than me."

I pressed. "Didn't you want vengeance?"

He answered thoughtfully. "No. I figured everybody should have a trial before being executed."

I still wasn't satisfied. "Nobody gave you a trial, or your brothers and sisters a trial."

He answered emphatically, "That is precisely how the Germans behaved. I was different. I figured maybe Osten-Sacken didn't do it. He can't be responsible for what other Germans did. I had to be sure that he was the guilty one."

Binem walked over to Osten-Sacken, who was lying in the street in front of the police station in a pool of his own blood. Osten-Sacken looked like a mortally wounded animal. He was still conscious, despite the terrible beating. He was trembling with fear.

Binem addressed the arresting officer. "Leave the German to me, I'll take care of him!"

The officer probably assumed that Binem, who was known to be Jewish, would show the alleged Nazi Gestapo agent no mercy. Giving Binem a knowing nod, he gleefully handed over Osten-Sacken. Binem, in an apparent display to his fellow officers, dragged Osten-Sacken to a cell and closed the door behind himself.

Binem looked around the eight-by-ten foot cell. He saw that there was a pail of water in the far corner of the room.

He carried the bucket over to Osten-Sacken who was laying on the cell floor near the door. Binem ladled a portion of the water into a cup and encouraged Osten-Sacken to drink. Osten-Sacken drank the water as if he had just emerged from the desert. When he finished, Binem dipped a rag into the pail and gently wiped Osten-Sacken's face until it was clean from the blood and grime. Binem then tried to comfort him by offering words of encouragement. He told him not to be afraid. All was not lost. He lied and told Osten-Sacken that he had a sure fire-plan to gain his release.

Binem racked his brain trying to come up with some way to save his protector. Finally, he decided that the best course of action would be to talk to the station chief. Binem felt that the Chief was a fair man, and seemed honest. So he left Osten-Sacken in the cell and went directly to the Chief's office. Binem knocked on the door and the Chief gave him permission to enter. The Chief was sitting behind his desk looking at a file.

The Chief looked up and smiled at Binem as he entered the room. He said, "Binem, sit down."

Binem did not sit down. Instead, he got right to the point.

"The prisoner that was just brought in, his name is Osten-Sacken and he helped me to live over the war. He deserves a break."

The Chief stared back at Binem. "I've been told that this guy named Osten-Sacken is not only a Nazi but also a traitor."

Then the Chief continued, "I don't know anything about him being a Nazi. But if you say he should be treated fairly, then O.K. You are in charge of him."

So for the next several weeks, Binem visited Osten-Sacken daily and made sure he was provided for. As a result of Binem's humane treatment of the prisoner, the other officers also treated Osten-Sacken well. They were thinking, "If a Jew can treat this man with dignity, then why shouldn't we do the same?"

Finally, the date came for Osten-Sacken's trial. The evidence against him was overwhelming. Binem testified on his behalf. In open court he told the story of how Osten-Sacken had saved him from certain death. He described in detail how Osten-Sacken had hid and fed him, and added that he was sure that Osten-Sacken was "a nice man."

It should be noted that in the Spielberg interview, my father said that he testified on behalf of Osten-Sacken only by way of a written statement.

Osten-Sacken was found guilty. However, the tribunal was swayed by Binem's testimony. In most cases, Volksdeutsche collaborators were killed without a trial. When an actual trial would take place, the typical sentence was death by either hanging or a firing squad.

Osten-Sacken received an unusually lenient punishment. He was sentenced to exile and forfeiture of his estate. Exile meant living outside a specified radius from Radziejow.

Osten-Sacken was dumbstruck by the incredibly charitable sentence. He had already resigned himself to the most probable outcome of the trial, that he would be executed. Due to Binem's testimony, he left the courtroom a free man. Both Osten-Sacken and his wife thanked Binem profusely. That same day, they boarded a train and went into exile. They eventually settled in a large Polish town, Torun, just outside the area that he was ordered to be exiled. Later the Osten-Sackens were joined by Wanda and her brother.

In the Spielberg interview, my father said that for a long time he did not visit the Osten-Sackens because the town was too far away. Then, one day, the Princess showed up in Radziejow specifically to meet with Binem. She told him that in the town where they settled, the neighbors had discovered that her husband was German and were threatening to kill him.

Binem had a soft heart for the Princess, for she had selflessly saved his life, and still felt obligated to fulfill the vow he had made to her son. He requested a short leave from his post. Binem accompanied the Princess on the long trip to the town. When Binem arrived, the neighbors saw him in his police uniform. Seeing that Osten-Sacken had connections to the government, the neighbors decided to leave him alone.

I asked my father, "What happened to Osten-Sacken and the Princess?"

He answered, "I know one thing, when I left [Poland] they were still alive. Later I was in more danger then they were. They were far away from the turmoil that struck Radziejow."

I asked, "What happened to their son?"

He said, "The Osten-Sackens had no idea what happened to him."

My father explained that after the war, there was a struggle between Polish communists, backed by the Soviet Union, and the resistance group known as the Home Army, backed by England, for political control of Poland. As a Jew, he was caught in the middle of these two factions that were committing horrendous attacks against each other on a daily basis.

I asked, "Which was the better side for Poland?"

He answered, "I didn't know or care. It wasn't my war anymore."

History bears out my father's recollection of events in post-war Poland. The Jews were in an untenable position. "Unfortunately, the killing of Jews in Poland did not stop with the end of the war. One report stated that 350 Jews were killed in Poland within seven months after the end of the war." Members of the Home Army were the main perpetrators of these anti-Semitic killings. They justified their crimes by accusing Polish Jewish survivors of imposing communism on post-war Poland. To prove their point, they pointed to several Jewish officials in the newly formed communist government.

The Jewish survivors were faced with a deadly dilemma. Either ally themselves with the communists for self-preservation, or abandon Poland and join the millions of post-war refugees. "The anti-Semitic campaign... drove out of Poland 100,000 Jews."

I asked my father which side was he on. He stated that he was on the Russian side. He said that all the members of his unit sided with the Russians. He remembered that there were several Jewish officers in his militia, and the militia was working with the Russians.

I asked my father, "Were you a communist?"

He laughed. "Oh no. I had no interest in politics. I was just a Jew trying to survive."

In the beginning, Binem had little to fear. The Home Army had limited influence in Radziejow. As a member of the police, he was protected by his position and by his fellow officers. Binem felt that the comradery among police officers was sufficient to make him impervious to any threats from anti-Semites. Moreover, many members of the police's upper command had communist leanings.

The focus of the rank-and-file officer was on police matters and not political infighting. For the most part, Binem's fellow officers were indifferent to politics. The officers were waiting to see "which way the wind would blow."

A few months later, Binem was reassigned from the Radziejow station to the police station located in Alexandrow, a larger town located about 20 miles away. This post was much more active, both in routine police work and in arresting those who had collaborated with the Nazi occupation forces. It was the latter objective that Binem was not prepared for.

Binem in the Polish Police

For the most part, those labeled collaborators were Volksdeutsche, ethnic Germans that had lived in Poland for many generations. The procedures for dealing with these "traitors" often did not go by the book. Rather, the officers felt it was preferable to cut through the tedious red tape by using other methods. In Binem's unit in Alexandrow, many of the officers were not concerned with the need to gather evidence against a suspect, but rather were simply out for revenge against the Germans.

Binem wanted no part in the illegal and immoral behavior that was prevalent at his new post. He understood exactly how his fellow officers felt about Germans, who had raped, tortured, and murdered hundreds of thousands of Poles during the occupation. Sometimes, when he remembered how the Nazis wiped out his entire family and turned his life into a living hell, he became so angry that he could crush a glass in his hand. However, as the son of a pious Jew, he abhorred such behavior.

Binem maintained that individuals did not have the right to take the law into their own hands. He felt that anyone suspected of traitorous behavior should have a chance to prove his innocence in court. Binem thought, "First give the suspect a trial, and then, if he is guilty, let the court sentence him."

There was another reason why Binem did not rush out to seek vengeance against the Volksdeutsche. For the most part, this ethnic group of Germans had historically always been friendly to Jews.

Binem's convictions were placing him at odds with his fellow officers. As the struggle between the two political and paramilitary factions escalated, Binem found that members of his unit were behaving more and more like criminals. Even worse, at night, they engaged in unspeakable acts of violence. Binem surmised that his superiors were either actively encouraging or at the very least closing their eyes to the violence.

Binem realized that circumstances would not allow him to simply be an honest, productive citizen of post-war Poland. So he began thinking about the possibility of just running away and leaving Poland altogether. But to do so would be an act of desertion, because he was a member of what constituted the military of Poland.

He thought, "I'm a draftee. To just run away meant being branded as a deserter. Being caught as a deserter meant certain death."

Binem observed that members in his unit were becoming bolder and bolder as they engaged in acts of vengeance against the Volksdeutsche. At first he could only identify a few officers who were responsible. As time went on, random acts of extreme violence against the Volksdeutsche became a common practice among most of the officers. Binem thought that there must be some justification that he was missing. He constantly asked himself, "Did all Volksdeutsche commit treason by in some way cooperating with Hitler and Germany during the occupation?"

Binem came to the conclusion that the law required each Volksdeutsche be judged on the actual evidence. Therefore, he would never acquiesce to joining these officers who were acting outside of the law.

But what actions could Binem take to stop these terrible acts? He understood that no matter how he felt or behaved it would have no influence on his fellow officers. To them he was a "stinking Yid," or as the Germans had called the Jews, an *untermensch*, or subhuman.

Binem observed that superior officers refused to investigate complaints concerning this "ethnic cleansing." Policemen engaging in such activities found that no one would testify against them. Therefore they understood that they were free to act without the fear of repercussions.

One cold, rainy night Binem was assigned for the first time to the midnight shift. The shift leader ordered Binem to accompany him and several other officers on a night raid. When Binem asked for details, he was told that they were going to the house of man "on the list, who was a very bad German."

Binem was told that his duties included to assist in "cleaning him out." Binem wasn't sure exactly what that meant, but he had a gut feeling that whatever this action was he did not want to take part. However, an order was an order. At the time, the universal attitude of military and paramilitary subordinates was that expressed in Alfred, Lord Tennyson's poem, *The Charge of the Light Brigade*: "Theirs not to reason why; Theirs but to do and die."

Having no choice, Binem boarded the truck and accompanied his shift supervisor and fellow officers on the raid. They arrived at the farm house of the suspect which was a short distance from Alexandrow. The officers piled out of the back of the truck as if they were regular soldiers. Binem was the last out and he slowly and reluctantly trailed behind.

When Binem finally caught up with them, he watched in horror as they dragged the badly beaten suspect out of his house and forced him to stand next to a trench that was only a few meters away. Then, the officers opened fire on the suspect.

Binem was aghast. He thought to himself, "How could policemen that are sworn to uphold the law act in such a lawless manner?"

Binem could only compare what he saw to what he had witnessed during the darkest days of the Holocaust. During his entire service with the Polish Police, the thought never even crossed his mind that his fellow police officers could be cold-blooded murderers. He wanted no part of this. He would never participate in something so evil. He remembered how just a short time ago he was hunted by the Nazis. He remembered the fear of being a cornered animal.

Binem knew that there was nothing he could do for that poor soul laying at the bottom of the ditch. He just hoped that he would not be forced to witness such cruelty again.

At that moment he vowed to himself, "I will never be forced to behave like a Nazi!"

Unfortunately, luck was not with Binem. He was now assigned permanently to the midnight shift, which meant he was ordered to accompany his fellow officers on these raids. Binem was now in the middle of a deadly dilemma. If he refused to participate, he would be labeled a Jewish coward who knew too much. In such cases, the common "solution" to this problem was to murder the non-cooperative officer.

After the first raid, Binem feigned that he was too ill to leave the town, so he was left at the station. Binem knew this excuse couldn't last very long. If he continued this ploy, his fellow officers would catch on. Again he contemplated going AWOL. But where would he go? He knew he would eventually be caught, which would result in his own execution.

He thought, "What other options do I have? I can't run and join the anti-communist Home Army, for they would kill me just for being a Jew!"

Having no alternative, Binem decided that he would just wait and hope for an opportunity to escape. He made himself a vow that if he was ordered to go on a raid, he would passively accompany his fellow officers. If they performed their duties as prescribed by the law, then he would assist them. But if they did anything against the law, he would pretend to be one of them but would not actually participate. Binem knew that this strategy was fraught with danger. If his fellow officers caught him in his deception, he would be killed. Even among his friends that were police officers at the Alexandrow Station, there was no one that he could trust.

I asked my father, "Weren't there any other law-abiding officers to turn to?"

He answered, "No. Even if they were nice to me by day when I faced them, how would they react at night when I wasn't facing them?"

Just like when he was on the run, Binem developed a set of rules of survival. The first rule was that during the raids he would always remain a few steps behind his fellow officers. His other rule was that if he was ordered to shoot the Volksdeutsche, he would obey the order to fire but only after aiming the weapon at the ground.

This strategy worked for a short time, until he almost got caught. During a raid, Binem was given the order to shoot, so he shot off a round into the ground. This time his aim was too close.

The team leader shouted at Binem, "What the hell are you shooting at? You have to be the worst shot I've ever seen. Keep shooting like that and your going to get one of us killed!"

Binem, his face flushed, stared back at him with an embarrassed look, but didn't reply.

A few days later, a similar incident occurred with a different team leader. The officer joked with the others, "Hey, he's trying to kill us!"

Binem became concerned that his fellow officers would remember the first incident and suspect that he was not participating in the executions. Suddenly he had an idea.

Binem laughed and said, "Comrades, I wasn't aiming at you. The gun, for some reason, misfired!"

His fellow officers stared at Binem for a long moment. Then they all began to laugh, probably thinking, "the lazy Jew didn't clean his gun."

After the second incident, Binem knew that his fellow officers would be scrutinizing his every move. Knowing this, he decided to simply not show up. He invented excuses for not being able to participate in the raids. Such excuses included, "I'm sick," "I hurt myself today," "I have an important date with a lady friend," or even, "I must visit an injured friend."

One evening, after Binem had once again successfully excused himself from a night raid, he was stopped by a civilian on a quiet side street in Alexandrow. Binem looked at his face, which didn't have any distinguishing features. He thought to himself, "I know just about everyone that lives in this district, but I can't place this man." At that time, there were few visitors to Alexandrow.

The man spoke up and addressed Binem in Polish. He stated as a matter of fact, "You are Jewish."

Binem was perplexed. It was his job to ask questions. Why would a Pole dare say such a thing to a uniformed police officer? Instead of becoming angry, Binem just replied, "How do you know?"

The man stared into Binem's eyes and said, "Because I am Jewish, too."

Binem thought to himself, "Could this man be a *lantz-man* (fellow Jew)?"

Binem smiled, then asked. "What is your name?"

The man replied by changing languages from Polish to Yiddish. "It is not important what my name is, what is important is that I know your name. I am under orders to tell you to go deep into Germany. There are camps there for displaced Jews. From there, they will send you to Israel. No Jew should live in Poland, because all Poland is one big Jewish cemetery. No Jew should live in Poland anymore."

It was dark, moonless night, and most of the townsfolk were already asleep, so there was little light illuminating the street.

Binem heard a sound behind him, so he briefly turned around to see what it was. When he turned back, the man had disappeared. The man had literally vanished into thin air. Binem searched the vicinity for him, but to no avail.

Binem thought to himself, "I know every street and hiding place in this town. It is impossible for him to disappear, but he did."

I asked my father, "Who do you think that guy was?"

My father appeared to be revisiting the same question he had been asking himself for nearly half a century. He finally spoke up. "All I can say is that he was a mystery man."

Binem took a transport truck to Radziejow. The whole ride, he couldn't get his mind off the strange encounter.

He thought, "Maybe I was dreaming, it couldn't be true that I met such a man."

Even after he arrived in Radziejow, he continued thinking about the message the strange Jew had delivered to him. Binem tried without success to unravel the mystery. In the end, he never mentioned the incident to his roommates and instead dismissed the advice.

As time passed, anti-Semitic Polish leaders increasingly used diatribes against the Jews to rally their followers. Binem started hearing rumors that fellow Jewish police officers were receiving anonymous letters warning them to quit. The letters explicitly stated that if the Jewish officer did not heed the warning, he would be ambushed and killed in a gruesome manner.

These letters were not being sent in a vacuum. Deadly events against Jews were taking place throughout Poland. In the town of Ociency, just a few miles from Radziejow, there was a pogrom against the Jews. Members of a group known as the Anders Army entered the town and killed several Jewish survivors of the Holocaust.

Pogroms were taking place throughout Poland. In Kelz, dozens of Jewish survivors were killed by members of anti-communist parties supported by England. The reasons for Jews being killed included banditry, political loyalties, and the fact that Jews were trying to reclaim their property from before the war.

Then the inevitable happened. Instead of being sent a letter, Binem received a warning through a Polish officer who was his best friend in his police unit and his off-duty drinking buddy. The officer approached Binem outside of the station after Binem had finished his shift.

He told Binem with a grave look on his face, "I just got the news. There is a contract out on you. Tonight, they are going to kill you."

Binem was taken aback. He asked, "What should I do?"

His friend said, "Take my advice, run!"

Binem was in shock. "How can I run? I don't even own civilian clothes."

Binem's friend answered, "Switch your uniform with me and I will give you my clothes. No one will recognize you."

The two found a secluded corner and Binem exchanged his uniform for his Polish friend's civilian clothes. Binem thanked his friend, knowing that this would probably be the last time he would ever see him. Instead of using the transport truck, Binem hired a civilian wagon to take him back to Radziejow.

Upon arriving at the Naiman building, Binem gathered his fellow survivor roommates in the kitchen and told them what had just happened. He told them that he had no alternative but to leave Radziejow. He also told his friends that they should be careful, because the way things are going, they are also in danger. All of the roommates were aware of what had recently happened to survivor Roman Rogers, who had been arrested on bogus charges shortly after his return to Radziejow around March of 1946. Rogers' arrest had already put the roommates on edge. Now that Binem received his warning, they were now ready to make a decision about their future.

Binem's roommates were all in agreement that they too must flee. They had heard of a Jewish refugee camp near Hamburg, on the grounds of the former concentration camp Bergen-Belsen. Though the war was over, no one was quite sure whether it would be difficult or even possible to cross into Germany. Still, it was worth the chance.

Each roommate packed what few belongings he or she had accumulated since liberation. When it was light, the friends set out towards the German border, a good two days away by foot. They walked along the side of the road as they travelled west.

Not long after departing, a wagon stopped next to the group. The driver, a strapping young Pole, asked them if they needed a lift. The group was already tired, so they found this offer to be a blessing. They all thanked him. The driver, with a big smile on his face, told them to throw their luggage up onto the back of the wagon and then hop on board. As soon as the wagon was loaded with all their belongings, the driver snapped the reins and the wagon sped off, leaving the survivors standing dumbfounded. Binem and his friends gave chase, but the wagon soon left them far behind.

As Binem returned to the group, he could see on the faces of his friends a look of despair. After some time, they realized that there was nothing they could do, so they continued towards the border minus their earthly possessions. They were now leaving Poland with literally only the clothes on their backs. The only upside to this event was that it was now a lot easier to walk without their packs and suitcases.

The beleaguered group of survivors reached the border and found it open for all to cross in either direction. Binem thought it was ironic that he and his fellow Jews were entering Germany to seek refuge. They were not alone. The highway going west into Germany was filled with hundreds if not thousands of disheveled people walking or riding on wagons. Binem could hear them speak to one another in several different languages. Many had been slave laborers for the Germans. Others were Germans themselves that had been forcibly evicted from other countries.

As they walked, the group met several Jewish refugees. Since all spoke the same language, Yiddish, with varying dialects, they were able to communicate with one another. These refugees had also been told that the best place to go for assistance was Bergen-Belsen.

BERGEN-BELSEN

Bergen-Belsen was a place of great suffering for Jews during the war. Up until March 1944, it was used to incarcerate influential Jews who the Nazis considered to have ransom value. During the early years of the war, the conditions in the concentration camp were somewhat better than other concentration camps in Germany. Those conditions changed radically in December of 1944, when Josef Kramer, a former commander of the infamous Auschwitz-Birkenau extermination camp, took command. Soon after, the camp population quickly expanded from 15,000 inmates to approximately 95,000 inmates. As the Third Reich entered its last days, tens of thousands of prisoners died via exhaustion from forced marches, epidemic illnesses, and starvation.

On April 15, 1945, the British Army entered Bergen-Belsen and liberated the remaining 60,000 inmates, the vast majority of whom were Jewish. Most of the inmates were barely able to walk, while the rest were barely alive. The soldiers were shocked by the inhumane conditions and incredible suffering. Despite concerted efforts by the British medical teams, another 10,000 died in the weeks following liberation.

After the war, the Allies designated the camp as a refuge for displaced non-Germans. At first, refugees from all countries were housed together. This proved to be a disaster. Many of the refugees were anti-Semitic and used their time to beat and even kill Jews. Other ethnic groups were also targeted by a criminal element that festered in the camp.

This behavior resulted in a great deal of tension and turmoil. General Dwight D. Eisenhower, then Commander in Chief of the American Forces of Occupation in Germany, was alerted to the terrible situation by President Truman. Truman had received complaints from Jewish leaders in America responding to reports sent by relief workers assisting at the camp. Eisenhower dealt with the matter by issuing a number of orders, the most important of which was to create a separate camp for Jewish refugees. The camp administration went one step further and divided the the remainder of the refugees into several groups based on ethnicity.

The newly formed Jewish camp was supported the United Nations Relief and Rehabilitation Administration (UNRRA), the American Jewish Joint Distribution Committee, and the British Jewish Relief Unit, among others. It was self-administered, and even had its own police force made up of Jewish residents.

Despite these measures, anti-Semitic violence continued. In May of 1946, eight Jews were stabbed by Polish refugees after a "friendly" soccer match. During the incident, another Jew was shot and wounded by an officer of the Polish camp police. The conditions deteriorated to such an extent that the Central Jewish Committee at Bergen-Belsen petitioned the authorities not only to arm their police officers, but also to augment security with a military unit of the Jewish Brigade. The Brigade was made up of Jews from Palestine.

Binem and his friends arrived at Bergen-Belsen in early 1946. After they were processed, they were assigned to the Jewish camp. Binem was shocked to learn that he would be living in a building that had served as Nazi barracks just outside of the former concentration camp.

Binem at Bergen Belson

Binem's first objective was to get into touch with his brothers, Harry and Max. Binem had never met his older brother Harry, and did not remember Max. What he did recall was that his eldest brother lived in Milwaukee which was somewhere in America. Assisting Binem in his efforts were caring members of different volunteer groups, comprised of both international organizations and local residents.

Binem's name was placed on the United States list with a reference that his relatives lived in Wisconsin. Harry told my father that he was able to locate him after listening to a radio broadcast that read off the names of a survivor's list from Bergen-Belsen.

Harry and Max Neuman

Harry, a prominent member of the Jewish community of Milwaukee, was elated that his youngest brother was still alive. He made every effort to help his brother. The two began a regular correspondence. Harry sent Binem packages filled with items that Binem requested.

Although Harry was thankful that at least one member of his family survived the Holocaust, he was heartbroken upon hearing the fate of his other brothers and sisters. Harry had tried to persuade his family to move to the United States before the war. He even sent money for tickets. "Why didn't they listen to me?" he asked himself.

Binem was provided a large room where he stayed with three other Jewish survivors from Radziejow. Joyce (Yetka) Wagner stated in her book that she lived with Binem in this room along with Binem's first cousin Manes and a mutual friend named Luba. Later that year, in October 1946, Yetka married Michael, another survivor from Radziejow. Yetka and Michael stayed in a draped-off section of the room.

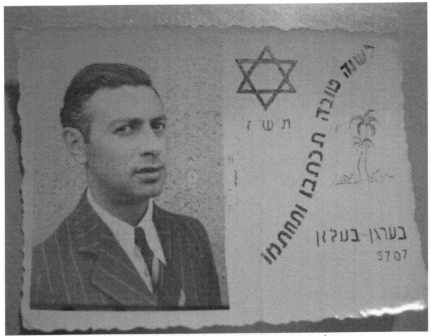

Rosh Hashanah Card from Bergen Belson

When I asked my father about his daily routine at the refugee camp, he was vague. He remembered bartering items he received from his brother Harry's care packages, including coffee, cigarettes, and chocolate. He must have been quite successful, as a number of expensive items in my house when I was growing up had been acquired at Bergen-Belsen. These items included a gold watch, a Leica camera, and a complete set of oversized sterling silver flatware.

I was informed by survivors who had been at Bergen-Belsen that some of the refugees became wealthy by bartering. In fact, some unscrupulous refugees even dealt with items stolen from the camp. The Jews involved rationalized that they had to in order to survive. In some cases, these black market transactions allowed certain refugees to accumulate large sums of cash, which was converted to diamonds and ultimately used to finance new businesses after the refugees were relocated to South America, the United States, Canada, Germany, France and Australia.

Binem at a Zionist Meeting at Bergen Belson
(5th from Left)

Late in 1946, David Ben Gurion, then the head of the
Jewish Agency in Palestine and soon to become the first Prime
Minister of Israel, came to Bergen-Belsen on a series of visits.
My father attended one of the mass gatherings of Jewish resi-
dents of Bergen-Belsen to honor this new leader of the Jewish
people.

Ben-Gurion told the large audience that Jews were
going to establish a Jewish Homeland in Palestine. He stated
proudly that we must be prepared to fight to claim the Jewish
land of our ancestors. He challenged those survivors who were
ready to do battle against our enemies to sign up. He said specifically that Israel needed men that knew how to use a gun.

Binem was enthralled by Ben-Gurion's words that went
directly to his heart. The speech had awakened Zionist sen-

timents that he had harbored as a member of the Hashomer Hatzair before the war. Binem saw this call to arms as an opportunity to repay God for saving him, when so many of his friends had been murdered by the Nazi scourge. As a former Polish police officer trained in the use of both handguns and rifles, he felt that he was qualified for the challenge. He signed up, and was informed that arrangements would be made for his transportation to Palestine. After making this commitment he was pleased that he would be serving a higher purpose, helping establish the State of Israel.

After a few weeks of waiting for his transport to the Holy Land, Binem's initial enthusiasm faded. He was not sure if it was the right thing to do. So he wrote to his brothers informing them of his decision.

Harry wrote back emphatically, "Don't do this. You are the only one of our family that lived over the war. We give lots of money to Israel and there are many volunteers from the United States that didn't suffer as much as you. They are going to fight for Israel. You don't have to do it. It will be done anyway. We want to see you. You are the only one that lived over the war, I can't let you do it. For the money I give to Israel, they can hire someone to take your place."

After reading the letter, Binem was torn. He mulled over the pros and cons of his initial decision to go to Palestine. After a few days, he wrote Harry back and told them that he would take his advice seriously and would "think over what I am going to do."

Binem's life was at a crossroads. While he was contemplating his decision, Ben Gurion returned to the camp to give yet another speech. After the speech, several of the volunteers that had signed up with Binem were processed to be illegally transported to Israel. The Jewish Agency had picked the strongest volunteers who could contribute to the anticipated war with the Arabs. Binem was one of the chosen ones.

At the same time, Max and Harry were actively working with several Jewish organizations in the United States to bring Binem to America. They kept Binem apprised of their progress. Binem just couldn't decide. He asked himself, "Should I go to Israel and fight and possibly die to help establish the rebirth of the Jewish State, or should I follow the sound advice of my brothers to move to America and live a normal life?" Binem felt that both paths were correct, however, he could choose only one. In the end, Binem decided to listen to his brothers Harry and Max and immigrate to the United States.

After nearly three years as a refugee at Bergen-Belsen, all arrangements were finalized for Binem to join his brothers in the United States. He boarded the SS Marine Jumper out of Hamburg on February 4th, 1949, and arrived at Ellis Island on February 15, 1949. Once processing by immigration officials was completed, he was told that his brothers were outside waiting for him.

Binem's HIAS Travel Papers

A NEW LIFE IN
AMERICA

Binem was enthralled about the prospects of his new life in the United States. It did not matter to him that he neither spoke nor understood English. He knew that his Yiddish would go a long way with communicating with his fellow Jews in his new country.

In the visitor reception area, he saw a group of people waiting. One man came up to him and presented himself as a representative from the Hebrew Immigrant Aid Society. He told Binem in Yiddish that he would take him to his brothers. Binem followed the representative to a pair of men who had great big smiles on their faces. Binem sort of recognized the faces from pictures that had been sent to him.

He said to himself, "If I wasn't introduced, I wouldn't even know they were my brothers."

It was a joyous reunion. Harry and Max were sincerely grateful to God that at least one of their brothers had lived over the war. They repeatedly hugged and kissed Binem. They talked excitedly in Yiddish. Binem could tell by the true joy that his two brothers exhibited that they would do everything possible to help him.

From the port, the three men boarded a ferry to Battery Park in New York City. From there, they drove by cab to Grand Central Station. Binem couldn't believe his eyes. New York City was the most amazing place he had ever seen. The throngs of people, the skyscrapers, the thousands of stores. Binem thought there must be room for one more Jew in America. The hustle and bustle of pedestrians was in Binem's eyes truly marvelous. At the station, they boarded a train to Milwaukee, Wisconsin.

When Binem arrived, he was warmly received by his many uncles, aunts, and cousins that had come to the United States prior to World War II. Binem's arrival was significant enough to be announced in an article in the Wisconsin Jewish Chronicle, which stated that Binem was the first Holocaust survivor to take up roots in Milwaukee, Wisconsin. The brief article, which was riddled with errors, shows how American Jews at the time knew little to nothing about about the Holocaust.

THE WISCONSIN JEWISH CHRONICLE

First Jewish DP Under New Law Arrives Here

The first Jewish DP to settle in Wisconsin under the new immigration law is Dinem Newman, 28, who arrived here recently to live with his brother and sister-in-law, Mr. and Mrs. Harry M. Newman, N. Sherman blvd.

Originally from Poland, Mr. Newman escaped from the infamous Bergen-Belsen camp when it appeared that he was headed for the gas chambers. For over a year he hid on a farm, protected by friendly Christians.

Mr. Newman is reticent about relating his experiences overseas, prefering to forget them as a bad dream. All members of his family were murdered by the Nazis. Now he is striving to learn the English language and hopes to become a useful American citizen.

Binem soon learned that Harry was a prominent member of the Jewish community of Milwaukee. He was also one of the highest ranking Masons in the State of Wisconsin. Harry had a heart of gold when it came to Binem's welfare. Despite his busy schedule, Harry seemed to have all the time in the world for his youngest brother. He pampered Binem. At first, he implored Binem to only rest. Binem wanted no part of that. He was curious to explore his new country, and anxious to begin his new life. So, without telling Harry, he started searching for a job. When Harry found out, he mildly scolded Binem. "You didn't live over the war to work in a factory. I know that I could just give you a lot of money, but that would not be healthy. You would probably just go out and spend it. So what I am going to do is put you into business, any business you want."

Harry had Binem accompany him to meetings with different wholesale merchants. Harry told the wholesalers, "Give him any merchandise he wants, I'll pay." So Binem was able to acquire all the merchandise he needed to start a business. After listening to Harry's advice, Binem decided to open a store that would sell flowers, toys, novelties, and lamps.

His next task was to find a location for the store. Harry had an idea. He owned a giant building where he had a supermarket. There was plenty of room to add a store. Binem liked the idea of being close to Harry, so he agreed. Harry had contractors come in and divide a section of the building that would have its own entrance and front window display. The space was also easily accessible from the inside of Harry's supermarket.

When it was completed, Harry said to Binem, "This is your store - you are in charge of it. You don't even have to pay rent."

Thanks to Harry's business acumen, Binem's little store was a success. As Harry predicted, people shopping for food in his store would filter into Binem's section looking for bargains. In fact, Binem was so successful he soon determined that the local wholesalers could not supply him with the merchandise he desired. So Binem began to travel to Chicago where the world famous Merchandise Mart was located. There he found an endless supply of the latest products.

During one of these buying trips, Binem visited a fellow survivor from Radziejow who was living in Chicago, Yakob Zelik. His wife Angie offered to try to find Binem a *shidduch* (match). Binem was receptive. He was now independent and ready to live the American dream. So he gave her the go-ahead to make the necessary inquiries. A few weeks later, he received a call from Angie telling him that she had found a wonderful young woman for him. A meeting was arranged. Binem and Bernice Halevy immediately hit it off at their very first meeting.

Binem was now eager to travel to Chicago even more frequently. After a relatively short courtship, the two agreed that a prolonged dating period was not necessary especially considering the difficulty of travel. So Binem proposed to Bernice and she said "Yes." She agreed to come to Milwaukee where they would work together in his busy store.

Soon thereafter, there was a large wedding that took place in Chicago. Unfortunately, the wedding photographs were destroyed in a fire at the photographer's studio. All that could be salvaged were a few badly damaged negatives. Binem and Bernice hired an artist who specialized in drawing pictures in pencil that looked like photographs. Using the damaged negatives, he was able to recreate two of the pictures. These pictures can be found on the wall of my brother's house in the same place they have been on display for decades.

After the wedding, Bernice joined Binem in Milwaukee. Binem had already signed a lease for a beautiful apartment with a spectacular view of Lake Michigan. Each day, Binem and Bernice worked hard in the store.

As time went on, Bernice became depressed. She had been very close to her mother. The sixty miles separating mother and daughter was too much. After six months, Bernice told Binem that Milwaukee was "a hick town," and that if she had to stay in Milwaukee, she would need to make frequent visits back to Chicago. For Bernice, trips to Chicago were actually visits with her mother. The trips increased in frequency until Bernice was visiting her mother just about every week.

Binem had to close his store for at least two days a week in order to drive Bernice to Chicago. As a result, the business soon became unprofitable. Then, on a trip to Chicago during the winter, Binem had a car accident. Though their car was damaged, Binem and Bernice came out of the accident without injury. Still, they realized that the accident could have ended catastrophically.

After the accident, Bernice pleaded with Binem. "We just can't continue doing this. Let's move to Chicago."

Binem knew that for the sake of his marriage he would have to compromise. He thought to himself, "If the King of England can give up his throne (King Edward VIII had abdicated his throne in 1936 in order to marry American divorcee Wallis Simpson) for his love, than I can give up a store."

So Binem broke the news to Harry, who understood. They put up a sign in the store, "Going Out of Business." Over the next few months, most of the merchandise was sold. Binem and Bernice packed their belongings and moved to Chicago.

Bernice found an apartment on the north side of Chicago, near the beach on Marina Drive. Like the apartment in Milwalkee, it also had a wonderful view of Lake Michigan. Since there was not enough savings for Binem to set up a new business, he searched for a job. After trying several different jobs, Binem chose a profession that he was familiar with, selling shoes. Most of the major shoe stores were located in downtown Chicago. The first store he interviewed at, Mailings Shoes, hired him. Mailings specialized in high priced women's shoes. Binem planned to work there only for a short time to gain experience and save enough money to open his own shoe store.

I asked my father, "Why did you want to open a shoe store when you already proved successful in your toy and novelty store?"

He gave a practical answer. "Wearing shoes, not owning novelties, is a necessity in life."

Selling shoes on commission was not an easy way to earn a living. Mailings Shoes had dozens of salesmen. The salesmen waited in order to be called upon by a floor manager to assist customers. On a busy day, Binem might have the opportunity of waiting on up to five women per hour. On a slow day, it could be as little as one. The main way of increasing commissions was to make the sale as quickly as possible in order to get back in the line of salesmen.

Binem learned valuable techniques to make quick sales. But he soon discovered that commission sales was a cutthroat business. Some salesmen didn't play by the rules of the store. They considered Binem a greenhorn and took advantage of him. One particular salesman went too far, and came up with a method to steal Binem's commissions. After having several of his commissions credited to this unscrupulous salesman, Binem knew he had to do something. He discussed the matter with his wife. He knew that because Bernice was a native-born American she would know the proper way to handle the situation.

Since she was a little girl, Bernice had a reputation of being someone that no one dared to take advantage of. Her younger sister, Shirley, liked to brag about how Bernice was her block's gang leader in their neighborhood on Chicago's North Side near Humboldt Park, where she attended Tuley High School.

Shirley boasted about her sister, "One time she had a fight with our own brother David and broke his arm!" This was mind-boggling since we all knew Uncle David was a giant of a man weighing nearly 350 pounds.

When Binem asked his wife's advice, she was pregnant. They knew that it wasn't an option to change jobs because Mailings was providing their health insurance.

Bernice advised him, "Bullies only understand one

thing, which is pain. So tomorrow at work, take care of business."

The next day, Binem saw the salesperson stealing his commissions and told him the he would like to discuss something with him in private. The two stepped out the back door into the alley behind Mailings. This was not unusual. Salesmen were always going out the back door to smoke.

Instead of talking, Binem used skills that he had acquired years ago as a policeman in Poland. He was trained to use violence when necessary to deal with Polish drunks that became rowdy. By the time Binem finished with his colleague, he would never bother him again.

My sister Helene was born in 1952. Three years later, on September 13, 1955, I was born. That same year, my father became eligible to become an American citizen. He studied hard to pass the test and was successful. He proudly took the oath of allegiance to the United States. At that time of the ceremony, he was given the opportunity adopt an American name. So he changed his name from Binem to Ben. Four years quickly passed and in December of 1959 my brother Keith was born.

Soon after, Ben and Bernice decided to try their luck and open their own shoe store. In 1962 they opened Ben's Shoes, on Milwaukee Avenue in the Wicker Park neighborhood of Chicago, which at the time was located next to the largest Polish community in the world after Warsaw. Their landlord was a Polish man who had a jewelry store in the same building. He rented to my parents a small store. Ben worked long hours and was therefore able to scrape together an income sufficient to support the family.

After a number of years in the small store, Ben and Bernice had an opportunity to buy a building on the same block. The property had three stores and twelve apartments upstairs. Being a corner lot, it looked eerily similar to the Naiman building of Radziejow. The building was in poor shape and was not too far away from being condemned.

My father chose the center store for the new location

of Ben's Shoes. Over the decades, the other two stores were rented out to various tenants that included a bar, bridal shop, thrift store, lamp store, voodoo store, et cetera.

The apartments upstairs proved to be a headache. The tenants were low income families, some of whom did not pay their rent and eventually had to be evicted. My father hired a man named Pedro to manage the twelve apartments. Their relationship with Pedro could be summed up with my mother's famous words: "He's robbing us blind." After several building violations and a lawsuit filed by the city building inspectors, a judge told Ben and Bernice that if they didn't close up the apartments the fine would exceed the value of the building. So, without any argument, Ben and Bernice evicted the tenants and boarded up the apartments.

Ben's Shoes remained at this same location for over forty years. It was truly a family business in that the employees, save a few instances of experimentation with outsiders, were my parents and their children. When we reached the age of twelve, it was time to start working in the store on the weekends. I remember being paid five dollars a day. Eventually my father raised my pay to ten dollars.

Ben's new life as an entrepreneur was filled with interesting events and colorful people. These included my mother's friend Loretta the lush, Walkie, the walking policeman, Ismal, the bookie for the underground Puerto Rican lottery, Pedro the crook, Junior the bouncer, and Mrs. Zislis, the old lady who ran the lamp store that was constantly being robbed when she would doze off.

Over the years, the customers changed. First it was the Poles. Ben refused to speak Polish with them. One day I was working in the store and a Polish man was giving my father a hard time. He claimed that he didn't believe the shoe was made from real leather. I saw my father lose his temper. He shoved the shoe into the mouth of the Pole and said to him, "Take a bite, this is a *buciki* (a real shoe)!" My father then cursed out the customer with a long tirade in Polish. It was as if my father had been transported to the Naiman Shoe Store in Radziejow. The Poles were interested in quality shoes and did not insist they be stylish.

As time went on, there were fewer Poles and more Hispanic customers. The majority were from Puerto Rico. The rest were many from Mexico with questionable legal status, and a few were from Haiti. The men bought work boots and waterproof high boots for their jobs in the meatpacking industry of Chicago. Bernice noted that the Hispanic men would be dragged into the store by their wives on Fridays. Friday was usually payday or the day they received their welfare checks. The couple would bring in their children to buy shoes for school and church. My mother would smile and added that it was always on Friday, "Before they spent the rest of their money at the bars!" The busiest season for the Hispanic community was Christmas and Easter. The parents would buy white dress shoes for the girls and black patent leather shoes for the boys.

Then the customer base changed and more African-Americans started to shop at the store. They were mostly loyal customers and fairly easy to sell to. Generally, they insisted on more color and style in their footwear.

The most feared customers were the gypsies. I remember working in the store when a gypsy family invaded the store. They were easy to spot. The women actually wore gypsy-style clothes, colorful dresses with lots of pockets! Upon spotting them, my father would immediately sound the alarm for us to be on high alert. They would spread out throughout the store, making it impossible to keep our eyes on all of them. When they left, there was always at least one empty shoe box.

If the Gypsy attacks weren't bad enough, Ben and Bernice were victims of several robberies. One robbery in particular stands out in my memory. A drifter had stopped at the outside display window. He entered the store and asked my father to come outside. Then he pointed to a pair of shoes that he wanted to try on. This was a typical method of picking out shoes. My father located the shoes in the back of the store. The drifter entered behind him. Suddenly, the drifter pulled out a "Saturday Night Special," a cheaply made gun, and pointed it at my father. He told my father to keep calm as he came behind him and pushed the gun into my father's back. He instructed my father to walk to the cash register. My mother was behind the counter manning the register. Ben took a bag and handed it to Bernice.

He told Bernice, "Fill the bag with the money in the register."

Bernice did not understand the unusual request, so she said, "Ben, what are you talking about?"

Ben then repeated his previous instructions. Bernice suddenly understood. She then unexpectedly announced, "The hell I will!"

With her face red and full of anger, Bernice rushed out from behind the counter in a fit of rage and pounced upon the would-be robber. The robber was momentarily stunned by this unexpected move, but he quickly recovered, removed the gun from Ben's back and aimed it at Bernice. He then pulled the trigger. But the Almighty intervened. The gun didn't fire - it was jammed. Ben rushed out the front door of the store to get help.

He ran into the bar next door. Junior, a part owner of the bar and its official bouncer, was behind the counter. Seeing my father's face flushed with panic, he asked, "Mr. Ben, what happened?"

Ben explained the emergency in a few words. Junior was a giant of a man who was known as the Puerto Rican version of Hercules. He also had a reputation of being fearless. Upon hearing that "Mrs. Ben" needed help, he rushed to the store. The drifter didn't know what hit him when Junior tackled him at full speed. In a few moments, the police arrived and hand-cuffed the drifter.

As the drifter was handcuffed by two uniformed police

officers, the detective on the scene asked Bernice, "What happened?"

Bernice simply answered, "I wasn't going to give him a damn thing!"

The detective then looked at the drifter and was surprised that he did not looked distressed. In fact, the robber appeared to be relieved.

The detective asked the drifter, "What are you so happy about?"

The drifter replied, "Just keep that woman away from me!"

When the children were older, Ben and Bernice would travel during the slow sales month of February. They traveled to Europe, the Caribbean, and Israel.

As soon as they were both eligible for Social Security, in 1989, they finalized their retirement. They turned over the business to their youngest son, Keith. He kept the name of the store Ben's Shoes. He successfully continued to run the business for an additional twenty-two years until his own retirement.

Bernice Neuman died of a stroke a few years after the business was sold to Keith. After her death, my father complained that he was again suffering as a survivor. He lived an additional ten years with Keith. He would insist on accompanying Keith to the store to make sure that his son was not alone. When I asked my father what he, as an eighty-year-old man, could possibly do to protect Keith, he said simply, "I can watch."

I eventually settled in Michigan. I made it a point to visit my father on a regular basis. It was a five hour drive each way, but it was worth it. We would eat out and talk. Often times we would discuss his experiences during the Holocaust.

One time I asked him, "Aren't you curious to find out what happened to the Osten-Sackens and Wanda?"

He answered, "Of course. I think of them sometimes."

So I asked, "Why didn't you ever visit Poland and make

an effort to find them?"

His answer was not what I expected. He said, "That's a good question. As time went by, I didn't even know how to start to find them. Later on, I had my own troubles. I was establishing a family. Besides, I couldn't go back to Poland. I ran away. I am considered a deserter from the police. If I did go back to Poland, I would probably get arrested."

I then slightly changed my approach and asked, "Why didn't you nominate them for the Righteous Gentile Program at Yad Vashem?" The Yad Vashem Holocaust Museum in Jerusalem has a garden dedicated to gentiles who righteously saved Jews during the Holocaust.

My father replied, "It's not so easy. Who should I pick as my savior? Osten-Sacken? The Princess? Wanda? Or perhaps all the poor Polish peasants that put me up sometimes for one night sometimes for more? Better yet, those who gave me the equivalent of gold, a piece of bread. These people had more at risk than the Princess."

He continued. "There are just too many people for me to submit to Yad Vashem. If it was only one person that saved me, then I should. But there are so many people that I have to be thankful for. Who should I thank more?"

It was clear that my father had asked himself the same question.

He then blurted out, "I am thinking about some day to go back [to Poland]."

My father never returned to Poland. He died a few short years later. In his final years, he reverted back to his fervent religious beliefs that he had prior to the Holocaust, when he lived in his small town of Radziejow. He became an observant Jew who attended prayers three times a day. He reaffirmed his belief in God and the traditions of his father. He never once, in my presence, blamed the Holocaust on God. Finally, he was not bitter about his fate on this planet. In fact, he took pride in raising a family in which all his children grew up to be proud Jews who married within the faith.

As a result of my father's attitude, I never had cause to blame God for the Holocaust. Because it was clear to me that if my father, who had suffered so greatly, found no guilt in the Almighty, who am I, a skinny little Jew from Chicago, to dare judge the Creator of the Universe.

EPILOGUE

On April 28, 2003, at about 7:00 p.m, I was out shopping with my daughter Ruth. We were about to enter the Farmer Jack supermarket located just a few blocks from our house in West Bloomfield, Michigan, when I received a phone call from my father. He asked me to come see him right away. I told him that it was late and I would leave in the morning. He laughed and said it would be too late. I regrettably dismissed his comment, thinking, how could it hurt if I left early in the morning? Surely that would be soon enough.

I was wrong.

At 4:10 a.m., my father died. It was Holocaust Remembrance Day, April 29, 2003. He was 83.

At his funeral, both my brother and I gave eulogies on behalf of his children. This despite being informed that the funeral was taking place in a period of the Jewish calendar year when eulogies are not typically given. Moreover, my father was the son of a Radomsker Chassid, and Chassidim normally do not give eulogies at funerals. The reasoning behind this custom is the concern that praising someone at their funeral may cause God to inquire as to whether the statements made are actually true.

Still, I felt it necessary to speak that day and relate to the hundred or so people in attendance the true miracle of my father's life. So, after some persuasion, and pointing out that there are accepted leniencies to the "no eulogy" rule, the Rabbi grudgingly relented.

My father was a quiet hero. He was a true survivor in so many ways. His life was filled with many tragedies as well as triumphs. He lived through the worst nightmares we can imagine and persevered.

Dad grew up in a very religious home in the village of Radziejow in Poland. He was the second-youngest of eleven brothers and sisters. His brothers and sisters, like so many in Poland at the time, were less religious than their parents. But because my father was the youngest son, he was the one my grandfather pushed to maintain the traditions.

My father went to public school from early morning to early afternoon. As soon as the school bell rang, he rushed to attend cheder for his Jewish studies. When he finally arrived home in the evening, he would study with my grandfather Talmud until late into the night.

The Nazis invaded Poland when my father was twenty years old. He observed how my grandfather reacted to the invasion of the anti-semites. My grandfather's name was Shimon Naiman. He was beloved by all, and was the most trusted member of the Jewish community. With the Nazis imposing their will on his fellow Jews, Shimon refused to allow them to change his religious ways. For example, my father begged him to shave his beard lest the Nazis use it as a pretext to beat him. My grandfather only agreed to a tragically laughable "compromise." He wore a handkerchief over his beard.

The Nazis' first act of occupation of my father's hometown was to execute laws that served the purpose of humiliating the Jews. This was done by enacting, changing and modifying an endless set of laws that had no other logic but to degrade the Jews. These laws included daily roll calls in which all Jews were required to attend. After roll call, the Jews were forced to perform humiliating tasks. By degrading the Jews, several Poles of Radziejow were encouraged to openly exhibit their anti-Semitic feelings. My grandfather refused to follow the edicts issued by the Germans. Instead, he intensified his Talmud learning, spending most of his day with a Gemara open in the living room despite the family's pleas for him to stop.

Within the first few months of the occupation, my grandfather became ill. He died at home surrounded by his still-intact family. He was buried by the community with all honors afforded to a great member of the community. More than one of the attendees commented that Shimon Naiman's death was a blessing from God, for God allowed him to pass away at home rather than endure the surely certain death that was in store for all Jews.

Two years later, the Radziejow ghetto was liquidated by the Nazis. During the liquidation, my father was away from the town for more than a year. He was conscripted as a slave in a forced-labor camp with one of his brothers. When they learned what happened to the Jews of Radziejow, his brother told him that they were doomed, but as the youngest brother, he must somehow survive.

So my father escaped the surrounded camp and returned to the area by Radziejow. There he hid in the fields. He was an unusual hero. He had no food, no shelter, and no plan. Being hunted and constantly starving for food, soon life became unbearable. So unbearable that he decided to end his misery. Late one night he crept into the Jewish cemetery where my grandfather and grandmother were buried. First he prayed and then he cried. When he was done he re-

moved his belt and wrapped it around his neck. He then pulled as hard as he could at the belt, trying to end his misery. But to his astonishment, nothing happened. So he took out a white shaving bar that was in his pocket and thinking it was poison, he swallowed it. Again, nothing happened. While contemplating other methods of suicide, he suddenly made out a voice in the wind moaning, "Get out of here." Scared and dejected, he followed the command of the wind. He ran away, feeling that he failed at even trying to kill himself.

And thank God that he did run, because somehow he survived. He stated that he became driven by the thought that he must bear witness when the Nazis too will suffer as he and the Jewish people suffered. His vision was actuated when with his own eyes he observed the Russians not only liberating him but more satisfying he witnessed the Russians administer the most barbaric vengeance on the Nazis.

After the war, he did not know where to go or what to do, so he returned to his town. The Russian officials drafted him as a police officer. He moved back into the house of his birth. There were no longer any Jews left but him, but soon a few others returned. He soon discovered that the Poles of his town were not so happy that the Nazis had failed to kill all the Jews. Within a year, a friend on the police force warned him that there were people plotting to kill him.

So my father took flight from his beloved Radziejow, never to return again. He ended up near Frankfurt, Germany at Bergen Belsen, an infamous concentration camp now-turned refugee camp. There, his name was published on a list of survivors that was sent around the world.

An older brother, Harry Neuman, who had left Poland when my father was four years old, located him. My father had already signed up to go to Palestine to help establish the State of Israel, Harry convinced him through letters that he had already lived through hell, and it was time to begin living a normal life. He decided to listen to his brother's advice and immigrate to the United States. He moved in with Harry and his wife Ida in Milwaukee, Wisconsin. There his brother set him up in business, and most importantly gave him the tools to live a normal life.

Soon thereafter, my father decided it was time to find a wife. He took dancing lessons at the Fred Astaire Studio. He was set up to meet Bernice Halevy, from Chicago, Illinois. They couldn't have been more different. She was born and raised in the United States, spoke Yiddish, but knew little about the Jewish religion. She was always known as tomboy. During the war, she had volunteered in the spirit of "Rosie the Riveter" and became a welder in a munitions factory. She matured into a woman who was lovely but always remained tough as nails. On the other hand, my father was a quiet man. He was still experiencing the after-effects of the Holocaust. But they fell in love and got married.

My mother forced my father to give up his business in Milwaukee and move to Chicago. He knew how to sell shoes from his family business in Poland, so he went to work at Mailings Shoe Store in downtown Chicago. One of the salesmen took advantage of my father because he was a greenhorn. He stole my father's customers and robbed him of his commissions. After discussing it with my mother, my father took the salesman into an alley and taught him a lesson. That salesman never took a penny away from my family again.

As a child, I watched my father sleep in an odd manner. When he slept, his legs would constantly be moving. My mother said he was dreaming that he was running from the Nazis.

My parents ultimately decided to open their own shoe store, Ben's Shoes, in the 1960s. Through robberies, shakedowns, slow business, and thriving business, my father raised three American children that grew up to be proud Jews.

After my mother died, I watched my younger brother Keith care for my father until his last days. My father's health deteriorated. His lungs were bad. He had heart problems, His hearing was impaired. He could barely see. Still, as long as he was alive, I always felt I was someone's child. But today, at age forty-seven, I realize that I now have to fully grow up and play the role of a mature adult as my father did.

My wife, my children, and I will miss Grandpa because we know that if he did not survive the Holocaust we would not be here today.

After I finished speaking, I returned to my seat satisfied that I honored my father. While the Rabbi spoke, my mind wandered. I finally stared at the casket that was about ten feet in front of me. Completely at ease, I experienced a waking dream. I saw my father hovering above and behind the casket. He was in a standing position. The entire area around him was basked in a soft, calming light. He was dressed in a shroud and wore a shimmering *tallis*, or prayer shawl. He stood between two similarly dressed apparitions. The vision felt natural, as if I was experiencing a very pleasant ceremony. I felt enveloped with a feeling of peace and tranquility. The vision ended as naturally as it had begun. It suddenly occurred to me to turn to my sister and brother and ask them if they were watching the same thing. Unfortunately, they both answered that they did not see a thing.

POSTSCRIPT

Months after publication of the first edition of this book, I received an unexpected e-mail from someone claiming to be a relative of "the Princess." I talked to her over the phone for about an hour, and later I spoke with her brother and another relative. They told me that they were related to Halina Fudakowska (maiden name Daszkowska), who they said was the sister of the Princess, and that Halina knew my father even better than the Princess did. She said that Halina was still alive and living in Canada. I was skeptical for a number of reasons. Still, I felt it worthwhile to report the information they provided.

According to these sources, the Princess's name was Maria (Marychna), and she was born in 1907. Her husband's name was Wiktor, and he was born in 1892. Their estate was known as the Klonowek farm, and was located near Kwilno. They describe it as less than palatial. However, the picture of the house they emailed me appeared to be quite large, especially by Polish standards, and almost certainly would have appeared to my father as a mansion. They also sent me pictures of one of the barns on the estate.

They described Wiktor Osten-Sacken, who was the head of the association of sugar growers in Poland, as identifying as a Pole and not a German. They believed that he was charged with collaboration with the Germans, but were unaware that he had been physically assaulted. They stated that after his trial, in which he was sentenced to forfeiture of his property, he moved to Torun and later wrote a play about the war. He died in 1951. They stated that Maria, though a member of the Polish gentry, avoided fancy clothes and hid her jewelry before the war. She died in 1975. The Osten-Sackens are buried together in St. George's Cemetery in Torun, Poland.

They also asserted that the Osten-Sackens' son, whose name was Andrew (Andresz), was conscripted at age 19 to the German army and was not an officer. Rather than being killed at the Russian front, they claim he was sent to the Western front where he deserted the German army and joined Polish forces in in Italy.

Finally, they suggest that when my father referred to "Wanda," he was really talking about Maria's sister Halina, who they say often brought him food when he was in hiding.

I reviewed the interview tapes and found that the city the Osten-Sakens moved to after the trial was in fact Torun. And my father had in fact referred to Osten-Sacken on one occasion as Victor. However, many of the claims they made were inconsistent with my father's account.

For example, my father said that he knew Wanda from primary school in Radziejow, which makes it clear that she is a different person than Halina. They also do not know who Wanda's brother was or his relationship to the Osten-Sackens. There are additional inconsistencies in their claims regarding the timeline of events of my father's taking refuge in the barn, and the extent of Wiktor and Andrew's cooperation with the German authorities during the German occupation of Poland.

I suspect there is some truth mixed in with their narrative, however, a desire to protect the family legacy may have contributed to a certain degree of revisionism and a possible whitewashing of events. Therefore, I have not deviated from my father's account in this edition, spare some minor changes.

Regardless, now being able to identify the Osten-Sackens with some confidence, we have submitted their names to Yad Vashem's Righteous Among the Nations program for recognition, which we hope will be forthcoming.

ACKNOWLEDGEMENTS

First of all, I would like to thank God for saving my father's life, and for all the blessings He has bestowed on myself and my family.

I would like to thank my wife, Gila, and my daughter, Ruth, for their constant support throughout many years of work on this book.

I would like to thank my son, Adi, for his work on the website *polandinjustice.com*, and for his thorough editing of this book from my raw manuscript.

I would like to thank Steven Spielberg and the Shoah Foundation for recording the histories of Radziejow survivors, including my father, from which I drew extensively.

Finally, I would like to acknowledge the Radziejow library and its librarian for their contribution of photographs.

REFERENCES

BBC On this Day: September 1, 1939

Deathcamps.org

German crimes in Poland: Central Commission for Investigation of German Crimes in Poland,1946. Extermination Camp Chelmno.

Gilbert, Martin. The First World War: a Complete History, 1994.

Jewish Virtual Library: Einsatzgruppen.

Montague, Patrick. Chelmno and the Holocaust, 2012.

Munoz, Antonio. Generalgouvernement: Internal Security in the Eastern Occupied Polish Territories, 1939-1945, 2004.

Munoz, Antonio. Hitler's Green Army, 2006.

Piotrowski, Tadeusz. Poland's Holocaust, 2007.

Sztetl.org.pl

United States Consumer Product Safety Commission

United States Holocaust Museum

Wagner, Joyce. A Promise Kept to Bear Witness. 2007. Browning, Christopher. Ordinary Men. 1998.

About the Author

S cott M. Neuman grew up in Chicago, Illinois. He holds a degree in criminal justice from the University of Illinois at Chicago Circle, as well as a J.D. from Thomas M. Cooley Law School of Western Michigan University.

He is a veteran of the Israel Defense Forces, where he served as a combat medic and fought in Operation Peace for the Galilee, otherwise known as the 1982 Lebanon War. He is also a black belt in Tae Kwon Do.

He is currently a practicing attorney in Michigan.

44082451R00189

Made in the USA
Middletown, DE
02 May 2019